D1562377

Building a Superior
School Band Library

Building a Superior
School Band Library

Lawrence J. Intravaia

Parker Publishing Company, Inc.
West Nyack, New York

© 1972 BY

PARKER PUBLISHING COMPANY, INC.
WEST NYACK, NEW YORK

LIBRARY OF CONGRESS
CATALOG CARD NUMBER: 78–174588

PRINTED IN THE UNITED STATES OF AMERICA
ISBN–0–13–087031–5
B & P

Foreword

Lawrence Intravaia has prepared a book which fills a great need for all band directors regardless of years of experience. *Building a Superior School Band Library* is an important and convenient reference source. Some vital subjects covered in this excellent book include the acquisition of new music (concert, marching, for developing performing skills and musical "know-how"); filing, indexing, and cataloging; housing and storage of music; training librarians; and provisions of the Copyright Law (1909) and some provisions of the new law now under consideration.

Before entering a laboratory, the research scientist begins his work in a library, one which reveals the necessary sources to carry on his experiments. Our great centers of learning are built on the foundations of their libraries. Musical organizations are also completely dependent on an adequate library. The band especially needs a well-organized, efficiently-managed library to perform its varied functions as well as to save time for the harried band director.

We are fortunate that Dr. Intravaia, an experienced teacher and director, has provided us with the tools to build just such a superior music library.

Raymond F. Dvorak
Emeritus Professor of Music
University of Wisconsin

5

What This Book Offers

The "band library" is usually interpreted as including all the music for the entire instrumental music department. Totally speaking, this music comprises the band's "course of study." The band director must consider the building, developing, and improving of his library as a continuous, on-going process in order that the student, in his "course of study," may have a full opportunity for adequate musical incentive, challenge, musical growth, and the development and appreciation of worthwhile music.

In actuality, the term *library* means the total collection of musical literature contained in the band director's files. The term *building* refers to many aspects including enlarging the library through proper selection of literature, where and how to locate literature, selecting performance and training literature, organizing the library including systematic acquisition, budgeting and ordering, practical filing techniques (indexing and cataloging), care and control of the literature (checking in-out system, mending, repairing music sheets), and aesthetic considerations such as how the right literature will contribute to the student's musical growth, knowledge, and understanding of music. This book will cover all these aspects, as well as others, in detail and in a practical manner.

I recognize that the busy, experienced band director's life is a harried one at best. He is interested in practical, specific information that he can adapt to improve his current library and often does not have time to design new administrative practices—and he does not want to waste his limited time reading about a theoretical utopian system. This book will assist him in keeping up with current trends and eliminating some of his major library problems through practical, tested and proven ideas, suggestions and guidelines that any band director can adapt no matter what size his current library and what his musical needs may be.

In the building of a superior library the proper and judicious choice of literature is perhaps the most crucial consideration. What the band director thinks is right, best, important, or even expedient is what should be included in his library. He must trust his own judgment, taste, the objectives set for his program, and his feeling for and knowledge of his students. The choice made by the director must vary from that of his colleagues according to his personal needs and the interpretation of the criteria and factors recommended herein. This book offers criteria for choosing concert and marching literature, advice on how to determine suitable training literature, and a survey of the development of the band's repertoire. These criteria are illustrated as part of a coordinated system that will result in training and performance continuity throughout all stages and levels of the band program.

In addition to all this, the book offers recommendations and advice from major publishers of band music and music dealers throughout the country on the most efficient and economical methods for ordering and purchasing music. A discussion of the Copyright Law will bring the band director up-to-date regarding the responsibilities and relationship of the school band to the Copyright Law.

All the more practical aspects of successfully managing the band library are covered in this book such as, proper indexing and filing as well as cataloging, which means efficient administration and better use of rehearsal time, and the proper use of students in the maintenance and management of the library.

Artistically, good literature teaches itself; the more mediocre or unsuitable the literature, the more skilled the director must be. To have a superior band, the director must develop and maintain a superior music library.

Lawrence J. Intravaia
Carbondale, Illinois

Contents

1

How a Superior Music Library
Will Improve Your Band

THE BAND'S REPERTOIRE

According to the Music Educator's National Conference, there are at least 50,000 school bands in this country; the potential as a media of musical culture is rather formidable.[23] * The growth and development of the American school band is a twentieth century phenomenon, but an adequate and representative repertoire for it has been a more recent development. In fact, until the past decade or two, repertoire has been a basic problem of the band since it consisted mainly of a great number of dubious original compositions and an even larger amount of transcriptions from other media. Several leading present-day composers have come to recognize the band as a serious medium of musical expression and have composed many excellent and worthwhile compositions for it.

A suitable repertoire is a strong contributing element in the development of bands and band music. It may be divided into three broad areas or classifications including: (1) original concert band and marching band compositions; (2) transcriptions and arrangements of compositions originally for other media; and (3) instructional and/or training literature.[5] This gives the band repertoire a contrast which is one of its most valuable assets.

---

* Numbers refer to items in the Selected References at end of the chapters.

SELECT IT WITH CARE!

Each year every band director faces the responsibility of selecting proper music for his organizations; it is one responsibility which must be regarded with a serious intent. This is even more true when one considers the care which other educational areas employ about decisions on instructional material used.[23] Careful selection of music for the band library will adequately supply the essentials for instructional and public performance requirements, and ultimately the educational and musical needs of all students involved as well.

Music is an aural art and to fulfill this function it must be publicly performed and heard. In contrast to one popular opinion, public performance is not the basic function and purpose of school music. Performances are an extension and reflection of class instruction and educational experiences derived by students as a band participant.[12] The band director should, therefore, be guided in his choice of repertoire by a multiplicity of considerations; some music is suitable for various types of performances and some for instructional purposes. Fundamentally, the band repertoire should be educational rather than audience oriented.[4]

Regardless of the size of the school band and the scope of its program, the emphasis on repertoire selected should be placed on quality and not quantity; in this case, measurement is qualitative not quantitative. We would all agree that, to a certain degree, the school band is a laboratory-type organization, educationally speaking. The students should have an opportunity to meet special basic educational objectives, including the development of necessary technical skills for effective performance, but also to further the development of musical understanding and value judgments concerning music.[21] The effect of this approach on the band library should result in a selection of a wider variety of materials.

THE MUSIC LIBRARY PROVIDES FOR
A COURSE OF STUDY

One of the most effective means of promoting music as an influential part of our culture to school band members is through organized, progressive, and sequential curricular experiences.[21]

This implies that the music library constitutes the band's "course of study;" the music which the band studies and performs stands for its "textbook." [8] Whatever musical and artistic merits are implicit in the repertoire will be mirrored in the end product, the performers themselves.

Sequence and Progress

Most instrumental music programs are conducted segmentally, that is, year by year and class by class, from beginning "band classes" through senior high school. Each level or phase of the program bears a singular function and relationship to the program as a whole.[9] It is incumbent on the band director to plan his program so that it achieves whatever musical and educational goals he has designed regarding student accomplishment. If the music library is considered the band's "course of study," it will allow the band director to think of his program in terms of "educational experiences" for his students that are naturally progressive, additive, restrengthening, and related.[9] The program must at the same time remain flexible enough to meet the needs of the individual student. The sequential character of the program can be brought about through the introduction and use of appropriate musical literature. The obvious role of the band director in his selection of a repertoire is a critical one; he must see to it that gaps or weaknesses do not exist in the music library.[8] The music library should contain literature for all levels of instruction in the program. This means that as each level of development makes increasing demands on the students' musical awareness and performance skills, the literature should become progressively more complex and refined. To these various ends one must begin by exposing the students to the very best literature available. There is good music, both original and transcribed, for all levels of ability ranging from easy to difficult, that can be used by the director for the promotion of music education without resorting to cheap, tawdry, and pretentious material.[11]

Development of Skills

Most of the academic disciplines in the present-day school curriculum have evolved into structured, coordinated programs.

Progress from one level of achievement to the next is based on an assimilation and development of knowledge, skills, and various experiences.[23] The same should be no less true for the band program. This factor is vitally important when one considers the fact that many band directors in this country have substantially the same students as members of their performing organizations possibly from three to eight years.

The band's program, or "course of study," must be developed around experiences, skills, activities, and the knowledge which lead to those objectives and goals established by the director. The band library should contain literature that will assist the director and students in achieving these desirable results. For example, development of performance techniques and skills is important, but of equal importance is the development of musical perception, understanding, and sensitivity. These can be presented, taught, and cultivated through superior literature involving melody, harmony, rhythm, musical form, and stylistic interpretation representative of various styles and periods of musical history.[12] To accomplish this, the music selected must be within the physiological, psychological, and musical capacities of all the students involved in the program.

Motivation

Many band directors whose programs include more than one level utilize the band's literature as a motivational device. Where certain levels of accomplishment are required on the part of the student for promotion or entrance into the organization at the next higher level, directors outline what competencies, technical skills, and musical comprehension are required.[18] Naturally, the specific elements may be selected from the band's current literature. For the student to know in advance what is expected of him gives him definite goals on which he can set his musical sights. The attainment of these goals provides both satisfaction and motivation for the student. This is in keeping with learning theories which suggest that a student's progress may be greatly enhanced through knowledge of his position in the educational process.[18]

The use of superior literature for motivation is also related to its use in the development of skills and the sequential character of the band program. In his endeavor to maintain proper sequence, aid the student to accomplish musical and technical skills, and motivate him, the band director should expose his student to good quality literature.

Effectiveness of Instruction

If the band director conceives his music library as a "course of study," he will generally have a good idea of what his student players should accomplish both musically and technically. The degree to which his students achieve these objectives can provide the means for the director to check on the effectiveness of his instruction. He may ask himself: How well have my students understood and assimilated all the musical fundamentals and knowledge I have explained and taught them?

One of the greatest dangers in the band program is *repetition* of musical styles, forms, elements, and types of music. The danger lies in the fact that a student may not receive any new musical experiences during his second or third year that he did not get his first year; the program might stagnate in this situation.[13] This does not imply that a director should not repeat good, worthwhile music every three or four years. It does mean that, through proper selection of quality literature, the director can keep his students progressing, moving, motivated, challenged, and on a steady course toward his program's objectives. Thus the students should become more self-sufficient as competent performers and discriminating consumers of music.[13]

SUPERIOR LITERATURE HELPS
ATTAIN YOUR OBJECTIVES

The value of the music located in band libraries goes hand in hand with the individual band director's interpretation of the objectives for music education generally, for the school band in particular, and for the function of his band program more specifically.[20] This diversity of interpretation perhaps accounts for the broad scope in the quality of music performed by bands. Only that literature which will fulfill these objectives and purposes can be justified for use by any band.

Musical Objectives

One of the purposes of education is to guide or change the student's behavioral pattern. In music education, this idea is translated as the acquisition of desirable traits of musical behavior. The music, or band program must specify those consequences and experiences which its students must have to attain these results.[25] It follows, then, that musical information, knowledge, literature, and methods must be selected to create the context in which the projected learning should take place.[26] The student's mode of behavior, experiences, information, and knowledge are so closely interrelated with musical literature that the band director can do no less than be very selective about the materials he chooses for his band library. In this way he is able to assert control over the educative environment of his students in order to produce the intended results of his program. It must be remembered that the primary function of the band is to serve as a medium for promoting a musical education to the student players.[1]

Nationally there is an unfortunate lack of complete agreement on the objectives and purposes of the instrumental music program in our schools. Regardless of conflicting philosophical concepts, the following selected list of objectives will apply to practically any instrumental program; the only major differences would be in breadth and scope.

The objectives or goals of an instrumental music program, via a superior music library, would be to:

1. Perform a wide range of musical styles.
2. Discover meaning in many types of music.
3. Develop a knowledge of stylistic characteristics which distinguish music of one period from that of another and an ability to recognize them when heard.
4. Organize discussions with students about their varying reactions to compositions.
5. Develop the skill in performing and listening to music—hearing and following the main elements of musical composition.
6. Develop a greater accuracy in sight-reading.
7. Develop taste through discriminating judgments of value and quality in good music.

8. Recognize the values which distinguish truly artistic and educative music from music which is merely entertaining.
9. Develop an ability to distinguish between the personal taste of an individual (himself or another) and the merit of a musical composition which may or may not coincide with that taste; an attitude of musical broadmindness.
10. Develop an understanding of instrumentation (arranging) and how one's part is related to the composition as a whole and other parts specifically.
11. Develop an understanding of the elements of good musical interpretation.
12. Develop habits of selecting good recordings, searching for more musically satisfying radio and T.V. programs, and attending worthwhile concerts.
13. Extend, clarify, and refine the broad musical competencies which have grown out of previous general music instruction in the elementary school.[6, 8, 9, 14, 20, 21, 26]

In the past, instrumental music was justified on the basis that it made a contribution to non-musical ends and values. This was due to the fact that music was not justified on its own merits. The picture is rapidly changing; music educators are defending and promoting the quality content of the music program on its own intrinsic values. Non-musical values could be included but only if they do not deter the musical objectives of the program.[2]

Coda

The quality of the instrumental program plays a vital role in the success of the total school music program and, among other factors, is highly dependent upon the quality of the literature found in the library.[26] The band exists primarily for the creation of a musically sensitive individual. The ultimate selection of literature for the band library will depend on what the director conceives to be the function, purpose, and objectives of his band. In summary, the director must select literature for the benefit of his students. Directors realize that they select music with an awareness of its suitability for various types of performances, but the decision is not made entirely on this basis.[8] There should always be a close relationship between the band's literature and the objectives of the program.

Good literature teaches itself. All aspects of good music, the melodic, tonal, and rhythmic configurations, style, and inherent beauty have an appeal, accord, and rapport with and to the director and players that are almost immediately apparent. This is conducive to a stimulating, interesting, and effective learning experience. On the other hand, poor, mediocre, or unsuitable literature taxes the band director's teaching skill; it is difficult indeed to glean any meaningful values from music of low quality.

The late Erik Leidzen once stated that too many bands are playing "badly written music," and that "The only thing worse than performing such music badly is performing it beautifully." [20]

Selected References

Books

1. Bachman, Harold B. *Program Building,* Chicago: Frederick Charles, Inc., 1962.
2. Colwell, Richard J. *The Teaching of Instrumental Music,* New York: Appleton-Century-Crofts, 1969.
3. Goldman, Richard F. *The Concert Band,* New York: Rinehart and Company, 1946.
4. Goldman, Richard F. *The Wind Band: Its Literature and Technique,* Boston: Allyn and Bacon, Inc., 1961.
5. Green, Elizabeth A.H. *The Modern Conductor,* Englewood Cliffs, New Jersey: Prentice-Hall, Inc., 1961.
6. Hartshorn, William C. *Music for the Academically Talented Student in the Secondary School,* Washington, D.C.: Music Educators National Conference, 1960.
7. Hind, Harold C. *The Brass Band,* London: Hawkes and Son, Ltd., 1934.
8. House, Robert W. *Instrumental Music for Today's Schools,* Englewood Cliffs, New Jersey: Prentice-Hall, Inc., 1965.
9. Leonhard, Charles and Robert W. House. *Foundations and Principles of Music Education,* New York: McGraw-Hill, 1959.
10. Music Educators National Conference. *Music in the Senior High School,* Washington, D.C.: Music Educators National Conference, 1959.
11. Music Educators National Conference. *Perspectives in Music Education* (Source Book III) (Bonnie C. Kowall, ed.), Washington, D.C.: Music Educators National Conference, 1966.

12. Sur, William and Charles Schuller. *Music Education for Teenagers*, New York: Harper, 1966.

Periodicals

13. Baird, Forrest J. "Let's Sell Our Music Program," *The School Musician*, Vol. 35, No. 1, Aug.–Sept., 1963.
14. Fowler, Charles B. "Music Education Through Performance," *The Instrumentalist*, Vol. XIX, No. 4, Nov., 1964.
15. Hullfish, William and Jack Allen. "Let's Teach Music Appreciation in Band," *The School Musician*, Vol. 36, No. 9, May, 1965.
16. Labuta, Joseph. "High School Band Curriculum," *The Instrumentalist*, Vol. XXI, No. 2, Sept., 1966.
17. Sperry, Gale L. "The Importance of a Band Course of Study," *The School Musician*, Vol. 34, No. 1, Sept., 1962.

Unpublished Literature

18. Cecil, Herbert M. *Fundamental Principles of the Organization, Management, and Teaching of the School Band*, Ph.D., University of Rochester, 1953.
19. Fjeld, Marvin W. *A Survey and Evaluation of Music Performed in Public Concert by Indiana High School Bands*, Ed.D., Indiana University, 1959.
20. Garner, Gary T. *Transcriptions for School Band of Selected Music Written Before 1800*, Mus. A.D., University of Southern California, 1967.
21. Griffith, Donald N. *Remarks in Coordinating Committee Panel Discussion*, College Band Directors National Association, 15th National Conference Proceedings, Feb., 1969.
22. Haines, Harry H. *Problems in Writing Curriculm Materials for School Bands*, Mus. Ed.D., University of Oklahoma, 1968.
23. Henderson, Hubert P. "Straws in the Winds," *An Address to the College Band Directors National Conference*, 15th National Conference Proceedings, Feb., 1969.
24. Pugh, Russell O. *The Band Compositions of the Contemporary Music Project for Creativity in Music Education*, Ed.D., University of Arkansas, 1966.
25. Shaughnessy, Robert M. *Harmonic and Contrapuntal Elements in Selected School Concert Band Compositions*, Mus. A.D., Boston University, 1963.
26. Stewart, Robert L. *The Musical Taste of the Secondary School Instrumental Music Teacher in Relation to the Character and Success of His Program*, Ph.D., University of Kansas, 1965.

2

Eight Criteria in Selecting
Outstanding Concert Literature

AN HISTORICAL PERSPECTIVE

There was a time when the band's concert repertoire consisted of a conglomeration of "descriptive" compositions, musical
"knickknacks," assorted dance forms (polkas, two-steps, waltzes),
marches, and a large amount of transcribed material. One of the
obstacles which loomed in the band's path toward acceptance as
a serious medium of musical expression was this repertoire; it
was considered mediocre and monotonous. While band concerts
may have been entertaining, musically they left much to be desired. This does not intend to minimize those programs specifically
designed for musical entertainment, such as outdoor "pop" concerts nor the efforts of all the historical predecessors of the contemporary concert band. However, in some instances, the only
thing symphonic about band music labeled as "symphonic band
music," at that time, was the title.

Although such eminent 18th and 19th century composers as
Beethoven, Gossec, Mehul, Catel, Berlioz, and Mendelssohn had
written music for the wind-band of their day, their compositions
were not generally available for performance. Consequently, in
order to expand the band's repertoire, it was necessary to rely
on transcriptions of orchestral music and arrangements of music

originally composed for other media. A major reason for this situation was the band's flexible and evolving function. From its earliest inception, the band's basic activities were relegated to outdoor performance whether for military, civic, utilitarian, or concert purposes. Any original material, therefore, was composed and developed in keeping with this perspective. A lack of sufficient original band music brought about the general usage of transcriptions and arrangements.

The present-day picture is not quite as dark as has been suggested above. Moving the band indoors, along with the growth and development of the school band, has altered and improved the band's artistic position through the creation of an environment conducive to the production of a new repertoire and exploitation of the band's myriad timbres and colors.[34] There is a definite feeling that something new has been developing in the province of band composition. Many leading musicians in the band field agree that the band is at last beginning to accumulate a repertoire which will help it achieve its deserved place in the musical world.

Years ago a band director had to rely only on a few conpositions by Holst, Vaughan-Williams, Grainger, and Respighi to give his concert library an air of respectability and genuineness.[37] Since 1950 an ever-increasing number of prominent composers have been supplying the band with concert music in various idioms which, needless to say, has decidedly enriched its repertoire. No less an important composer of music for band than Frank Erickson ". . . feels that the concert band is (now) an 'expressive unit' which stands on its own merits rather than a substitute for the orchestra media."[39] The result is that the band repertoire now consists mainly of original 20th century compositions, the several original works from the 18th and 19th centuries, and transcriptions or arrangements of music from all periods of music history notwithstanding.

AREAS OF RESPONSIBILITY

Scratch a band director's convention and you will usually uncover a "bull session" about the amount of trash and trite band literature on the current market; inevitably the discussion is directed toward establishing the guilty party for this condition.

There are three main areas of responsibility for the type, standard, and quality of band literature today: (1) the publisher, (2) the composer and/or arranger, and (3) the band director.

The Publisher

The publisher is often criticized for deficiency in works of artistic merit and musical worth. Directors claim that he publishes only that music he *hopes* school bands will purchase, not what they actually should have or need. Bear in mind that the publisher is a businessman; occasionally the editor-in-chief is an ex-conductor or ex-professional performer who advises the publisher on prospective publications. Through various administrative channels the publisher attempts to remain sensitive to trends in what is selling best; at times he has only to look at his sales record to determine this factor. Discussions with publishers' representatives indicates the following point of view: *if band directors are discouraged because of the great amount of cheap literature on the market, the directors as an educational body should encourage their colleagues not to purchase it.* Eventually publishing houses will find a surplus of this type of literature on their shelves and perhaps change their editorial policy.[29] The publisher, however, is not always at fault. Often when he does publish music he considers of value or intrinsic worth, he finds a limited market. He considers it necessary to offset losses in this case and publishes music of a simpler, more naive character; more often than not, he finds a good, ready market.

The Composer and/or Arranger

Everyone realizes that there are many instances when the composer/arranger's product is determined by demands from both the publisher and director. The publisher might require that the composer/arranger write in specified key signatures, meter signatures, limited rhythmic patterns, and limited complexity of musical components making up his composition; further, that he include parts for *all* instruments even though his original instrumentation does not require it. The person has yet to be discovered, but years ago someone recommended that it was an educational axiom for every player in the band to be kept busy throughout each composition. At best, the only possible result is a constant drone of sound. There are a few composers who tend to "write down" to school bands as they feel these players are incapable of producing the more subtle and sensitive musical nuances. Unfortunately, there are composers who make little attempt to prove anything musically or artistically, but simply compose to sell. Fortunately, there are a considerable number of composer/arrangers who write what they feel and for the instrumentation or musical medium they wish; the responsibility for determining its suitability is left to the director.

Composers have often stated that their past reluctance to write for the concert band was due to the lack of a standardized instrumentation; the principle of instrumentation is the reason why they have felt more secure in composing for orchestra. Not knowing what numbers of different groupings of instruments will perform their music for concert band tends to be somewhat discouraging. They suggest that the best approach to developing more interest among *important* composers is for the band directors, publishers, and composers/arrangers to agree on a standardized instrumentation.[38]

The Band Director

In a manner of speaking, the band director has perhaps the greatest responsibility for the type, standard, and quality of band literature on the market. He must remember that he is guiding the musical tastes of his students and audience, for the band is by tradition a popular medium and the first acquaintance with live music for many persons is through the band. If he wants to give his students and audience variety and succeed at his job, the director must have an extremely broad knowledge of and familiarity with styles embracing all types of music. In other words, the competent band director must have universal adaptability.

The director must exert his own musical taste as to what he thinks is best, right, suitable, or pertinent to his organization. Rarely should he rely *entirely* on having the music selected for him or *always* depend on someone else's recommendations; the director should assert a certain amount of independence in this matter. The experienced person who resorts to indiscriminate selection of literature, or who does not develop his own capability for evaluating what music or arrangement is best, will not build a creditable library for his band as a long range policy. Another inexcusable approach is for the director to select music that he feels he *ought* to include in his library simply because its inclusion might "look good" on a concert program, but yet he is not truly convinced of its worth. An extension of this concept, with similar weaknesses, is for the band director to select *only* what the students or audience likes; this would be a disservice to music and education.[5]

THE CRITERIA

The application of a set of criteria for the selection of band literature is a highly subjective matter. It is not surprising to learn that individuals will vary considerably not only in *what* they consider to be the important criteria, but also in the *number* of them they employ. In order to meet the flexible requirements of the band's functions, one should apply different criteria for each style or type of music. For example, one does not look for the same exact characteristics in serious concert music as in popular music. So, the director must familiarize himself with the standards in each type of music to assure himself of selecting the best quality literature.[1] In the following description, selective factors are grouped into large, broad areas of criteria, with secondary or sub-factors as criterion within them. In this way, the key points most band directors should consider when selecting literature will be covered. The criteria are not necessarily listed in order of their importance.

Artistic Values

In essence, the writer is referring to "quality" in music when discussing artistic values. It is the most comparative and relative yet the least absolute of all the criteria.[6] There is no disagreement with the admonition that bands should perform "good," "quality" music, but there is with the definition of what constitutes "quality" music. The subjective aspect is so strong in this matter that it defies the structuring of steadfast rules or principles by which one may arrive at a definition which is completely acceptable to everyone. Even the esteemed conductor Eugene Ormandy exclaims that life would be tremendously easier if there were a positive answer to the question of what is "good music."[9]

Quality in music is not synonymous with its difficulty; at all levels of difficulty one may find quality. The portrayal of interpretative and expressive elements in one composition are just as challenging as are digital requirements or the complexity of rhythmic or metrical problems in another. What is more important is the manner in which the musical elements are integrated. Good music gives one the impression that these elements are equally balanced so as to create a feeling of expressive content, a feeling that all musical forces are logically put together.[8] The challenge to the director and players is to comprehend and express the depth of meaning residing within the total composition.

Musical compositions are often classified according to their effect or nature as serious, heavy, light, entertaining, profound, abstract, subtle, novel, exalted, brilliant, and so on.[28] "Good" music is usually characterized as being subtle, profound, or abstract not only in the musical ideas expressed but also in their development. The principle propounded is that music of high quality is not as apparent at first hearing as music of lesser stature. However, music often must be evaluated in terms of its purpose or use. For example, if a work is classified as "entertainment" type, then it will be obvious or apparent by any standards. Serious music, on the other hand, is designed to challenge, stimulate, or appeal to the the intellect and is by nature more subtle, abstract, or profound.[8] One could say that a director should not use a piece of music for any other purpose than what the composer intended for it.[1]

Craftsmanship is normally associated with quality. Craftsmanship gives the necessary impulse to melody, harmony, rhythm, and form by integrating them into an expressive whole.[30] Without craftsmanship, these elements sound trite, mediocre, and banal. With it, the elements are blended in such a manner that no one of them predominates but are balanced in a way that the results are likely to produce "good music." The superior composer with creative imagination will invest his musical materials with logic and coherence so that they endow his composition with a character and expression beyond the ordinary type of musical work.[8, 30] While the ordinary type composition may be more easily comprehended at first hearing than the abstract type, it does not tend to hold one's interest over a long period of time. The degree to which the more abstract music challenges, stimulates, or appeals to one's intellect, or holds one's interest varies with the individual person.

Good music will have a sense of durability, a lasting quality about it. Durability in a musical work means that it wears well; director and students will want to perform it again, and the audience will enjoy hearing it again. A guiding principle might be that one should grow *into* good music rather than out of it.[30] What gives music this quality of lasting value? One obvious reason is that certain compositions have been performed repeatedly. Therefore, they have withstood the test of time, so to speak. In band literature, this allows one to judge a work by comparing it with others that have become "standards"; we then can use this repertoire as a model upon which we base decisions concerning new works about which one may not be thoroughly familiar or informed. The quality of durability cannot be determined immediately but only after many, many hearings.

Most compositions will contain the principle of tension-relaxation, stress-release, or unity-variety, especially in the melodic and rhythmic elements. Good music does not overwork this principle into tired, worn-out clichés or trite and meaningless repetition of melodic phrases, rhythmic patterns, and harmonic progressions. It tends to impart to the performer and listener a sense of feeling and fulfillment. Since reactions to music are highly subjective, these responses may be aroused by any type of music, from light to serious.

Although a composer strives for contrast among his musical ideas, he nevertheless attempts to relate them stylistically. In good music the different ideas and the manner of shaping and utilizing the musical elements seem to come from the same stylistic source to produce what may be described as structural consistency.[30] In other words, the style of melody, harmony, rhythm, plus the type of form, texture, and timbres are all related to each other; all aspects of the composition are integrated into a meaningful totality.

Another factor which causes difficulty in differentiating between good and poor quality music is that the director's standards change with age and musical maturation. Music which appealed to him when he was in a high school or college band may not do so by the time he has assumed the responsibility for his own program.

Leonhard and House, in describing the differences between *good* and *great* music, make a distinction by stating that *good* music ". . . calls forth specific feelings," while *great* music "expresses the 'life of feeling,' a general state of feeling." *Great* music gives us an ". . . insight into the form and structure of human feeling," the symbolic expression of the "life of feeling which cannot be expressed through language or any other medium of human expression." [8] What Leonhard and House are implying is that great music is more abstract, objective, and symbolic, thereby making it difficult to describe in terms of absolute or specific responses but more subtle and nebulous in character. Good music, on the other hand, lends itself more easily to subjective, specific terminology and conjures up descriptive responses, emotions, reactions, or moods.

Reputation

It is virtually impossible for a director to peruse all available band music. He must, therefore, depend on certain evaluative factors as guides to the selection of music. Many directors practice the habit of "buying name brands" when choosing music by a particular composer or arranger. Obviously, one expects the music by recognized, "top-drawer" composers to be of superior quality. As stated in the previous criteria, the test of time does produce a quality of durability on good music; this time factor allows a perspective for better evaluation of a composition. The director should feel secure in the selection of music composed by historically-significant or important modern composers.

If a director is to balance his library, then he must consider new as well as earlier composers. It is not always necessary to look to works by traditional, established composers to find these qualities. Music by contemporary composers who are recognized in the band field, but relatively unknown otherwise and have not as yet established their niche in the musical spectrum, contains all or

enough high quality characteristics to make their selection worthwhile. Ormandy offers up a prayer that ". . . Heaven defend us
from programs made up solely of masterpieces . . . The honor
we pay a masterpiece will be greater for a share of that honor
bestowed upon a lesser work." [9]

A few problems which arise when considering music by reputable composers, especially the Europeans, are that their works may
be: (1) scored for a group of unspecified wind instruments; (2)
scored for obsolete instruments; or (3) written for modern wind
and percussion instruments but scored for a small wind group
rather than a large band instrumentation. This is mainly true of
wind music from the 18th and 19th centuries and in several examples of 20th century music written prior to 1950 (item #3
above). The music in items *1* and *2* above must be either arranged
or rearranged, or transcribed for use with present-day instruments.

Why are these such problems? First, all directors are concerned
with the matter of achieving contrast on concert programs. Contrast not only refers to style and type of music but instrumentation
as well. We must give our audiences relief from any possible
monotonous repetition of one selection after another all scored
for complete instrumentation. One may learn from Whitwell's
invaluable studies that, "There is original wind music from all
periods, all styles, all countries. There is music for wind groups of
varying size and instrumentation. Why should everyone play all
the time?" [31] The band instrumentation is full of a variety of
colors and timbres which should be exploited. The music described in all three items above is scored for less than full instrumentation and would aid the band director in achieving the
desired relief in his concert programs as well as demonstrating the
variation of instrumental timbres in the concert band.

The information in Richard Franko Goldman's three definitive
and significant books devoted to the band,[4, 5] and David Whitwell's series of articles on some 127 major composers and their
music for wind instruments,[32] indicates that there is a wealth of
music for wind instruments written by front-rank composers during various stages of music history. Goldman opines that there is
no music prior to 1760 which can be classified as band music, but
more properly as wind ensemble music.[5] Providing one has the
instrumentation and capable players, there are many marches,

divertimenti, sinfonias, serenades, and other types of music by K. P. E. Bach, J. C. Bach, Josef Haydn, Mozart, Beethoven, von Dittersdorf, and other composers of the Pre-classic and Classic periods. What may be regarded as band music during the late 18th century is found in the form of marches, overtures, and *sinfonias* by the leading composers of the time including Michael Haydn, Beethoven, Gossec, Catel, Méhul, and Paer.

The 19th century shows a lessening of activity in composing expressly for the band. What exists is of varying quality and interest, both musically and historically. A partial list of composers includes Beethoven, Spohr, Hummel, Mendelssohn, Rossini, Cherubini, Berlioz, Wagner, Meyerbeer, Bruckner, Grieg, Tschaikowsky, and Rimsky-Korsakov. One must remember that this was the era when the band as a concert medium was just beginning its impetus. Lacking sufficient repertoire for concert performances on a large scale, band directors turned to arrangements and transcriptions of music for other musical media as a source of supply. There is also an amount of original, nondescript music written by obscure directors which has, fortunately, passed into obscurity. While the number of compositions seem infinitesimal compared to orchestral music of the same period, they are important to the director and performer of band music.

It is not within the scope or purpose of this book to name all the composers who have written music for the concert band during the 20th century. Suffice it to say that the first works of prestige were composed early in this century by Holst, Grainger, Vaughan-Williams, Fauchet, Hindemith, Hadley, Respighi, Roussel, and Stravinsky, to name a few. Later in the century Prokofieff, Barber, Milhaud, Copland, Harris, Creston, Jacob, Schoenberg, Gould, Riegger, and others made noteworthy contributions to the concert band repertoire.

In addition to the previously-named composers, Whitwell's research lists Ibert, Berg, Webern, Ives, Villa-Lobos, Piston, Sibelius, Poulenc, Schuman, "Richard Strauss, Giannini, and Persichetti. These composers, ". . . regardless of age or place of residence, individually began to explore the wind field at the same time." [33] While many of these works are for various small ensembles, there are a sufficient number of band compositions of the highest calibre. Other composers of distinction who have written specifically for the concert band include Still, Cowell, Thomson, Mennin, Robert Russell Bennett, Hanson, and Dello Joio.

Programmability

Due to its traditionally utilitarian and flexible function, the band concert may be one of a wide variety of types. These include: (1) in-school activities such as concerts for the general public or school, exchange concerts by bands from localities of similar size, interdepartmental collaboration in the production of musical activities, and closed-circuit and educational television programs originating from the school itself; (2) out-of-school activities such as exchange concerts by bands from localities of different size, P.T.A. meetings, meetings of school associations or music education professional meetings, competitive and non-competitive festivals; and (3) community activities including holidays or special occasions, special performances for civic, church, and young people's organizations, benefit concerts, and the rather questionable practice of performing at political events.

One need only give a cursory glance at these types to realize the fact that each requires individual consideration when selecting the most appropriate literature to perform. Choice of literature in each of these instances will be determined to a great extent by possible effect on the audience, effect on the performers, and the all-inclusive factors of balance in types of music, contrast, climax, tempo, and program pace. There is no reason why one cannot find a certain amount of worthwhile quality in music selected for any type of performance. Good composers are capable of expressing themselves at varying levels of feelings depending on the purpose of the particular composition. Obviously, music not intended to appeal to the intellect will be of a lighter nature, but should not necessarily be of a lesser quality.[6]

The band library must contain enough variation in types of concert music to cover all the above-named types of performances. A selection may be considered suitable for one occasion but not have that element of "programmability" in another. Generally, the director must choose music which gives primary consideration for the musical and educational welfare of his students. Performance is a musical/educational demonstration of student accomplishment, especially in the case of serious, formal school concerts, and must be programmed as such with music selected accordingly. For occasions in which pure entertainment is the uppermost objective, without concern for the musical/cultural indoctrination of the audience, then *audience reaction* should be regarded as highly important.

Contrast and Variety

The band library should include examples of the best available literature in each of the various classifications (see Chapter 8 for a listing of classifications); the scope of the literature selected, therefore, should not be limited.[6] The primary purposes are to give the students a balanced diet of musical experiences and the development of playing styles. Too many bands limit their libraries chronologically and stylistically. This tends to give their concert programs a sameness, an uninteresting and banal effect. The probable result on the students is to implant in their minds a narrow view and concept of music literature in general and band music in particular, regarding styles, types, and forms.

To provide invaluable musical experiences for his students, the director must select as much serious music (original, transcribed, arranged) as possible, but within the technical limitations of the band. One often hears the remark from the band director that he wishes to program serious music but does not because his *public* would not appreciate it. Since there are as many publics as there are varying functions of the band, this comment is without validity. Most audiences who attend formal band concerts, at least junior and senior high school bands, are not as concerned with *what* music is performed as with *how* it is performed.

Tarwater, in an analysis of major 20th century compositions for band, offers a list of factors which could serve as a basis in checking for contrast and variety in literature. The factors are: musical forms; harmonic structures; type and treatment of thematic materials; proportions between polyphonic and homophonic textures; degrees of contrapuntal texture; expression of mood; functions of instruments; scoring; adherence (or lack of adherence) to tonalities, modes, or tonal centers; levels of technical difficulty;

instrumentation required; and mixtures of solo and ensemble colors.[41]

Early Original Wind Music. As noted before, there are a number of serious compositions originally written for band prior to the 20th century by "prestige" composers consisting of marches, overtures, *sinfonias,* and a few solos with wind-band accompaniment. Some of this music has been rearranged for use by present-day bands and may be located in various publishers' catalogs. There is an even greater amount of true wind ensemble music from the 18th and early 19th centuries. These should be included in the library not only for the sake of contrast in concert band programs but for the musical and stylistic development of the students. Although the original purpose of these works was for either outdoor or indoor performance as entertainment, background, or functional music, today they hold a place of honor as high quality chamber music for winds.

Transcriptions. The bulk of the published band music representing the 17th, 18th, and 19th centuries appears in arranged and transcribed form. The main musical media which serve as a source of supply are the orchestra, piano, and organ. Solos originally accompanied by orchestra, but transcribed for band accompaniment, also may be included in this classification. It is somewhat unfortunate that a large quantity of these works lay on publishers' rental shelves unknown to many band directors.

Light Music. This type of music has probably undergone the greatest change during the 20th century. At one time it consisted of "novelty numbers," two-steps, polkas, waltzes, patrols, serenades, "trombone smears," and other compositions of similar style. Currently these have been replaced by selections from musical theater productions (it seems no longer proper to refer to this type of production as "musical comedy"), background music and "hit" tunes from movie and television scores, true and pseudo-Latin American (or Spanish) numbers, and arrangements of popular hits. While a large percentage of this classification is more suitable for the marching band, it nevertheless fulfills the need for "entertainment" music by the concert band. Considering the short life span of popular music and "hit" tunes from movie and television scores, the band director should be rather conservative in his expenditure of funds in this case.

In addition to the above, there are light concert pieces in a variety of forms such as song, chorale, overture, or free forms. There are enough of these that merit a high-quality rating on the basis of thematic ideas, harmonic construction and variation, rhythmic interest, and scoring techniques all blended in a crafts-man-like manner, to negate the need for works of inferior value which prove little musically or educationally. It is equally possible for the band director to show discrimination and taste in light concert music as in serious band music.[11] One must choose works from this classification with a high degree of selectivity and sensitivity; their use must be restricted according to the nature of the performance.

Educational Music. The decades of the 1920s and 1930s were the periods when the school band movement was gaining momentum in terms of growth, expansion, and interest. True, there was a sparsity of good, original band music that was technically playable by many of the new, young bands at that time. Most of the published band music simply was not intended for performance by teenage musicians although several school bands throughout the nation amazed their audiences with superior performances of many of these works. A few American composers aided this situation by writing music expressly for these bands. Among the most notable of these composers were Yoder, Buchtel, David Bennett, Lake, Fillmore, King, and O'Neil. The school band will be forever indebted to these and the many other unnamed men like them.

Since 1950 there has been a parallel growth and increase in instrumental music in this country alongside the number of publications for band. Due to this literature, many more bands can aspire to achieve the accomplishments that were thought to be the exclusive domain of but a few during those early years of the school band movement.

There is a certain amount of band literature referred to as "educational material" hiding under a cloak of easy training repertoire. Its *raison d'être* is claimed to be that it fills an educational "need" or that it meets the technical requirements of school bands. The major criticisms against this music are that: (1) the melodic lines are lacking in creative imagination and are usually trite; (2) any development of melodic or thematic ideas is likewise limited by a mediocre compositional ability; and (3) the character and style (melodic and rhythmic patterns, meters, keys, harmony, form) is the same from work to work and only the title changes. Since most of this music is of easy to medium grade in level of difficulty, it may be acceptable as training material for very young bands, but hardly as a steady musical diet.[7]

Original Contemporary Band Music. This classification constitutes all serious, original band music written since the beginning of the 20th century and includes compositions by distinguished, near-distinguished, and new but highly competent composers. Much of the credit for the growth of what is fast becoming an impressive list of original band music is due to the recognition of such a need on the part of individuals, publishers, and organizations who have sponsored or commissioned these works from leading composers.

A musical composition may not necessarily receive a chronological classification of "contemporary" simply because it was written in the 20th century, or even current times, according to some band directors and composers. There are any number of concert band works that are "backward looking" in terms of style and use of musical idioms. A few contemporary compositions exist that are considered too advanced, too *avante-garde,* or perhaps too dissonant for performance by high school bands. However, there are many works within the capabilities of school bands which are challenging and interesting enough to be included in the library.[7]

Musical Criteria

The musical criteria should provide for continuity in each student's musical, technological, and educational development from commencement of instrumental study to matriculation from high school or college. The individual components of this criteria may be thought of in terms of melodic, rhythmic, harmonic, and textural qualities or values. Music must be selected that is in keeping with the band's particular stage or level of development within each of these components. There must be literature in the library that takes the band from one level to the next higher in a logical, thorough process. The effects and results of these components will be important and should become evident after the music has been studied and performed, that is, some change or improvement in the musical behavior (condition) of the student should take place.

Melodic Quality. This quality is perhaps the most intangible, subjective, and subtle of all the components to define as to what is considered a "good" melody; to a very great extent it is a matter of personal opinion. It is rather interesting that most musicians will agree on melodic quality at its extreme opposites, i.e., a truly great work of merit as contrasted with a poor, commonplace composition. Most differences of opinion are concerned with the vast number of melodies which fall somewhere in the regions between this polarity.

Music education materials, clinics, and workshops have often advocated that a good melody must: (1) be pleasing; (2) arouse some emotional quality or reaction in the listener or performer; (3) stimulate the listener's or performer's intellect; (4) have symmetrical balance in construction; and (5) contain logical development of melodic or thematic material. The relevancy of these factors to melodic quality is determined to a great degree by the music's predisposition. The application to the evaluation of melodic quality will depend on the individual band director's interpretation of their meaning. The most effective means for judging an unfamiliar composition is to hear it performed, such as on the piano, a recording, or live performance. Although there will be a difference in tonal characteristics when the music is played on piano, it does give the director an opportunity to determine the general logic and structure of the melodic line.

One cannot determine the quality of a composition on the basis of the melodic component alone, but also in the interrelationship among all the musical components including rhythm, harmony, form, and texture as designed by the composer. However, the melodic quality seems to be the fundamental source on which interest toward a new or particular piece of music is founded. There are many examples of compositions which have interesting rhythmic or harmonic treatment, but little melodic or thematic development. An interesting, pleasing, or attractive melody will certainly enhance the enjoyment of a composition.[12]

Balance and proportion are salient factors in a melodic line. There should be a balance between and among phrase groups which provides for contrast within the contours of the melodic line. For instance, the phrases may be related stylistically but contrasted in spirit, movement, rhythm, or the mood suggested. Proportion in a melody should give a feeling or sense of completion and satisfaction. Some melodic lines have so many secondary or false climaxes built into them that the real or intended climax loses its effectiveness. A meaningful quality is achieved through a smooth interlocking of melodic ideas.[11] Unity and cohesion are equally important factors with the preceding ones. Many composers are creative enough to unify their ideas through sequential patterns both intervalically and rhythmically. The purpose is to bind the ideas organically into a cohesive entity. Trite or mediocre ideas may be recognized because redundancy or repetition tends to replace creative imagination. While sequence may give the melodic line unity, and contrast gives it interest or variety, stylistic uniformity among all these will give it cohesion.

Harmony has a strong influence on melody. The type and quality of harmonic structure in certain cases dictates the melodic contour; therefore, the melodic intervals should balance or relate with the harmonic structure. Melodies in contemporary works indicate more independence from harmonic structure as may be evident from their fundamental contour. They tend to be more or less strikingly dissonant than music of previous historical periods; the degree of dissonance often determines the acceptance or rejection and amount of appeal for the performer as well as the listener.

Rhythmic Quality. One cannot disregard the amount of interest that rhythm can create toward a piece of music. It is a fact, though not as we would like it to be, that it is impossible to choose music containing an equal amount of rhythmic interest in each and every composition. A guiding concept might be that as more independence is expected of individual players, then rhythmic patterns may be progressively more complex or difficult. Similarity to the other criterion may be noted in the fact that, from the consideration of rhythmic problems point of view, music should be chosen which allows for continual musical and technical growth on the part of the students.

When possible, the director should select pieces which employ a variety and complexity of patterns. The director whose band is capable of assimilating and performing a wide range in types of rhythmic patterns will discover that he has more flexibility in his choice of music. If it is a matter of aspiring to higher levels of ability, but the players are not quite ready, perhaps the best approach is to select pieces in which moderately difficult patterns occur in *all* parts *simultaneously* and are repeated throughout the work. When the players have gained sufficient confidence, experience, and understanding, then the director will be free to choose music in which more individuality is required of all sections concerning rhythmic patterns.[6] One advantage in repetition of patterns is that there is a reduction of time needed to study and learn the music; the same may be true of melodic patterns. The one danger is that repetition can be carried too far, perhaps even to the point of triteness and/or boredom.

There is a compelling quality about a piece of music in which the rhythmic aspect seems natural, without sounding forced, as though each pattern "belongs" to that particular work. Rhythmically, one of the basic differences between good and mediocre music is that there is an obvious lack of "padding" which the latter contain in order to create the effect of an extended work. Sensitive musicians feel that the real test of judging rhythmic quality is not in music of moderate to fast *tempi*, but in slower ones. The prestigious composer is one able to empower slow music with far more effective rhythmic momentum, vitality, and charm.[14]

It has been said that young students today are more attuned to the rhythmic complexities of contemporary music than are their directors. One should not be reluctant to select music which includes difficult rhythmic patterns simply on the basis of seeming complexity. Rather, one should attempt to determine whether or not the students can *eventually* develop a feeling and comprehension for such rhythmic structures.

Meter. Contrast, variety, and provision for musical development are as much the primary factors in meter signatures of band literature as in other elements. Reference is made not only to the types of meters used in a work, but also to the frequency of change in meters within it. The more easy the music, the more consistent the meter used throughout the entire movement or composition; the more difficult works employ frequent meter changes not only from simple to simple, but from simple to complex.

Naturally, the style and type of music will determine the frequency of meter change.

When considering a particular composition on the basis of meters, the director will naturally consider the musical comprehension and experience of his students. Obviously, lack of familiarity with meters will require an extended learning period for the students. However, this does not mean that he should limit his choice to meters his students can play at that moment, but rather what he knows they will be able to learn in the near future. For instance, some directors are averse to (but should not be) using music employing compound meters such as 5/4 or 5/8.[12]

In 1954, J. Philip Dalby initiated a project devoted to a study of the high school band regarding its instrumentation, technical competence, and musical activities. His fundamental purpose was to develop a set of recommendations for the arranger who scores music designed primarily for performance by high school bands. As might be expected, determining the technical competence of the high school band was somewhat complicated. Attainment of this factor was accomplished by: (1) specifying what criteria relating to musical difficulty or grading could be measured; and (2) studying the scores and individual parts of musical compositions which the respondents to the survey reported their bands as being able to play, as well as music reported by publishers as having sold successfully. The problems of musical performance were classified into groups or areas that were thought to be those over which the arranger has a certain degree of control. They were: compass (pitch), dynamics (loudness), and rhythm (duration). Music was divided into three grades of difficulty, A, B, and C in order that the technical limitations of each could be specifically analyzed.

Rhythmic complexity was scaled into types of rhythm patterns as follows: *Type I*—note values and rests of one or more beats in length; *Type II*—divisions of the beat into two equal parts, simple time; *Type III*—divisions of the beat into three equal parts, compound time; *Type IV*—syncopation, by tying a weak beat or weak part of a divided beat into the next strong beat or strong part of a divided beat; *Type V*—subdivision of a beat into four parts; *Type VI*—subdivision of the beat into six parts; *Type VII*—syncopation within the subdivided beat; *Type VIII*—superimposed background, the compound division of the beat in simple time, or the simple division of the beat in compound time; *Type IX*—superimposed meter, the superimposing of an entire measure of one meter on one of another meter; and, *Type X*—subdivision of the beat into five, seven, eight, or more parts.

Dalby then made the following recommendations to the arranger of band music with regard to rhythmic patterns used in each of the three grades of music: *Grade A*—patterns *I* through *X; Grade B*—patterns *I* through *VIII*, and *X;* and *Grade C*—patterns *I* through *V*, and *VIII*. The band director should be able to apply these recommendations to the rhythmic criterion in his selection of music for his library.

Harmonic Quality. Because of evolution in practices and codification, harmonic usage has changed from period to period in music history. Combinations of sound which had an acceptance during one era were found to be out of favor with the advent of new rules or practices of a succeeding era. New harmonic structures and progressions that were considered highly dissonant or harsh and difficult to comprehend at first, gradually became accepted as sounding quite normal. The process was usually due to general usage on the part of composers and growing familiarity for the performers and audience.

Selecting music in which the harmonic treatment is varied will help to achieve and maintain player and audience interest. This should also provide contrast and freshness within a particular composition as well as among the various works in the library. There are numerous examples of band music, especially those classified as "easy" grade level, in which the harmonic structure is limited to the same few fundamental chords, thereby giving them a striking, but boring, similarity.[12] What is perhaps worse is the composition with an harmonic structure totally unrelated to its style and idiom. The band director must be aware of any mixture of harmonic style in one piece of music, such as the use of romantic and contemporary idioms in the same work. One may say then, that for the harmonic treatment of a given composition to be regarded as "good," "excellent," etc., it must at least be consistent and suitable with the style and idiom employed by the composer.[14]

Some directors show a reluctance to select certain contemporary band works because they consider the harmonies to be a bit too dissonant or *avante-garde* for their students to assimilate or comprehend and perform capably. With sufficient time and effective teaching methods, the students should be able to grow into these new harmonies.

Textural Quality. Textural quality is involved with such other factors as contrast and variety of classifications in the repertoire, a wide range of types and styles of music from all periods of musical history, and providing for the musical development of the students. These factors are all interrelated. Some works are transparent in the polyphonic manner of the Baroque; there are those exemplifying the clarity, balance, and objectiveness within the homophonic style of Classicism; others are the thick, lush, warm, lyrical, super-expressive, and subjective type of Romanticism. The 20th century is an amalgamation of past and present forms, compositional techniques, musical idioms, textures, and timbres, but with contemporary sounds and modes of expression. Therefore, careful regard for varying textural quality in compositions will help in the selection of a wide range in types and styles of music from different periods of musical history.

Providing for the musical development of the students via textural quality is accomplished in many ways. The most obvious one is that mentioned above, an exposure to a chronologically extensive repertoire. One of the most constant criticisms of today's band music is that too much of it is mainly a *soli* (sections) and *tutti* (entire ensemble) sound. While the band *tutti* can be full, deep, rich, sonorous, and at times glorious, it would be a breach of programming techniques to feature this texture exclusively. If nothing else, it tends to produce monotony for the performer and audience. Music for the very young and training bands could be an exception in this case.[18, 23]

There are an adequate number of compositions in which the composers have exploited the profuse, distinctive single colors of the band to afford the band director a selection of works with a light, thin, transparent texture. This is not only to enable the players to hear themselves, but also for the audience to distinguish more clearly the diverse timbres of the instruments in the band. The latter point is perhaps the most important step in the process of developing self-confidence and musical maturity on the part of the players. For example, how better to develop individuality and self-initiative than through a work which utilizes polyphonic texture or contrapuntal style exclusively? The achievement of confidence in the players, both in solo and exposed sectional passages, will allow a greater flexibility in the selection of music for the library by the band director.

Instrumentation and Scoring

Instrumentation means not only the presence in the band of the instruments indicated on the score, but their balance and distribution as well. The director must consider the number of players in his full band instrumentation that would play each part of the score because the potential effectiveness of a work is partially based on the probable projection of the individual parts. Therefore, the director should see to it that all parts in the music are "covered" by his instrumentation. Often, such matters are not in the director's control, in which case he would be wise to choose repertoire accordingly. The resourceful director will select music which exploits the full potentialities of his band and subordinates its weaknesses. A case in point would be to avoid a composition if it contains important or solo passages for instruments not included in the band's instrumentation, or if the instruments are present but the players lack the necessary experience to perform the parts efficiently.[11]

For very young bands simpler music requires less individuality in the separate parts and less dependence of each part to the other. Doubling is both necessary and helpful for inexperienced players; it gives them musical confidence and boosts their morale. Naturally, the same need not be true for advanced players.[6]

Scoring. Several years ago, Richard Franko Goldman wrote that ". . . in band music the instruments are not chosen for their appropriateness to the music, but that the music must be adapted to fit the instruments."[4] Regardless of whether or not this remains true today, it appears that until recently band music had a characteristic feature which seemed to limit the sort of musical idea composers conceived for it. These limitations possibly may have been due to the large groupings of woodwinds, brasses, and percussion and the diversity in types of instruments within these groups. One contemporary composer remarked to this writer that prior to writing his first work for band, he studied the layout of instrumentation on the score page and felt utterly baffled as to what he was going to do with so many instruments! He had not even considered the probable number of performers who might be playing each part.

Much band music has been reared in a traditional atmosphere of scores that are heavily doubled, completely cross-cued, and continuously full sounding. Bilik feels that it is no wonder then that students are generally fearful of solo and exposed passages.[20] Even many solo passages are over-scored in the accompaniment, probably to bolster the security of the soloist. The tendency, however, is to negate the sense of personal responsibility which the performer should assume. Many band directors have practiced the art of "re-balancing" passages (especially in transcribed or arranged music) by deleting certain instruments in cross-cued melodies, or overly-doubled melodies and accompaniments. It becomes the obligation of the band director to choose music for his library which contains an adequate amount of contrast in scoring procedures to allow different solo instruments and sections to be heard. Regarding sections, the contrast should be not only between woodwind and brass, but also between the high and low register instruments and varying timbres within these sections.[20]

There are directors who need to accustom themselves to more transparent, varying tone colors in band music and select works which offer these effects. Their hesitancy may be due to the fact that lightly-textured music might not particularly enhance the sound of their band which, for a number of reasons, is somewhat insecure in this type of scoring. An attitude of confidence can be taught and established by the director in such a situation mainly through exposure to music scored in a manner which will help instill it.[18]

Most textbooks on the subject of band scoring point out that the most prominent and strongest instruments are located in the middle area of the band's *tessitura.* One of the greatest sins committed in band scoring is that too many composers and arrangers utilize only this thick middle register as well as the middle range of the instruments located in it. This is neglecting the band's complete and colorful range. One should refrain from selecting music which is constantly scored in this manner, except for very young and training bands. All instruments are entitled to melodic recognition at one time or another; it certainly aids the individual to develop the feeling that one is important to the ensemble.[10]

The band has unique problems regarding tonal weight, diverse tone colors, flexibility of part-writing, and shadings of expression.[40] *The effective composer or arranger employs the full tutti sound sparingly and utilizes the band's varied tone colors proportionately more of the time throughout the score.* Edwin F. Goldman was a staunch advocate of the concept of building up a band to a *good* arrangement rather than resort to a cheap, mutilated, and simplified arrangement of the same work on the grounds of expediency. He felt that the latter is the quickest road to a band's musical ruination.[24]

Whatever the style and type music, it is important that the scoring be top-notch. A few factors one may apply to determine the quality of an arrangement are: (1) Is the workmanship in good taste?; (2) Is the arrangement well-balanced, that is, between solo and accompaniment, between sections, and within sections?; (3) Are the exposed passages written so as to be effective in performance?; (4) After listening to the arrangement, is it effective?; and, (5) Is there sufficient interest in all parts to adequately balance the responsibilities of all instruments in the overall arrangement? True, one cannot expect to find complete satisfaction in all these factors, but the more of these that exist in an arrangement, the more suitable it will be to the library.

Key Signatures. Key signatures for both band and orchestra seem to be a matter of practical function and tradition. Sharp keys are considered easier for string instruments, so orchestral music is traditionally based on them. Wind players aspiring for orchestral experience are generally trained to perform in sharp keys. Most band instruments are constructed in flat keys and, therefore, function best in them. Therein appears to lie the justification on the part of composers/arrangers for setting the larger percentage of band music in flat keys. However, there is no reason why an advanced, experienced ensemble cannot be trained to perform in "concert keys" which would place the transposing instruments in easy to moderately difficult sharp keys. Occasionally, especially in the case of woodwinds, it is a matter of teaching the students alternate fingerings. One or two compositions on a concert program which do not contain flat keys throughout the entire work would be a refreshing change in tonality, sonority, and melodic and harmonic color. The fundamental problem is that students are in the habit of playing in flat keys ever since they received the first instruction in band ensemble experience from method books.

Dalby's report recommends that key signatures should be ". . . kept within the experience and capability of high school band musicians. . . ." Therefore, *Class C* music may be restricted to the concert key signatures of from one to five flats, while *Class B* and *A* music may contain one sharp, no sharps or flats, and one to six flats.[22]

Ranges. Students will not come up to or not progress much beyond their level of ability unless stimulated or challenged. Carrying this principle to an extreme could have a reversal effect; if the student is challenged in excess of what he might be reasonably expected to achieve, he could lose his musical poise.[17] To help the student advance, develop, and improve, he should be exposed to the sort of musical confrontation which he can attain with proper instruction and time to meet it or overcome it.

If school band players hope to increase their playing range, then the major portion of music in the band library should not constantly limit individual instruments to a particular *tessitura*. The library should contain enough literature which helps to gradually develop and increase the playing ranges for all instruments while at the same time teaching control. Selection of literature must be made on the basis of the players' technical abilities in relationship to range at the time the choice is made. For instance, range especially affects facility and intonation, and for some instruments a choice of fingerings. Naturally, one expects the selection to change as the range improves. The wider the overall range required in a composition, the greater the variety of timbre and tonal colors available in it. One of the factors contributing to the dull, grey, heaviness which much band music is accused of producing, is that the scoring for the strongest instruments is in their middle, thick registers.

Based on the conclusions in his project, Dalby makes the following recommendations with respect to the written tonal range that may be used for each instrument in the three classes of music. The practical compass is indicated in white notes, the extreme compass in dark notes. (See the following *"Recommended Ranges."*) [22]

RECOMMENDED RANGES

CLASS A   CLASS B   CLASS C

Suitability for a Particular Group

If the music in the library is to aid in furthering the students' musical education, it must be suitable to the particular band for which it is intended. Suitability comes in many forms, a few of which are the students' musical understanding, the students' technical ability, and grade of difficulty assigned to the music itself.[6] There is little musical or educational value for a band to attempt the performance of a composition which does not fulfill these requirements. The unanswered question is whether or not the performance of a composition can be musically rewarding even if it is technically too difficult and yet of good quality. There are band directors who wish to expose their students to good music and will allow them to attempt such performances on that basis.

Students' Technical Level. The band library should include that which *eventually* can be performed well by *all* the players.[7] The late Edwin F. Goldman once recommended that "all selections should lie within the players' capabilities." [24] Although not always possible to find in each and every composition, the director should select music that will challenge the best players without taxing the weaker ones. This requires careful consideration of the band's unique strengths and weaknesses. Perhaps the best approach is to select music that includes a *reasonable* amount of challenge to all players.[2] The director who painstakingly and sensitively analyzes the literature will do much to increase the effectiveness of the program for his students.[7]

There may be one method for determining whether or not a musical composition is technically suitable. When sight-reading a work, if the band is able to perform it from start to finish without any problems whatsoever, it may be considered easy or too easy. If the band stops every few measures because of its inability to continue, then the work may be considered difficult or too difficult. Then there is the music which the band is able to read through with a minimum number of stops or stumbling. This is perhaps the type referred to as that which *eventually* can be performed well by *all* the players in the band.

A rather questionable attitude is for the director to decide that it is much easier to select and perform music below his band's ability level year after year. It would certainly tend to limit the musical improvement and progress of his students as well as possibly curb their enthusiasm toward the program. Then too, the director (especially the novice) might go to the other extreme by setting his standards too high and select music that his students are simply incapable of comprehending, learning, or performing due to technical and musical limitations.[2] A happy medium between these two situations is the ideal solution.

Recent results of new techniques and experimentation with learning theories have indicated that children are capable of assimilating and retaining abstract knowledge at an earlier age level than ever thought possible years ago. These findings have transcended into the field of music education. While there is a limit to which adolescent students are able to handle music of profound abstractness, their maturity should be challenged in the same manner as their technical abilities.[6] Although most adolescents prefer light, entertainment-type music, the director will help foster discrimination, appreciation, and gratification on the part of his students by choosing music that is stimulating and challenging in a variety of ways.[10]

Grade of Difficulty. Most band directors rely on some form of grading system for band literature in making their selections. Several factors on which grading is usually based include: the degree of complexity in each of the musical elements; digital requirements; range of individual parts; key and meter signatures and their frequency of change; relative exposure of sections; instrumentation; and form. Wareham's study regarding the matter of grading in band literature revealed the following situation: (1) graded lists from various states indicate a confused situation as they vary in the number of grades used and the means of marking the grades; (2) the principal reason for the variety of grade levels appeared to be the result of contest organization; (3) a survey of 26 band music publishing companies also indicated confusion especially in the number of grades of difficulty assigned while some companies ignored the idea of subjective grading; and (4) while N.I.M.A.C. (National Interscholastic Music Activities Commission) assigned grades to music, it was with the understanding that the grades listed should be regarded as no more than a guide based on the opinions of the committees who were responsible for the preparation of the lists.[42]

There is much good music that cannot always be measured in terms of technical requirements or musical complexities. In a composition of a slow, sustained nature, interpretation, tone, intonation, and phrasing can be major problems. Players and audience will appreciate a good performance of a fine work in which the texture is lighter, thinner, and the level of difficulty easier, but which demands control of tone, phrasing, and the subtleties of expression rather than a slipshod, laborious, stilted performance of a work that is beyond the players' abilities.[12] Along with these factors, consideration of available rehearsal time in relation to difficulty of a composition must be given serious thought in order to allow proper preparation for public performance.

There are many band directors who do not agree with the practice of grading music into various levels of difficulty; they feel that there is entirely too much fuss made over the grade level system and that no valid basis for making such judgment exists. As substantiation for their view, they point to the lack of agreement in grade assignments of the same compositions between state instrumental associations.[42] For them, quality of music, quality of performance, what the music can do for the students, and the lasting effect of the music on the students' attitude toward music in general is much more vital.[25]

Fundamentally, grade levels were designed to afford directors with some general idea of the comparative rating of difficulty among band compositions. While all will agree that it is an educational necessity, a grade level assigned to a work will not testify to its quality, which, in the final analysis, deserves primary consideration.

Age Appeal. Some of the music in the band library should have age appeal, that is, it must be selected with the players' ages and general interests in mind. Not only should it appeal to them, but also possibly provide some worthwhile musical experiences. Since most of the bands in this country are made up of adolescent musicians, pleasing them is one minor factor in selecting music.

While this style or type of music may not be at quite the artistic level the director prefers, there is no reason why it should not be musically substantial and sincere.

Length and Endurance

Length in music is closely related to attention span, mental fatigue, physical endurance (especially the embouchure), time involved in learning a piece of music for performance, and the musical attractiveness of the work in maintaining student interest over a long period of time. The older, experienced, and more advanced players should be capable of performing music in large form (symphony, suite, concerto). All things being equal, the longer the work, the more time it will take to learn it. If the music is of high quality, there need be no concern about loss of student interest during a lengthy rehearsal time period in learning the music.[6]

The directors who champion the cause of the band's acceptance as a serious medium of musical expression believe that the band repertoire needs more compositions in extended form. At present, the repertoire contains a multitude of brief compositions of four to five minutes in time. Many years ago, the traditional band concert was made up of a series of short works. This sufficed when the repertoire lacked compositions of length and substance. While music in short form may be excellent and worthwhile, brevity in a composition will not likely allow development of thematic ideas; musical maturity is difficult to build on a diet of fragmentary, partially-developed musical thoughts.

Likewise, short forms do not always lend themselves very well in demonstrating the various colors available in the band's instrumentation; the best one can hope for is a continuous stream of blends of sounds.[19] Short forms might be suitable for outdoor or light entertainment type concerts, in which appeal to the audience's musical sensitivity is not an essential factor. The eminent composer Roy Harris thinks that band compositions *should* be short and concise. It is his opinion that the band produces such a continuous brilliant shading of colors and powerful intensities of sound that it causes a desire for a shortening in length of music on the part of the audience.[41]

Endurance is related to the age and playing experience of the players as well as the physical limitations imposed by a wind instrument. Younger, less experienced players lack the physical stamina (constant wind pressure, breath support, embouchure control), in addition to a shorter attention span to study and perform works of lengthier form such as the symphony or suite. So, it becomes a matter of a building-up process throughout each stage of musical, educational, and physical development of the student from short to extended form compositions.

Coda

What the band director thinks is right, best, important, or even expedient is what should be included in his library. He must trust his own judgment, taste, the objectives set for his program, and his feeling for and knowledge of his students. Selectivity should broaden as he gains experience in learning, rehearsing, and performing band music. The choice made by the director must vary from that of his colleagues according to his personal needs and the interpretation of the criteria and factors recommended here.

It is a propitious time for the band director to examine his entire concept and approach in the selection of a concert repertoire. This may present a rather perplexing problem because the school band is a multi-purpose organization with a variety of functions and, therefore, various publics. Consequently, the "band" is interpreted in different ways by these different publics, so the ". . . band director must walk a tight rope among several possibilities."[8] It is obvious, then, that the band operates in two broad areas, namely, education and entertainment, or service. It seems unlikely that one may ignore either of these because on the one hand the band must depend on maintaining public interest, and on the other it must have a basis for its justification in the school curriculum. The band's library should reflect the fact that it serves both these areas equally through a balance of types of musical compositions by which it will gain the support of its student members, the school, and the community.[11]

A balance of composition in the band's library connotes a

variety in types, styles, and forms from as many historical periods as possible; in addition, there should be a variety of technical demands, timbres, and ensemble responsibilities. Today, the band director can make his selections from several general classifications (as will be described later).

Several studies have been undertaken in an attempt to analyze the type and quality of literature performed by school concert bands; they are almost entirely limited to surveys within a single state. At this writing, an exhaustive national survey and evaluation of the subject has not been made. Most of the studies were based on a comparative analysis of compositions listed on concert programs. The general impression seems to be that, while school concert band programs include a modicum of original, serious band literature, the majority of the works performed are "unknown" overtures, marches, and "programmatic" or "entertainment" music (show tunes, novelty numbers, and popular music).[36] The recommendation is that what is needed is more serious music that is interesting and challenging, yet playable by school bands. At one time serious music was considered the domain of the symphony orchestra and the band was accused of practicing pretense in performing it.[26] This situation is no longer valid.

Regardless of the type and technical level, *quality* in music is a vitally important factor. To study and perform band music of low quality is committing an injustice to students and audience alike.[9] Each of the musical elements in the composition must have intrinsic merit and value to be considered worthy of a place in the library. It is also helpful to one's evaluation of a particular work if it is significant enough to have received many nation-wide performances. Another evaluative factor is the composer's relative reputation based on the recognition of his contributions to the concert band as well as other musical media.[41]

In many localities the concert band (usually high school) is the only instrumental musical and cultural contact available in such cases. The artistically sincere band director should want the concert band to be regarded and accepted as a satisfying sound medium of musical expression. To this end he must select and program a repertoire of such calibre and quality not only for the educational and musical benefits of his students, but to attract and hold an attentive and perceptive audience as well.

Some time ago, Van Bodegraven and Wilson wrote that ". . . all music used in the public schools should: (1) Fit the ability of each section of the ensemble; (2) Hold the interest of the members of the ensemble; (3) Be conducive to finer technical and musical performance; and (4) Be educational as well as entertaining." [42]

Fluery designed the Music Classification Form which follows as an objective method for measuring group instrumental music. [37]

MUSIC CLASSIFICATION FORM

Procedure: Examine the musical selection carefully and note each item that you find listed on the form below. The scoring range is from 1 to 5 on each item, with 5 being the high value. The descriptive statements are to be valued as a guide rather than a limiting qualification.

Name of Selection: _____

Criteria	1	2	3	4	5
A. *Range*					
1. Minimum vocal range—one octave					
2. Vocal range—one octave plus					
3. Full vocal range—1½ octaves					
4. Instrumental range—not extreme					
5. Extended instrumental range					
B. *Rhythms*					
1. 𝅝 𝅗𝅥 𝅘𝅥 exclusively					
2. 𝅗𝅥. and 𝅘𝅥 simple syncopation					
3. Alternation of rhythms and contrary rhythms					
4. (rhythm notation example)					
5. Variety of difficult rhythm patterns					
C. *Meter*					
1. Simple duple or triple rhythm, with simple change					

   2. 6/8 time or 9/8 time

   3. Involving change

   4. Compound and less common meters

   5. Change, alternation, accented change

D. *Harmony*
   1. Melodic and consonant, basic chords

   2. Consonant, harmonic, secondary chords

   3. Modulations, color tones added
       melodically

   4. Dissonance added, chromaticism

   5. Dissonant, atonal, contrapuntal

E. *Articulations and Dynamics*
   1. Normal, slur, tie, "f", "p", short phrases

   2. Accent, legato, staccato, crescendo,
       decrescendo

   3. Sustained accent, sforzando

   4. Legato-staccato, "fp", crescendo,
       long phrases

   5. Difficult phrasing, frequent change in
       dynamics and articulations

F. *Scales (Keys)*
   1. F, B♭, E♭

   2. C, A♭, more than two keys

   3. D, A, easy minors, 3 or more keys

   4. E, D♭, G♭, more difficult minors

   5. B, F♯, C♯, C♭, atonal

G. *Tempo*
   1. Slow tempi with few ♪

   2. Slow ♪

   3. Moderate with ♪ and ♪

   4. Moderate fast with figurations

5. Awkward figurations at moderate to
    fast; vivace

H. *Orchestration*
    1. Minimum instrumentation required

    2. Full instrumentation, tutti, cued

    3. Full instrumentation, few alternate cues

    4. Isolation of solo instruments

    5. Complete instrumentation, open
        voicings, color instruments

Total Score: _____

Additional Factors to Be Considered:

1. Suites, collections of numbers: evaluate each part or separate piece and arrive at an average which recognizes the most difficult parts and fatigue factor.
2. Length of composition: consider the fatigue factor and evaluate under phrasing. The longer the selection the more difficult to prepare and perform.
3. Selections with solo passages: evaluate the difficulty of the solo passage as a separate selection and decide upon a compromise which recognizes the difficulty.
4. Unusual effects: note them and evaluate them under appropriate headings.

Scoring:

Class E (Grade I) . . . . 8 to 14 points
Class D (Grade II) . . . . 15 to 20 points
Class C (Grade III) . . . . 21 to 26 points
Class B (Grade IV) . . . . 27 to 32 points
Class A (Grade V) . . . . 33 to 40 points
Class AA (Grade VI) . . . . 33 to 40 points

Selected References

Books

1. Bessom, Malcolm E. *Supervising the School Music Program,* West Nyack, New York: Parker Publishing Company, Inc., 1969.
2. Duvall, W. Clyde. *The High School Band Director's Handbook,*

Englewood Cliffs, New Jersey: Prentice-Hall, Inc., 1960.
3. Fennell, Frederick. *Time and the Winds*, Kenosha, Wisconsin: G. Leblanc Corporation, 1954.
4. Goldman, Richard Franko. *The Concert Band*, New York: Rinehart and Company, 1946.
5. Goldman, Richard Franko. *The Wind Band (Its Literature and Technique)*, Boston: Allyn and Bacon, Inc., 1961.
6. Hoffer, Charles R. *Teaching Music in the Secondary Schools*, Belmont, California: Wadsworth Publishing Company, Inc., 1964.
7. House, Robert W. *Instrumental Music for Today's Schools*, Englewood Cliffs, New Jersey: Prentice-Hall, Inc., 1965.
8. Leonhard, Charles and Robert W. House. *Foundations and Principles of Music Education*, New York: McGraw-Hill, 1959.
9. Music Educators National Conference. *Perspectives in Music Education* (Source Book III) (Bonnie C. Kowall, editor), Washington, D.C.: M.E.N.C., 1966.
10. Norman, Theodore. *Instrumental Music in the Public Schools*, Philadelphia: Ditson, 1941.
11. Righter, Charles Boardman. *Success in Teaching School Orchestras and Bands*, Minneapolis: Schmitt, Hall and McCreary Company, 1945.

Monographs

12. Bachman, Harold B. *Program Building*, Chicago: Frederick Charles, Inc., 1962.
13. Hartshorn, William C. *The Study of Music as an Academic Discipline*, Washington, D.C., M.E.N.C., 1963.
14. Neilson, James. *What Is Quality in Music?*, Kenosha, Wisconsin: G. Leblanc Corporation (no date).

Periodicals

15. Akers, Howard E. "The March Is Music Also," *The School Musician*, Vol. 35, No. 1, Aug.–Sept., 1963.
16. Akers, Howard E. "What Is Good Music?," *The School Musician*, Vol. 37, No. 7, March, 1966.
17. Beeler, Walter. "Know Your Band Arrangements," *The Instrumentalist*, Vol. VIII, No. 2, Oct., 1953.
18. Beeler, Walter. "More Band Color," *The Instrumentalist*, Vol. XIX, No. 1, Aug., 1964.
19. Beeler, Walter. "The Next Twenty Years," *The School Musician*, Aug.–Sept., 1968.

20. Bilik, Jerry H. "A Missing Ingredient in Music Education," *The School Musician*, Vol., 35, No. 8, April, 1964.
21. Butler, John H. "Concert Band: Real Hope for New Music," *Music Journal*, Vol. XXVII, No. 7, Sept., 1969.
22. Dalby, J. Philip. "The Arranger and the High School Band," *Journal of Band Research*, Vol. IV, No. 1, Autumn, 1967.
23. Effinger, Cecil. "A New Look at the Concert Band," *Music Journal*, Jan.–Feb., 1950.
24. Goldman, Edwin F. "The Function of the Band," *Etude*, Nov., 1952.
25. Hullfish, William and Jack Allen. "Let's Teach Music Appreciation in Band," *The School Musician*, Vol. 36, No. 9, May, 1965.
26. Johnson, William and Donald McGinnis, Gilbert Mitchell, and Charles Payne. "From the Four Winds: A Symposium on Audience Reaction to Contemporary Band Music," *Journal of Band Research*, Vol. I, No. 1, Autumn, 1964.
27. Mathie, Gordon. "Wind Ensemble or Band?" *The Instrumentalist*, Vol. XXI, No. 5, Dec., 1966.
28. Neilson, James. "The Aesthetics of Programming," *Journal of Band Research*, Vol. I, No. 1, Autumn, 1964.
29. Satz, Ralph. "Actions Speak Louder Than . . ." *Music Journal*, Jan.–Feb., 1949.
30. Thompson, E.D. "Is It Good Music?" *The Instrumentalist*, Vol. XX, No. 5, Dec., 1965.
31. Whitcomb, Manley R. "The College Band of the Future," *Music Journal*, Vol. XXV, No. 7, Sept., 1967.
32. Whitwell, David. "The Contemporary Band: In Quest of an Historic Concept of Aesthetics," *The Instrumentalist*, Vol. XXIII, No. 9, April, 1969, Vol. XXIII, No. 10, May, 1969.
33. Whitwell, David. "Three Crises in Band Repertoire," *The Instrumentalist*, Vol. XIX, No. 8, March, 1965.
34. Wagner, Joseph. "Dilemma of Concert Band Programs," *Music Journal*, Vol. XXVII, No. 1, Jan., 1969.

Unpublished Literature

35. Cecil, Herbert M. *Fundamental Principles of the Organization, Management, and Teaching of the School Band*, unpublished dissertation, University of Rochester, 1953.
36. Fjeld, Marvin Wendell. *A Survey and Evaluation of Music Performed in Public Concert by Indiana High School Bands*, unpublished dissertation, Indiana University, 1959.

37. Fleury, Robert Myrl. *Objective Measurement of Group Instrumental Music,* unpublished dissertation, University of California, Los Angeles, 1963.
38. Lang, Philip J. "Band Repertoire," A Report for the College Band Directors National Association, National Conference Proceedings, Dec., 1960.
39. Pugh, Russell Oris. *The Band Compositions of the Contemporary Music Project for Creativity in Music Education,* unpublished dissertation, University of Arkansas, 1966.
40. Shaughnessy, Robert M. *Harmonic and Contrapuntal Elements in Selected School Concert Band Compositions,* unpublished dissertation, Boston University, 1963.
41. Tarwater, William H. *Analyses of Seven Major Band Compositions of the Twentieth Century,* unpublished dissertation, George Peabody College for Teachers, 1958.
42. Wareham, Duana Emerson. *The Development and Evaluation of Objective Criteria for Grading Band Music into Six Levels of Difficulty,* unpublished dissertation, The Pennsylvania State University, 1967.

3

Six Criteria in Selecting
Music for Marching Bands

THE PURPOSE OF THE MARCHING BAND

There are band directors who feel that it is possible for the marching band to provide both entertaining and cultural experiences to the players and audience. This is accomplished through a very careful selection of "quality" literature, development of sound ideas for field and street presentations, and a high standard in the execution of performances.[22] The combination of the visual with the audio should provide a stimulus for people to listen to music they ordinarily do not listen to at home.[9] Then there are band directors who caution us to be more realistic and admit that players and audience may gain very few, if any, cultural experiences from marching band performances, but they may possibly glean some educational ones. These persons do not discourage any band director from attempting to provide cultural experiences via the marching band, however, they strongly suggest that the main purpose of the marching band is "to entertain, not to elevate."[8] Even the venerable John Philip Sousa has been quoted as admitting that when he programmed selections by Beethoven, Wagner, Tschaikowsky, and other similar composers, his primary objective was to entertain his audience.

Perhaps the key to the problem is not a matter of justification but that the marching band should fulfill its place in the educational curriculum, as it is interrelated with its purpose and function in the school and community. One avenue to arriving at this goal has been previously recommended: to guide the student's development of discrimination and value judgments at his emotional, physical, and intellectual level of maturation. To do this, the band director must provide an atmosphere in which the motivation level is high.

FUNCTION OF THE MARCHING BAND

When most band directors think of the marching band, thoughts of pre-game and half-time activities in connection with football games enter their minds. Due to the flexible function of the total instrumental music program, the marching band may be more than this. Some factors which determine this are: the size of the community; the population of the school; the scope and variety of the curriculum; the diversity of extra-curricular activities in the school; the overall structure of the educational system in the community (number of schools, types of music programs); and the extent of any responsibilities the marching band has to its community.

The band has a functional heritage of outdoor activities, mainly military and ceremonial. With the advent of the school band movement, the major function of the marching band was the parade. Not until the increase in popularity of interscholastic sports was the marching band valued more for contributing to the "spirit" of these events than as a musical medium. Today, the principles and techniques of marching band performances at football games has evolved far beyond that of the 1930s, '40s and '50s. Likewise, the audience has become accustomed to the colorful and spectacular pageantry of the band's performances and go to see and hear them as much as they do the game itself. Not all band directors are pleased with the present-day style of some marching bands; they claim that the emphasis is on "flashy" movement rather than good, quality *musical* performances. As evidence, they describe marching bands as "gyrating, twisting, pulsating," prancing, and dancing, all at super-fast cadences but to the detriment of the music and sound.[14]

Hindsley is one of the strongest advocates for a more "rational and conservative perspective" of the marching band. He contends that the band is primarily a musical organization which marches and not a marching organization which happens to play music occasionally. The fact that a band marches merely testifies to its mobility as a musical medium. It is the responsibility of the band director to "develop in the band the best elements of both music and marching." [27]

One of the most unique innovations in the contemporary marching band has been the acceleration of tempo and a style of performance which is closely related to a stage show or night club.[18] One director of a very well-known midwestern university marching band points out that the audience listens with its *eyes* and not its ears. Another reminds us that regardless of any educational values accrued from marching band performances, when it performs in public, it is involved in *show business* and must design the sort of field presentations that appeal to the "interest and imagination of the audience for which it was intended." [15]

An all-encompassing picture of the functions of a marching band could include: school parades (homecoming, band festivals), local parades (civic, state, or national holidays and possibly political rallies), athletic events (football, basketball, soccer, and possibly baseball), marching band contests, and outdoor concerts (for local celebrations, county or state fairs). The degree of responsibility of the school marching band to these events varies from locale to locale. For example, some schools have extremely limited athletic programs and some schools restrict the appearance of their bands in community or non-school activities.

Fortunately, or unfortunately as the case may be, a considerable amount of public opinion about one's instrumental music program is based on the marching band's performances at outdoor activities and events. The strength of this opinion is founded on the total number of persons who view the marching band during one season of outdoor activities compared with the total number attending formal concerts and indoor events.[5] Entertainment and public relations values cannot be discounted, but these should be considered as "secondary by-products of its primary objectives," that of development of sound musicianship, discrimination and judgments "in dealing with music." [22] Since the marching band must march as well as play music, the liability for achieving an equitable relationship and balance between the two rests on the band director's shoulders. As long as the band must march, there is no reason why it cannot "march with precision and style," and since the band plays music, it should "play with artistry and good tone." [14]

As in the case of many other facets of the instrumental music program, band directors will probably continue to disagree on the musical and educational importance of marching band appearances, and will *do their own thing*, to use a popular contemporary phrase. The style and type of marching band developed by any one particular director is directly related to his concepts regarding its function. There is no reason why the marching band should not adhere to the same ideals and aspirations concerning musical performance as the concert band, but within the framework of the type of activities in which it engages and ultimately determines the choice of music. [21]

THE SIX CRITERIA

Musical Criteria

Within the broader classification of musical criteria, there are several essential criteria; they are fundamentally the same as those discussed in Chapter 2, namely, melody, harmony, rhythm (including meter and tempo), with the addition of counter-melody. The degree of quality expected in these criteria should be the same for marching band literature as that for the concert band. One major difference in the character of the literature for these two media might be less variety, contrast, and complexity as they apply to each of the criteria. Also, these criteria are perhaps more stylistically related in music for the marching than for the concert band. It is the basic nature of these two musical media which helps bring these conditions about. [2, 9]

If memorization of music is practiced by a band, the band director to whom it applies should constantly bear in mind that it decidedly affects his selection of music. Marching bands which utilize this technique for the street or field will require features in their music which should aid memorization.[9]

Melody. The melodic line in marching band music should be the strongest and most predominant musical element in the composition. The accompanimental features (harmony, countermelody, figurations, rhythmic figures) should not be so complex that they tend to obscure and detract from it. This is especially true in the case of marching bands whose presentations at football games feature formations of objects or abstract designs and depend on the audiences associating them with the melody for identification.[9] An intricate, highly ornamented melody will be rather difficult to memorize, for this type of performance. Whereas a motivic, fragmented type melodic line may be a desirable feature of some concert band literature, the same is not always true for the marching band, especially if it is to accompany movement or be associated with a formation. Since the marching band is working with a time-space factor, subtlety has little practical value in outdoor music; the musical ideas must "hit home" immediately. Therefore, a melody with an obvious or apparent quality or character is preferred.

Countermelody. The purpose of a well-designed countermelody is to add contrast and interest to a musical score. Its function should be to enhance the melody without interfering with it musically; its role, therefore, is of secondary importance to the melody. The following descriptions may be found in many band arranging books as "standard" procedures for creating a countermelody; they may also serve as desirable features of this criterion in marching band music. First, as its name implies, it is counter to the main melody in direction; when the melody moves upward, the countermelody moves downward and vice versa. Second, to achieve contrast in rhythmic activity, the countermelody moves when the melody is static, and vice versa; by "moves" is meant that the countermelody rhythmic patterns are in shorter time values than those of the melody. The third feature is that the countermelody should be scored in an opposite timbre from the melody, or at least for instruments of a different range or *tessitura* than the melody. The best test of a good countermelody is that it should sound "good" or be effective by itself. Actually, it is a second melody but embodying the three features just described. A characteristic weakness usually found in countermelodies created by students in band arranging courses may help focus attention on yet another feature. In their eagerness to design "interesting" countermelodies, students tend to over-score; the countermelody sounds and moves continually without provision for breathing places, musical (cadential points) or physical (for the players)! This causes conflicting rather than mutually interesting lines. If memorization "is your bag," you can realize what this would do to your players' efforts.

Harmony. When we analyze the harmonic structure of scores, we begin to realize the reason for those countless hours spent in developing techniques for correct "part writing" in our collegiate theory classes. We learned that all voices, or parts, should follow the rules of smooth resolution or "leading," and that all active tones must be resolved correctly. Clumsy intervals between notes of the harmonic structure can produce an impression of awkward chord progressions. Proper voice leading will not only provide an interesting harmonic line, but will be of great help to the player who must memorize those inner structural parts.[9] Most arrangers prefer to alter or add chords to the normal progressions found in popular music. Judicious use of this process is recommended; while this may produce a more colorful effect for an indoor performance, it is less so for one outdoors. There are any number of compositions in which chord enhancement is vitally necessary. An occasional alteration of or substitution for the regular chord in a progression can be effective, but a succession of altered or substituted chords tends to minimize the intended impact. Continuous complexity of harmony could provide its own downfall. The opposite extreme, however, would produce dull and boring results.

In summary, look for the following features regarding harmony: (1) the individual voices should be resolved properly; (2) the harmonic structure should be appropriate to the style and type of composition; (3) the inclusion of altered, added, or substitute chords should enhance the effectiveness of the music; (4) the use of "clashing" or dissonant tones within chord structures should be used rather judiciously in order to heighten the intended effect at that place; (5) whether or not the music is to be memorized, the individual lines which sound the harmonic structure should "flow" as smoothly as possible from pitch to pitch; and, (6) since the marching band must contend with the disadvantage of outdoor performance, the harmonic structure should be scored to give the band the fullest, most sonorous sound possible, especially for a small sized band.

Rhythm. Although marching bands play most of their music while in motion, they do perform a certain amount of it while standing or marching in place. The rhythmic criterion must be analyzed with these situations in mind. Generally, the rhythmic patterns for outdoor music need not be nearly as complex as that of indoor concert music, especially in music played to movement. Because the band's sound tends to become quickly diffused outdoors, there is a practical limit to the intricacy of the rhythmic patterns in the music. Distance between the marching individuals, whether on a street or field, is a criticial factor in the precise execution of the music and movements; complicated rhythmic patterns are difficult to coordinate between sections of the band due to this factor. Simplicity is the keyword which should guide the band director in his selection of music to accompany movements. Rythmically the music must be designed to afford the bandsmen adequate opportunity for attention to playing and marching at the same time.[20] Highly complex or excessively syncopated patterns could be a deterrent in this case, but perhaps not so in block band or concert type formations. Popular music is a favorite source of literature for marching band performances. Rhythmically the style of contemporary jazz and popular music is considerably more complex compared to that of former years. Band directors considering usage of this type of music must give careful consideration to the rhythmic factor, especially if the music is planned to be played while the band is in motion. One approach to resolving the answer to this problem is to determine how much experience the players have had to be able to play the music *stylistically* correct.

Rhythm is interdependent with tempo as it concerns music for the marching band. While the present practice of very fast cadences is frowned upon by many band directors throughout the country, an equal number of them condone or approve it. Critics refute this sort of performance on the grounds that it is difficult, or even impossible, to present a worthwhile musical interpretation of a piece of music played at an exceedingly fast tempo, especially one for which it was not originally composed. It is recommended, therefore, that music planned for performances at *tempi* beyond 138 or 140 beats per minute, should contain rhythmic patterns of much simpler structure than music of slower *tempi*. In general, the rhythmic patterns of carefuly selected music should help the band attain drive, spirit, and ensemble precision of execution in the performance.

Level of Difficulty

When the band director selects music for his marching band on the basis of difficulty, he should mentally classify it into two categories: (1) music for use while the band is marching; and (2) music for use while the band remains in place. As a general rule, music to be performed while marching, maneuvering, or accompanying any type movement should be approximately one grade level easier than concert music for the same band. Marching conditions impose certain physical limitations on the players, particularly bodily movement which does not help the player maintain normal tone control or visual focus for reading the music. There is no practical value in having a band play music on the march that would be taxing on a concert stage.[9] Since the physical limitations are removed when the band is motionless on the field, it then should be able to perform music of the same level of difficulty as concert literature.

Because easier music is less difficult to play, it allows the band to sound better. The players are able to execute the various elements of the composition with much more ease, thereby achieving more overall sonority in the band's total effect. Critics who decry this approach claim that it gives the audience the wrong impression of the band's true performing ability.

To determine whether or not the music is suitable for his band, the director must consider his players' capabilities. Since marching band performances are prepared over a much shorter period of time than concerts, the director is unable to rely on the possibility that his players will be able to learn and *eventually* play music that is beyond their technical level. The players should be able to overcome the technical demands inherent in the music far enough in advance so that they can fully concentrate on polishing the non-musical aspects of the performance (maneuvers, drills, alignment, etc.).

The available amount of rehearsal time is related to both level of difficulty and proficiency of the players. A band director may include a particular piece of music that he knows is slightly out of technical reach of his players simply because he desires to have it performed; however, due to lack of sufficient rehearsal time, the band gives the particular piece a sloppy, insecure rendition. It does his band little good in terms of audience response and reaction, and his players' *espirit de corps* regarding a sense of accomplishment.

The final feature to be considered within this criterion is the playing range required by the music. Compared to indoor concert music, a conservative playing range is generally recommended, especially for music to be performed to movement.[20] As outdoor performance demands more projection of tone in order to carry it to the audience, the music should emphasize the *tessitura* of the range which will allow this to happen. Music scored in the extremes of the playing range usually cause problems of tone control, intonation, blend, and balance for school bands. A richer sonority in the band's overall tone should fundamentally result from music scored in comfortable playing ranges. This applies to music performed while the band is marching. For music to be played standing in place, the director should feel free to select music with ranges an interval or two above and below his players' normal levels.

Instrumentation

The problem of instrumentation in marching band music is perhaps not quite as critical as for the concert band; there is a bit more leeway regarding the presence or lack of certain instruments in the band's instrumentation. The saving factor in this matter is that the composer/arranger, when scoring for marching band, is usually more concerned with portraying each of the musical elements as strongly and solidly as possible. He, therefore, resorts to more doubling of sections on each element and worries less about variety of timbre.

To attain a balance in all parts of the score during the band's performance, a major consideration regarding instrumentation is the relative numerical strength within each section of the marching band. This is quite important concerning the brass section since most marching band arrangements are weighted in its favor. The band director must study the individual scores carefully and partially base his selection on the music's adaptability to his in-instrumentation. The comparative musical strength of the individual sections is as vital as their numerical strength. On paper, a section may have an adequate number of players, but musically it falls quite short of one's expectations. The director must, therefore, compensate for this weakness through careful selection of music.

Also, as in the case of the concert band, a marching band may have adequate total numerical strength but lack good balance in representation between sections. For instance, in one marching band season, a band may be short of trombones, or clarinets, or percussion. If the director is unable to substitute or transfer players to correct this condition, then he must plan and select or edit his music accordingly.

Perhaps a director feels he has satisfactory musical and numerical strength, and balance in all sections of his marching band, then he must consider the overall size of his band in relationship to the type of arrangement available. Publishers have attempted to assist the band director by publishing arrangements that are suitable for small, moderate, or large bands. Through clever and imaginative scoring techniques, an arranger can help a small band sound full and solid; a moderately sized band sound rich and sonorous; and a large band make use of its varied instrumentation by exploiting its timbres. A more detailed discussion of this factor follows in the criterion, *"Scoring."*

Some band directors are fortunate enough to have control over their instrumentation. Differences between theirs and other bands (in the same situation) are based on individual beliefs concerning the function, purpose, and style of marching band they wish to produce. Bands that stress military or precision drills in their presentation can function with a "standard" marching band instrumentation. Those which feature concert music, Broadway musicals, or "production" numbers might need more varied wood-wind and percussion sections. A growing number of bands prefer a "stage band" style sound on the field and, therefore, require larger saxophone, trumpet, and trombone sections, the proper percussion equipment, and less variety in the other woodwind and brass sections. In each of these instances, the respective directors must select music accordingly.

Scoring

Since about 1950, several new techniques and approaches to scoring for the school marching band have become popular. Each of these methods is designed for: (1) a particular type and style of marching band; (2) a specific type of event for which the music is intended; (3) various sized bands and instrumentations; and, (4) a unique type of marching band sound. When considering music for his marching band, the director must carefully analyze the manner of scoring involved against the background of these factors.

The arranger should demonstrate in his score that he is aware of the technical and physical limitations imposed upon the marching bandsmen. The music must be arranged so that the band may produce a sound which has sonority and solidity while it allows the bandsmen to perform their movements as precisely as possible.[2, 9, 20] Arrangements that are designed to meet these conditions should be included in the marching band library. Fortunately, composers and arrangers have realized the growing diversity in styles of marching bands and have created scores which could meet the individual requirements of most bands.

The arrangement must not only be suitable to the outdoor idiom, but also make use of the full tonal possibilities inherent in the marching band.[27] The scope in variety of timbres within the marching band instrumentation is not as extensive as the concert band. In scores which require a performance time of from one to two or more minutes, there should be provision for changes of instrumental colors simply to avoid monotony. For the band that features only brief excerpts from compositions, with rapidly changing formations, drills, or patterns, a variety of timbre within one arrangement is not necessary; however, there could be a variety or contrast of colors between arrangements.[9]

Key signatures containing flats are more desirable in marching band music than concert. In music to be performed while marching, melodies and countermelodies should be as diatonic as possible; excessive chromaticism under these conditions is rather impractical. Concert-style arrangements of excerpts from orchestral or original concert band music, "production" numbers of Broadway shows, movie, or T.V. background music, intended to be played in place or semi-concert formation, may include sharp key signatures and chromaticism for contrast in musical effects.

Many current books and articles on the subject of scoring for marching bands recommend the elimination of the practice of assigning to wind instruments the beat-after-beat rhythmic patterns in the accompanimental parts and assign them instead to the bass and percussion sections. This technique frees more instruments to reinforce the harmonic structure and places these patterns in the sections who can best produce them. From a visual aspect, rhythm patterns in music for movement are easier to read when based on the half-note as the basic unit pulse in the meter signature rather than the quarter-note, especially if the arrangement contains many rapid figures.

It might be appropriate to interpolate a description and analysis of the various techniques, methods, and approaches in marching band arranging mentioned at the beginning of this criterion; included are the "5-line," "6-line," and "8-line" scores. Each of these types have two common factors: (1) the emphasis is on the projection of the individual musical elements (melody, countermelody, harmony, and rhythm); and (2) to effectively project these elements rather than individual timbres, the instruments are grouped in the score on the basis of register and function. Since performance takes place outdoors, volume is a primary necessity for carrying the musical ideas to the audience; this is the reason for regrouping the instruments. There is, then, much unison scoring for entire sections in order to produce adequate volume and bring out the elements. The most functional approach in scoring employed in any of these three methods is to regard the brass and percussion sections as the foundation and the woodwinds as reinforcing sections.

Assignment of Parts. The following list recommends the primary and secondary functions as related to the musical elements and register for each of the instruments.

INSTRUMENT	PRIMARY FUNCTION	SECONDARY FUNCTION
Piccolo	Melody 8*va* higher	embellishing figures
Flutes	same as piccolo	
1st Clarinets	Melody 8*va* higher	embellishing figures, harmony
2nd Clarinets	Harmony 8*va* higher	embellishing figures
Alto Saxes	Harmony	melody
Tenor Saxes	Countermelody	harmony, melody
Baritone Sax	Combination of countermelody and bass	
1st Trumpets	Melody	background figures
2nd Trumpets	Harmony	unison melody, background figures
3rd Trumpets	Harmony	unison melody, background figures
Horns	Harmony	countermelody
Trombones	same as tenor saxes	
Baritones	same as tenor saxes	
Basses	Bass line	
Percussion	Rhythm	
Bells	Melody (sounds 8*va* higher)	

Our analyzation continues with examples of several score layouts, followed by descriptive comments of possible results from each type score as well as recommendations for their best usage. All scores, with the probable exception of the *"Concert Score,"* should be in concert key and show actual sounding pitches.

5-LINE SCORE

Line 1: Melody in octaves	Piccolo, Flute, Bells (the upper octave), unison Trumpets (lower octave)
Line 2: Harmony in octaves (one voice)	Clarinets (upper octave) Alto Saxes, Horns (lower octave)
Line 3: Countermelody (unison)	Trombones, Baritones, Tenor Saxes (Baritone Sax)
Line 4: Bass Line	Basses (tubas), Baritone Sax
Line 5: Rhythm	Percussion

This type of scoring is appropriate for small high school bands, small or moderately sized junior high school bands, and bands of very limited or unbalanced instrumentations. The resultant sound effect is too thin for larger bands. Because of the grouping of so many sections to one line, this scoring limits the choice of music, or arrangement, to selections with simple harmonic (triadic) harmony. It tends to keep the instruments in their most playable, comfortable registers and is, therefore, suitable for bands of moderate technical ability.

6-LINE SCORE

Line 1: Melody in octaves	Piccolo, Flute, Bells (the upper octave), 1st Trumpets (lower octave)
Line 2: 1st Harmony part (in octaves)	all Clarinets (upper octave) 2nd Trumpets (lower octave)
Line 3: 2nd Harmony part (one voice)	3rd Trumpets, Alto Saxes, Horns
Line 5: Countermelody (unison)	Trombones, Baritones, Tenor Saxes (Baritone Sax)
Line 5: Bass Line	Basses (tubas), Baritone Sax
Line 6: Rhythm	Percussion

This type of scoring is suitable for moderately sized (50 pieces) high school or junior high school bands, bands with fair instrumentation, or bands with strong brass sections and weak woodwind sections. It is also a good style, or technique, for drill music or animated formations. The added harmony parts and more variety of part assignments results in somewhat more solidity of sound and musical effects, but not a big, "expansive" sound. With additional harmony parts, the director has greater freedom of choice in musical selections than in the 5-line score. Some arrangers insert occasional embellishing figures for piccolo, flute, and clarinet for contrast and interest.

8-LINE SCORE

Line 1: Melody in octaves	Piccolo, Flute, Bells (the upper octave), 1st Trumpets (lower octave)
Line 2: Harmony (unison)	all Clarinets (part derived from 2nd or 3rd Trumpet but written 8*va* higher)
Line 3: 1st Harmony part	2nd Trumpets
Line 4: 2nd Harmony part	3rd Trumpets
Line 5: 3rd Harmony part	Alto Saxes, Horns (may duplicate 2nd and 3rd Trumpets or added chord tone)
Line 6: Countermelody	Trombones, Baritones, Tenor Saxes (Baritone Sax)
Line 7: Bass Line	Basses (tuba), Baritone Sax
Line 8: Rhythm	Percussion

This type of scoring is appropriate for large (64 pieces and larger) bands and bands with balanced instrumentations. It is quite suitable for drill music and animated formations; with some modifications, it may be used for concert music and "special production" numbers. This technique allows a wide range in types of musical selections to be used by the band, including popular and jazz. The layouts for the preceding three types of scores give only the primary functions for all instruments. Naturally, there will be some variations from these assignments as suggested in the table "Assignment of Parts."

CONCERT SCORE

Line 1: Piccolo, Flutes	Figurations, embellishments, or melody 8*va* higher
Line 2: Clarinets	Melody 8*va* higher, figurations, embellishments (two parts or unison)
Line 3: Alto Saxes	Reinforce 2nd and 3rd Trumpets, countermelody with Horns (two parts)
Line 4: Tenor Saxes, Baritone Sax	Countermelody, melody
Line 5: Trumpets	Melody harmonized, rhythmic figures, embellishments (three parts)
Line 6: Horns	Countermelody or reinforce 2nd and 3rd Trumpets (unison or two parts)
Line 7: Trombones	Trumpet parts, 8*va* lower, countermelody, melody (two or three parts)
Line 8: Baritones	Countermelody, melody
Line 9: Basses (tuba)	Bass line
Line 10: Percussion	Rhythmic patterns, melodic line for definite pitch instruments

This type of scoring is suitable for bands of 80 or more pieces with very well balanced instrumentation and good players in all sections. It is appropriate for "special production" numbers and excerpts from concert music (orchestral). The effect tends to be wasted on drill music; it would be better to use the 8-line score

for that purpose. It can be effective in music for animated formations if not too widely spaced. There is more emphasis on individual timbres in this score.

STAGE BAND SCORE

Line 1: Piccolo, Flute, Clarinets	Melody 8*va* higher, embellishing figures (unison or harmonized)
Line 2: all Saxes (alto, tenor, baritone)	Reinforce Trumpets and Trombones, melody harmonized or unison, countermelody
Line 3: Trumpets (three or four parts)	Melody harmonized or unison, rhythmic figures, background
Line 4: Horns (two parts)	Countermelody with Saxes, reinforce 2nd and 3rd Trumpets
Line 5: Trombones (three parts)	Melody unison or harmonized (8*va* below Trumpets), rhythmic figures, countermelody
Line 6: Baritones	Melody 8*va* lower, countermelody with Saxes
Line 7: Basses (tuba)	Bass line
Line 8: Percussion	Rhythm

This type scoring sounds very idiomatic in popular music,
standard jazz tunes, or show tunes. Because of the harmonic
structure, 5-line and 6-line scores do not contain sufficient representation of the musical elements to portray this style of music.
The 8-line score, with division in the saxophone and trombone parts
could be used. The Concert Score tends to sound clumsy in this
type of music. Because of the intricacies involved in contemporary
popular and jazz music, it is recommended that this type of scoring be used when standing in place. For the more contemporary
"pop" tunes, a modification of this score would be appropriate:
(1) trumpets in 2–3 parts; (2) horns doubling alto saxes or
trumpets; (3) trombones in 2 parts; and (4) baritone doubling the
tuba an octave higher. Lines 1 and 2 remain as described.

For more information on the subject of scoring for marching bands, the following books are highly recommended:

Baker, David. *Arranging and Composition for Small Ensembles,* Chicago: Maher Publications.*

Delamont, Gordon. *Modern Arranging Technique,* Delevan, New York: Kendor Music, Inc., 1965.*

Lang, Philip J. *Scoring for the Band,* New York: Mills Music Co., Inc., 1950.

Spohn, Charles L. and Richard W. Heine, *The Marching Band (Comparative Techniques in Movement and Music),* Boston: Allyn and Bacon, 1969.

Wagner, Joseph. *Band Scoring,* New York: McGraw-Hill Book Co., Inc., 1960.

Types of Events

Earlier in this chapter, a description of the "Function of the Marching Band" alluded to the fact that the numerous events in which it may be customarily engaged are far more varied than the usual appearances at football games and an occasional parade. Although the titles or descriptive names of the events differ, they are quite similar in character or nature. For example, a parade, whether for a school function, civic celebration, or national holiday, is still basically a parade.

If we follow the line of thought that the music selected for the marching band is to be appropriate to the occasion for which it is performing, then one might conclude that it is possible to use music of similar style or form for events which are likewise similar. Therefore, street marches will be suitable to all types of parades. With the advent of the fast cadence style marching band, some composers and arrangers have been gearing their marches specifically for this type of band and tempo during recent years. Otherwise, the standard military style march can be used. Variations in types of music for parades include: a popular or "hit" tune arranged for performance on the march, such as Arthur Wilkinson's arrangements of the Beatles' songs for marching

---

* Although the Baker and Delamont books are concerned with scoring for the stage band, jazz combos, studio orchestra, etc., the techniques are adaptable for scoring pop and jazz tunes for the marching band.

bands; music of some historical or patriotic character for civic or state celebrations; and specially arranged music for a national or religious holiday (Thanksgiving, Christmas, New York's Day).

In many respects music to be performed at athletic events has similar characteristics; the medium is well known and will be discussed later. There has been a trend, especially in colleges and universities, to divide the marching band into smaller units, such as "pep" bands or "stage" bands, to provide music at basketball games, and sometimes soccer and baseball games. For these events, past and current popular tunes, standard and current jazz should receive considerably more play.

There are many instances of outdoor concerts performed immediately after a parade. In addition to the music noted above, light concert music and overtures or suites of selections from movie and Broadway musicals (rather than individual pieces) are suitable.

At one time the maneuvers, and to a certain extent the music also, for marching band contests was rigidly regulated; in some areas of the country they remain so. However, many contests now require that only a portion of the band's presentation be devoted to maneuvers accompanied by march music, while the remainder can be the director's choice, usually the type of show presented at football games. For all these events, the director must select the best possible quality music within the limitations of its style; it should be in good taste. Because a piece of music is suitable to an event, it may or may not be good or tasteful music.[18]

For most school marching bands, the greater percentage of their outdoor performances are devoted to the preparation and presentation of "shows" at football games. In fact, for many persons marching band shows and football games are synonymous; to them, a game without a marching band is like a day without sunshine or a fine dinner without wine! Revelli feels that the marching band has turned the football game into something more than an athletic event. There are many gridiron fans who go to be as thrilled by the exciting music, colorful pageantry, and intricate routines as by the game itself.[25]

Basic Types of Shows. The type of show the band presents will greatly influence its director's selection of music: (1) The *marching* show will feature either straightforward military (or

Marine) type drills, or the more recent precision type drill. Standard marches are good for the military type; for precision drills, show tunes or fast-tempo marches (designed for quick cadences) would be more suitable. The main point is that the music must be adaptable to the drill. (2) The pageantry show consists mainly of formations, augmented by props of all sizes and types (mechanized and non-mechanized); it may include some maneuvers. There may or may not be a central theme. One of the colorful aspects of this type of show is that the director can incorporate other non-musical groups into the performance, including mixed choruses, glee clubs, gymnasts, tumblers, school clubs, civic groups, etc. Floats also add to the total effect. Music in this case requires wide variety of styles, types, and forms from marches to folk songs. (3) The formation show usually incorporates letters, words, outlines or designs of objects. To enhance or encourage audience interest, parts or all of the formation moves, or bandsmen execute dance steps. In this type of show, a theme or unifying idea helps solidify the presentation. Many directors who favor this kind of show first select music of a central style, type, or idea (blues, evolution of jazz, a composer, etc.), then build their formations around the music. Show tunes, popular music, and jazz standards are all suitable in this case. (4) The variety or combination show contains some features from all the other three types, including an occasional concert selection. This type probably attracts more attention as it appeals to a wider scope of audience taste; with its greater variation of ideas, it is perhaps more interesting to watch. From the director's point of view, it requires more effort, planning, and careful selection of music.

Miscellany.   The type of show a director decides to design and produce, and ultimately his selection of music, are directly related to outdoor rehearsal facilities available for his band and also the kind of stadium in which it will perform. For a stadium with few and very low bleachers (with open end zones), the band would be wasting its time and effort performing music featuring varied timbres and formations of objects. The steeper the angle or pitch to the stadium seats, the more suitable it is to formations of maneuvers whose complexities depend on a high and expansive view for effectiveness. Stadiums with high rising seats and enclosed end zones tend to contain the band sound and enhance arrangements that feature a variety of dynamics, timbres, and musical effects. A band may have adequate stadium facilities, but little or no outdoor practice area available. If the band must use the streets around the school building or parking lots, it forces the director to design his show based on this situation.

The next criterion is the rehearsal time available to the band. Naturally, no director is going to attempt a show which involves a complexity of ideas, movements, and production on a short allotment of rehearsal time. Finally, the director must consider the musical, chronological, and educational levels of his students. In some bands there is a narrow gap or range between students with regard to these factors. This makes one director's decision far easier than another whose students indicate a wide range and mixture of these levels. For example, a combination of 8th or 9th with 12th grade students in the same band causes musical as well as physical problems, such as whether or not all students are capable of performing music of the same technical level, or if they are physically able to march in the same style and technique. In the final analysis, all of these criteria have a decided bearing on the director's choice of music.

Types of Music

While the nature and function of the marching band create certain limitations on the type of music it may perform, quality is not one of them. It is possible to locate and select literature of a high quality for any manner of activity in which the marching band participates. The range covers a moderately wide variety of types including street marches, concert marches (limited to coronations and assorted ceremonies), old standard "pop" tunes, new "pop" tunes, jazz "classics," folk music (traditional and contemporary), music from musicals, T.V. background music, film music, religious, patriotic, operatic, and concert music.

There are at least two types of music which must be discussed in detail because of differing opinions regarding their inclusion in marching band repertoires. First is the matter of new or current popular music. There are band directors who feel that this type of music is so much a daily part of the student's listening habit that it is needless to include it in marching band performances. Others shun it purely on an economical basis. The greater percentage of these tunes are promoted for the maximum amount of financial return in the minimum period of time. Consequently, their reign of popularity may be short-lived, perhaps a few weeks or less. A director can easily fill his library with one-season material of this type. However, the director must realize that the marching band must cater to a greater variety of musical tastes than the concert band. In the case of football shows, the band's performance will most certainly be enhanced by including music that all persons in the audience will recognize and enjoy hearing.[9] This means that *some* popular literature should be included. It is just as important for the director to develop value judgments regarding popular music in his students as it is for any other type of music.

The second type is concert music, either transcriptions from other media or original concert band literature. Critics of its inclusion at football games state that this type of music is definitely out of place at such an occasion. The mood of the audience, the atmosphere, and the environment do not lend themselves to the performance and reception of serious concert literature. The audience at a football game is there to be entertained, not culturally stimulated. Yet, there is evidence in the case of some bands, especially at the university level, who for years have included one concert selection (albeit brief) at each football game and whose audiences have learned to expect it and enjoy listening to it as much as any other type. These directors feel that if selection of music is based on appealing to many variations in taste, and at the same time exposing students to good quality literature, then serious concert music must be included.

Since the march is the band's own truly original musical art form and main source of literature for marching bands, it deserves special mention. Raymond F. Dvorak, to whom this writer owes a debt of gratitude for guidance in his early years in music, once made the following recommendations regarding the selection of a parade march.

1. One should keep in mind the march's adaptability to the group which will play it.
2. It should be easier to play than a concert march.
3. Melody, countermelody, and rhythm are the three most important elements of a good march.

  4. Good-sounding trombone parts are vital.
  5. Eliminate marches which tend to emphasize the band's weak-nesses.
  6. Marches with long first endings, *Da Capo* or *D'al Segno* signs and long or irregular repeat strains are hazardous to play on the march as they tend to cause confusion.
  7. A good parade march should have no weak strains or phrases.
  8. *Tutti* scoring is not necessary, some variety in instrumental color is desirable.
  9. Avoid marches with long or complicated "break" or "bridge" strains if they are played to accompany another marching group other than the band.
  10. Many favorite and well-known marches are not suitable for parade purpose; study the score carefully to determine its adaptability.[1]

After a survey of over 1,000 band directors from all parts of the country and from all levels of teaching, a list of "100 Most Popular Marches" was compiled and published in the October, 1964 issue of *The Instrumentalist* magazine.

Limited as the range of marching band literature may seem, the director must be certain that his library contains a sufficient amount in *contrast* and *variety* of types.

Entrances and exits should get the band on and off the field as quickly but precisely as possible. The music should be brief in length, spirited in character, and designed to allow the band to make a colorful entrance and quick exit (to borrow an old vaude-ville phrase). Transitional or "link" music must aid the bandsmen to march to their next spots quickly, but it must also be related to the general idea of the show. Music should be selected which allows the band to play in a variety of *tempi;* there is nothing more monotonous or dulling of audience interest than the per-formance by a band of one selection after another all at the same tempo.

Coda

And what of the future? Opinions vary. Band directors might take a cue from recommendations made by R. Stanwood Weeks. Television has created a considerable overexposure of marching band performances for its audiences. Marching bands of the future must create a new image by designing a mixture of types of shows within single performances at football games. He implied that marching bands have become hopelessly stereotyped; redundancy characterized a season of half-time shows.

Finally, Selmer in its periodical, *Bandwagon,* published a symposium in which a group of band directors were asked to offer opinions regarding half-time shows. As Robert B. Vezzetti, one of the respondents, stated, "The marching band is part of America and will be with us as long as football. As with the quality of concert organizations, the value and quality of marching performance will grow and develop into a cultural medium." [17] As for marching bands in general, their statements indicated that band directors are not totally in agreement on the matter of just how critical the role of the marching band is to the goals of music education.

While the marching band is part of a director's responsibilities, he should, to the best of his ability, maintain a high standard of musicianship and field or street performances all supported by good music. Rather than fret or worry about the marching band, one should be concerned with refining it and be constantly alert for new and fresh ideas. [4]

Selected References

Books

1. Dvorak, Raymond Francis. *The Band on Parade,* New York: Carl Fischer, 1937.
2. Foster, William P. *Band Pageantry,* Winona, Minnesota: Hal Leonard Music, Inc., 1968.
3. Hjelmervick, Kenneth and Richard Berg. *Marching Bands: How to Organize and Develop Them,* New York: The Ronald Press Co., 1953.
4. House, Robert W. *Instrumental Music for Today's School,* Englewood Cliffs, New Jersey: Prentice-Hall, Inc., 1965.
5. Jones, Archie (editor). *Music Education in Action,* Boston: Allyn and Bacon, 1960.
6. Lee, Jack. *Modern Marching Band Techniques,* Winona, Minnesota: Hal Leonard Music, Inc., 1955.

7. Marcouiller, Don. *Marching for Marching Bands*, Dubuque, Iowa: Wm. C. Brown Co., 1958.
8. Neidig, Kenneth I. (editor). *The Band Director's Guide*, Englewood Cliffs, New Jersey: Prentice-Hall, Inc., 1964.
9. Spohn, Charles L. and Richard W. Heine. *The Marching Band*, Boston: Allyn and Bacon, Inc., 1969.
10. Sur, William and Charles Schuller. *Music Education for Teen-Agers* (2nd edition), New York: Harper, 1966.

Periodicals

11. Andrus, Robert. "Marching Band Trends—Good or Bad?" *The School Musician*, Vol. 37, No. 2, Oct., 1965.
12. Ballou, Richard. "Preparing for Television Appearances," *The Instrumentalist*, Vol. XXIII, No. 3, Oct., 1968.
13. Blanton, Robert. "Music Reading and the Marching Band," *The Instrumentalist*, Vol. XXI, No. 8, March, 1967.
14. Downing, Edward. "Band, Marching," *The Instrumentalist*, Vol. XXI, No. 2, Sept., 1966.
15. Drake, Alan H. "21 Tips Toward the Production of Successful Marching Band Shows," *The School Musician*, Vol. 39, No. 1, Aug.–Sept., 1967.
16. Dunn, Earl. "The Marching Band Show, A Medium of Expression," *The Instrumentalist*, Vol. XXI, No. 2, Sept., 1966.
17. Izzo, Christopher, *et al.* "Are Half-Time Shows Doomed?" *Selmer Bandwagon*, No. 57, Fall, 1969.
18. Kisinger, E.D. "Good Music Is Our Aim," *Educational Music Magazine*, Sept.–Oct., 1949.
19. Long, Johnny. "A Short Evaluation of the Marching Band," *The School Musician*, Vol. 38, No. 1, Aug.–Sept., 1966.
20. Revelli, William D. "The Gridiron Marching Band," *The Instrumentalist*, Vol. XXI, No. 2, Sept., 1966.
21. Udell, Budd A. "A Statement of Purpose," *The Instrumentalist*, Vol. XIX, No. 4, Nov., 1964.
22. Werner, Robert. "A New Meaning for Marching Bands," *The Instrumentalist*, Vol. XXI, No. 2, Sept., 1966.
23. Whitwell, David. "Attitude Towards the Marching Band," *The Instrumentalist*, Vol. XIX, No. 7, Feb., 1965.

Monographs

24. N.I.M.A.C. *NIMAC Manual (The Organization and Management*

of Interscholastic Music Activities), Washington, D.C.: Music
Educators National Conference, 1963.
25. Revelli, William D. and George R. Cavender. *Marching Band
Fundamentals and Techniques,* Ann Arbor, Michigan: Les Strang
Publishing Co., 1961.

Unpublished Literature

26. Cecil, Herbert M. *Fundamental Principles of the Organization,
Management, and Teaching of the School Band,* unpublished dissertation, University of Rochester, 1953.
27. Hindsley, Mark H. "The Concert Band Conductor and the Marching Band," A Report for the College Band Directors National Association Conference Proceedings, Dec., 1960.
28. Weeks, R. Stanwood. "The College Band—Is It Time to Build a
Monument?" An Address delivered to the College Band Directors
National Association Conference, Dec., 1969.

4

How to Choose Among
Standard Works for the Band

A SHORT HISTORY OF TRANSCRIPTIONS

Compared to the symphony orchestra, regarding instrumentation, repertoire, and acceptance as a serious medium of musical expression, the concert band has been established for a relatively brief period of time. Although wind bands of various types and sizes have existed since the time of Lully, Goldman considers the true beginning of the modern concert band with the great National Festivals held throughout late 18th-century France commemorating the Revolution, based on present-day standards.[2] For these spectacular events, bands whose instrumentations included a good representation of woodwind, brass, and percussion instruments were formed to play serious compositions by such composers as Gossec, Méhul, Cherubini, and Catel. These pieces were in keeping with the style and forms of the times. Such an auspicious beginning notwithstanding, the basic function of the "band" remained a military one.

As noted in Chapter 2, there were comparatively few original compositions written for the concert band during the 19th century. This could hardly constitute a numerical sufficiency for a concert repertoire by a band of that time, whether European or American. Consequently, the majority of the band's repertoire consisted of transcriptions, including operatic overtures, non-operatic or "standard" overtures, movements from symphonies, and light "classics" (assorted orchestral pieces such as suites, and "descriptive" pieces). In addition, there were arrangements of piano and organ compositions, and instrumental or vocal solos with band accompaniment.

Until the school band movement began its upward surge, the band's repertoire changed little in content, style, and source, except for a growing body of original band music. Conductors and players alike came to consider this transcribed and arranged material as the standard band repertoire. One has only to think back to the old band journals published by Carl Fischer, Boosey and Hawkes, and Chappell, to name a few companies, to recall the status of the repertoire during the early 20th century. Neilson reflects on conditions then when he reminds us that ". . . the band repertory was slim indeed, consisting for the most part of inferior transcriptions from the orchestral repertory, instrumental solos accompanied by the band, and miscellaneous novelties or 'occasional' pieces of debatable value." [13]

Regardless of the fact that the number and quality of original band compositions have been increasing, especially during the past ten years, transcriptions and arrangements of works from other musical media have continued to be published, both in quality and quantity, as an important and necessary segment of the band repertoire. Whereas the source of music for transcriptions was mainly the 19th century, with scattered examples from late 18th-century symphonic works, the present-day selection is of a wider scope and variety in chronology and idiom. For example, there are many more works from the Baroque and even Renaissance musical periods available in transcribed or arranged form today than before. The 19th century continues to be a favorite source of supply except that the choice is a bit more varied than mainly orchestral works. There appears to be a concerted effort on the part of a few publishers of band music to supply compositions for the class "C" and "D" level bands.

Neilson once again describes the difference between the past and present situation when he writes that, "Present-day band conductors have an excellent repertory from which to choose:

original works for band in abundance plus an ever-growing list of excellent transcriptions and settings of music of all kinds and varieties from pre-Baroque through contemporary periods. The conductor who knows and adequately interprets this sizable repertory finds no important period of music beyond his reach." [13]

WHEN IS IT A TRANSCRIPTION OR ARRANGEMENT?

For quite a number of years there has been some confusion between the use of the terms, "transcription," and "arrangement," especially when applied to band music. In a transcription, the musical substance or ideas remain intact, that is, the arranger adds nothing new in the way of musical materials such as figurations, countermelodies, accompanimental features, altered or added chord structures, or change of form. The arranger transfers the entire work to a new medium, the band. On the other hand, an arrangement constitutes a complete reworking of a composition; this implies the addition of figurations, countermelodies, accompanying figures, new harmonies, and even slight modification of the melodic line and basic rhythmic patterns or even meter. A case in point would be an arrangement scored from a "lead sheet" which includes the melodic line with chord progressions and perhaps the words.

When working from an orchestral score, an arranger normally does not find it necessary to make any modifications other than raising or lowering certain tones or figures by an octave or more, if this is necessary at all. In the case of multiple stops in strings, the arranger finds it necessary to redistribute the chord tones or alter string devices. Also, he assumes that the composer's ideas as they appear on the original score are complete within themselves and there is no need for further additional material. When transcribing keyboard music (i.e., piano pieces by Chopin or Debussy, or organ music by Bach or Bruckner), the arranger finds it necessary only to transfer keyboard idioms into wind instrument techniques which does entail a certain amount of alteration.

Finally, in a transcription, the arranger makes an effort for the results to be consistent with the style (chronological period) of the composition. In an arrangement, the final result can be a completely new setting, especially stylistically. As an example, an "old standard" popular or jazz tune could receive any one of a number of treatments.

PROS AND CONS OF BAND TRANSCRIPTIONS

To reiterate, since about 1950 the concert band repertoire has increased in quantity of original contemporary compositions. Additional stimulus in quality and quantity has been given this growth through contributions by internationally-famous composers. There is a feeling on the part of many band directors that the time has finally arrived to eliminate transcriptions of "standard" works from the band's repertoire and concentrate solely on the study and performance of these original works.[2] Only by this approach can the concert band take its rightful place alongside the orchestra and other media as a formal concert ensemble.

Goldman, for one, feels that the band ". . . can no longer function as a poor man's orchestra, or purely as a medium for very light entertainment, at least in schools and colleges."[2] If it is to justify its place as an educational and musical ensemble, the band must rely on the development of fresh original literature, but retain some forms, such as the march, which are indigenous to it. In the final analysis, according to Goldman, these works are more suitable and, therefore, more becoming to the band's function. Directors who staunchly advocate emphasis on original literature claim that if composers had intended their works to be performed by the concert band, they would have scored for it. To these persons, it seems both illogical and impractical that a large concert band should attempt the performance of a work whose timbres and texture were designed for other colors and textures, especially lighter qualities. In other words, the band is not a suitable musical medium for the performance of much orchestral music.[11] Would it not be more effective for the band as ". . . an ensemble in its own right . . . (to continue the performance of) compositions written especially for it in a manner that no other musical group can imitate?"[12]

Among other reasons given in opposition to band transcriptions is that the ". . . standard band literature is old fashioned and no longer worthy of . . ." performance by contemporary bands.[11]

Further, since live or recorded orchestral performances of the masterworks are readily available, there seems to be little or no reason for the band to perform the same music. The implication is that the original is far more effective than a transcription. In fact, Carter, an important contemporary composer of music for band, has said that, ". . . generally speaking, a number written specifically for band is more desirable than a transcription of an orchestral number." [18]

It was previously recommended that the director give his students broad musical experiences which would maintain their interest, initiative, and responsibility. He must incorporate into his band library a repertoire that is wide and tasteful in range, meaning that it is historically and stylistically representative of all musical periods including the various types and forms. The band's repertoire is obviously deficient in this respect on the basis of quantity. Therefore, it is necessary to use transcribed and arranged music from all periods prior to the 20th century if the director wishes to expose his students to an historical variety of musical compositions. Desidero, who wrote a research study on teaching music history via the instrumental music program, concluded that secondary school instrumental students are weak in information and knowledge regarding music history. The far-reaching impact of this condition might be, he contended, that these same students will probably become music teachers ". . . and carry with them this basic deficiency," thereby creating a vicious circle.[20]

Bordo had an opportunity to investigate the effect of teaching music history through band literature during rehearsals. For the project he developed an outline and list of band music which included: rhythm; elementary form; elementary harmony; and the major musical periods from the 16th century to the present. Specific compositions from each period were selected to represent style characteristics, various typical forms, and major composers. The more significant factors which emerged from this project were ". . . that students liked the idea of discussing a certain aspect of music; and immediately playing an example in appropriate band literature." [10] Bordo pointed out that he and the students could make use of the information assimilated from one study in other related concert and festival materials; also, it was possible to devote a certain percentage of his rehearsal time to the study of music history without any detrimental affect on performance levels. He concludes that the potential success of the entire idea depends largely on the creativeness and degree of enthusiasm of the conductor.[10] Obviously, until the 20th century, the majority of the works listed on Bordo's outline were transcriptions and arrangements of instrumental music. Desidero supports Bordo's ideas. He states that the combination of factual knowledge with the study-performance of historical examples will enable the students to gain ". . . insight into the history of Western music and also acquire important correlative knowledge necessary for good performance practice." [20]

Garner made a study of transcriptions of works written before 1800 in which he directed attention to the need and use for transcriptions. Garner writes, "The repertory of the band is sadly inadequate to meet the demands of music education with respect to the presentation of music representative of all periods." [21] Sousa had far fewer original band works from which to select for his concert programs compared with the number available today. He thought that certain compositions of some composers sounded as well as, if not better than, the original orchestral version when transcribed for band.[17] Many students receive their initial, truly musical experiences in the concert band; they should not be denied these opportunities due to the fact that particular works were not originally written for the band medium. Critics of band transcriptions tend to dwell on one major factor and it is that the great 18th and 19th century composers did not look with favor on the concert band; this constitutes the basic aesthetic reason for the lack of sufficient original band music from these periods. What is not brought out is that these composers were not intensely interested in composing for the band because of the technical and mechanical limitations of wind instruments during those times. Also, the function of most bands then was a military one, except for the few professional and town bands which flourished mainly in the 19th century; the band had not established itself as a concert ensemble.

It is true that the sophisticated development of the phonograph, availability of recorded and broadcast music affords the serious music auditor far more opportunities for listening to orchestral works than ever before. While live orchestral performances are generally accessible, except for in small localities, a certain segment of the concert audience does not attend them as a matter of personal preference. For these persons, and those who are unable to hear live performances, the concert band is often their sole contact with formal concert music; if the concert band neglected to perform any transcribed music, the audience might never hear it.[17] Hindsley concedes to the fact that ". . . the future status of the concert band depends upon the development of an original and independent repertoire."[22] He also believes that the concert band achieved its place of music prominence through the performance of transcriptions. The "masters" simply did not have today's band for which to compose their music; but what is more important, they wrote great music that has remained with us through the years and should continue to be performed, heard, and enjoyed by player and audience alike. Comparisons are fewer concerning arrangements of keyboard music (from piano and organ); the main question is its suitability to the band medium, a factor to be discussed presently.

SOURCES OF STANDARD WORKS

Source material in transcribed and arranged form appears to be plentiful both in quantity and variety. A strong effort in choosing music from this type of literature should be directed toward careful selection and the music should reflect a high standard of quality. The band director may employ a three-pronged approach when considering sources of transcribed or arranged music for his library. The music should be representative of the very best examples of literature including: (1) the various style and periods of music history; (2) the various musical forms of each period; and (3) the principal media.

According to catalogs of published band music, the periods of music history should include the Renaissance, Baroque, Pre-Classic, Classic, Romantic, and 20th Century. The director must see to it that his library is chronologically balanced at least in quality if not quantity, keeping in mind that as one retrogrades in music history, the possibilities of source material become less. Garner's survey (1967), of music transcribed for the school band that was composed prior to 1800, shows that the principal pre-

19th-century compositions were written by Mozart, Haydn, Gluck, Handel, J.S. Bach, and Purcell. At that time he found less than sixty published transcriptions of music composed by other composers; they include: Arcadelt, C.P.E. Bach, J.C. Bach, Boccherini, Byrd, Catel, Clementi, Corelli, Couperin, Crüger, Frescobaldi, Gabrielli, Gervaise, Gibbons, Hasse, Jadin, Lasso, Locke, Lully, Marcello, Palestrina, Pergolesi, Rameau, Telemann, and Vivaldi.[21] The omission of Beethoven from this list is a curious one, until, perhaps, one remembers that all his symphonies were composed beginning in 1800; he composed marches which have been published for the modern band.

Bordo's outline for the 19th century shows the following composers: Beethoven, Schubert, Mendelssohn, Schumann, Brahms, Chopin, Dvorak, Wagner, and Debussy.[10] This group plus the addition of Tschaikowsky, Rossini, Verdi, Rimsky-Korsakov, von Weber, Berlioz, and Grieg would round out a good representation of "standard" or favorite composers whose music should serve as a major source of transcription or arranged material.

Generally, musical forms employed in transcribed or arranged band music encompass: (1) short forms—two and three part song forms, chorales, marches, (not originally for band, such as the operatic march), individual movements from dance suites, individual brief keyboard pieces; (2) extended or large forms and homophonic texture—overture, solo concerto, orchestral suite, symphonic poems, single movements from symphonies, theme and variations, and rondo; (3) contrapuntal form and polyphonic texture—fugue, chorale prelude, prelude and fugue, madrigals, Baroque dances (single movements and entire suites), Baroque operatic overtures, chaccone, passacaglia, and concerto grosso.[5]

Principal media would cover instrumental (non-keyboard)—orchestral, chamber music, strings only, winds only (where obsolete instruments are concerned), solo with instrumental accompaniment; keyboard—piano and organ; and vocal—operatic excerpts, madrigals, airs, arias, oratorio, and art songs.

If the student is to be helped to attain an acquaintance and contact with a wide range of musical literature, it is best that the library not overemphasize any one era or style of music. In addition to original band music, a good mixture of types of compositions, as suggested above, should likewise lead the student along the road to the development of musical taste.[4]

CRITERIA IN SELECTING TRANSCRIBED
OR ARRANGED MUSIC

Due to the nature of the musical material involved with transcriptions and arrangements, we are not concerned with exactly the same criteria as those described in Chapter 2. In most instances the original composition was written by a highly reputable and competent composer; therefore, an analyzation of the musical elements is not pertinent. There are cases, however, in which one must consider these elements with the same manner of scrutiny as recommended regarding original band literature. Bear in mind that one is confronted with the transference of musical ideas from one medium to another; our criteria and analysis should be concerned mainly with the method and suitability of transference.

There are three criteria to be considered as the basis for selecting music transcribed or arranged for band. They are: (1) the inherent value or quality of the original music itself; (2) the practicality and/or suitability of the music for the band medium; and, (3) the scoring approach, methods, or techniques employed by the arranger. Goldman writes that "The best arrangement is one which does not remind the listener that it is an arrangement. The musical result must sound natural to the performing medium." [1]

The Music's Inherent Value or Quality

Music historians have often written that one of the most important qualities in a musical composition is its ability to withstand the test of time, its durability or lasting quality.[9] While it is necessary to wait a number of years to apply this artistic yardstick in the case of original modern or contemporary band music, it is not necessary when it concerns transcribed or arranged music from earlier periods; the music has already proved itself. Eugene Ormandy agrees with this concept. After a considerable length of time as a conductor in countless countries and for greatly varying audiences, he says that "Time, of course, is the steadiest criterion . . ." in judging music. "Music which perennially makes its impact upon musician and listener alike cannot be called 'bad.' Fashions, in music as in mode, change, but certain composers have couched their message in terms which defy the test of time." [7] To fathom timelessness in music, one must look to both the man and his music. "The core of greatness in any person . . ." Ormandy continues, ". . . will be projected in one way or another . . . The granite strength of Beethoven . . . The sensitivity of Mozart . . ." [7]

Is a musical composition good simply because it was written by one of the *masters?* On the whole, decidedly yes. Arrangers in past years carefully selected the original source material from which they made their transcriptions or arrangements, especially with regard to "major" works by the major composers. As everyone knows, reputable composers wrote music which can be classified into various types such as functional, entertainment, and absolute, or from very light to very serious, and varying levels of quality. There are transcribed and arranged examples of very light music by established composers which were selected by the arranger more for their suitability to the band medium rather than quality. For instance, the music may be by Beethoven, Schubert, or Chopin but not *great* Beethoven, Schubert, or Chopin. Perhaps the arranger felt that a particular work would be a good "program" piece and would have some aesthetic value because of the composer's reputation. One might find this condition more in publications from the late 19th and early 20th centuries than recently. Then it was a matter of filling out the band repertoire due to a sparsity of original band literature. In the final analysis, the decision remains with each band director ". . . whose personal preference and judgement should be guided by good taste and sound values." [15]

Practicality and Suitability to the Band Medium

Because a composition was composed by one of history's most illustrious composers, does it mean that it will be at all practical or suitable to the band medium? Whether originally written for orchestra or piano, the factor of idiomatic writing enters into the picture of transcribed or arranged music at this point. In some musical works, the composer imbued his ideas with specific timbres or technical features which would be difficult to transcribe or arrange without destroying or distorting the character of the original.[19] In keyboard music, especially piano, the composer may demonstrate a particular pianistic technique through the music; to transfer this for wind performance would tend to negate the composer's intentions. Orchestral music contains numerous instances of idiomatic features for the string section that are difficult, if not impossible in some cases, to transcribe for winds and maintain the basic character or effect. In these circumstances, the band director must ask himself whether or not the music lends itself to transcription or arrangement.

How often have you heard or made the remark that a piece of music sounds better as a band transcription than it does in its original orchestral form? While this statement may or may not be true, the implication is that the composer could have written it for either medium. Goldman feels that one reason why some of these orchestral works sound effective as band music is that ". . . the originals never depended on subtleties of orchestration or intensity of expression."[2] Examples of this type of music might be operatic and non-operatic overtures from the 19th century. Wagner seems to be one composer whose music suits the band medium rather well. Fortunately such "Wagnerian" effects as a warm lushness of sound, intensity of emotion, emphasis on a large wind section, and an overwhelming power of tone are possible to produce in a band, some special string techniques notwithstanding.

Many examples from the Baroque and Classical periods are particularly suitable for the band, especially the small and moderate-sized ensembles. The main objection by opponents of band transcriptions is that the band is unable to reproduce the intended clarity of texture, tonal weight, and nuances in music of these periods. If such is the case, the band director who intends to have his band study and perform this music should make whatever adjustments are necessary to achieve these musical effects. Nevertheless, there are fewer idiomatic obstacles in music from these eras than the 19th century works. The director must remember that in the originals from the Classic period, the distribution of parts was not in our accustomed 1st-2nd-3rd-4th divisions. Most of the parts were grouped in pairs, except for an occasional trio of horns or trombones. The viola part could be considered a 3rd part in the string section. This pairing, then, should be emphasized in the director's distribution of parts to his players. The polarity of the outer (soprano and bass) lines of certain Baroque polyphonic compositions should also be given strong attention. Exceptions to this polarity are keyboard works (fugues, preludes, chorale-preludes) in which the individual lines receive equal emphasis. Concerning suitability to the band medium, 19th-century orchestration techniques and devices had changed radically from the 18th century and scoring had become far more idiomatic, mainly for the string section. Effects and devices were created and utilized which would be questionable from a practical viewpoint to transfer into wind idioms. Yet, a number of compositions containing such problems have been transcribed for band; they are as awkward to perform by professional and advanced players as by younger performers.

The factor of "difficulty" was discussed in Chapter 2. The same approach concerning difficulty should be applied with transcriptions and arrangements, especially regarding idiomatic effects and devices. Hind offers a suggestion, made by many other band directors as well, in reference to difficulty. He feels that each band library should contain a number of selections that are beyond the capabilities of the performers, at least at the time the music is selected. The main purpose is to give students contact with the music during rehearsals but not for performance. This music can be used as study or sight-reading material. Hind states that ". . . it does a great deal of good to 'tackle' (these) works. . . ."[3] If one follows through with the theory that one objective of the instrumental music program is to expose the students to music of all types and styles from the various periods of music history, then Hind's idea would be valuable.

There are directors who feel that, rather than attempt to play the more intricate, complex orchestral works, the band (conductor and players) would be better off to play "lighter" orchestral music which is not generally performed any longer by orchestras but popular among audiences nevertheless. Due to their inherent nature, these works, such as the old "standard" overtures, are thought to be more suitable to the band medium.[1]

A case for transcriptions and arrangements may be summed up

in the words of Leonhard and House. They advise the director to ". . . recognize that the band, like all school musical organizations, should be a *means* to the musical education of students and not an end in itself." [6]

Scoring Techniques and Practices

Scoring techniques, practicality, suitability, level of difficulty, and retention of the character of the original work are very closely interrelated. While it is possible to analyze these factors individually, a director often finds himself considering more than one simultaneously. As scoring practices and techniques are discussed, the factors previously mentioned will be alluded to or mentioned outright.

One procedure for ascertaining whether or not the arranger has retained the style and character of the original is to compare the scores of the original and the band version. It is at this moment when the matter of questionable scores arises. The American composer Joseph Wagner says that these scores are ". . . questionable to the purist when the original compositions appear to be hopelessly distorted." [16]

One of the strongest criticisms against band transcriptions, even by well-known arrangers, is that the method of simplifying and cutting employed in many scores results ". . . in the destruction of the original composition." [23] This practice has been justified occasionally on the basis that a little of a "great work" is better than none at all. The major weakness in such thinking is that it de-emphasizes the fundamental form of the composition, at least in the way it is presented in the transcription. Simplification and cutting eliminates much of the transitional or connecting material; it does not teach the students how the composer tied all his ideas together, balanced them, or achieved variety and contrast between them within the framework of the composition. Form and structure are as important to the student's total knowledge about music as are the other musical elements. Reference is not made to the many transcriptions which have been made of single works in which the arranger has kept the original form intact, but to those in which only the themes are presented, along with some transitional material and little else. Critics feel that such scores do not represent a true picture of the original concerning its style, character, and composer's creative imagination as portrayed through *all* his musical ideas.

Simplification is also found in alteration of the original melodic or rhythmic patterns as well as a change or elimination of chords. Publishers and arrangers claim that this practice is necessary if younger and weaker bands are to have the opportunity of performing these works. Goldman finds this ". . . an indefensible practice. It contributes nothing to the education of student or audience; on the contrary, it provides a false, and in many instances, a lasting impression that hinders rather than helps the development of musical taste or knowledge. . . ." [2] In this situation, it is mandatory that Mohammed must go to the mountain and not the reverse. In other words, bring the students up to the level of the music and not lower the inherent quality of the music through simplification. If the current publishers' lists are an indication, there should be an adequate supply of transcribed or arranged music of good quality that is suitable for younger or weaker bands.

Whether the publication is a transcription of an orchestral work or an arrangement of a keyboard piece, the scoring must be idiomatic for the band and should ". . . produce results that are 'best for the band'. . . ." [16] Several of the "old editions" of orchestral transcriptions are examples of attempts to make a band sound like an orchestra. The musical ideas expressed in the original score are but a starting point for the arranger. Since the band is made up of winds and percussion, it is almost impossible to duplicate all the original orchestral timbres designed by the composer. The best solution to this problem is that the transcription contain the same manner and degree of contrast between timbres as in the original.

Many arrangers score a transcription or arrangement so that it may be playable by bands of various sizes; this results in an over-scored work. The director must resort to the comparative approach once again; that is, comparing the band with the original score. He should edit or revise wherever necessary to retain the clarity or transparency of the original, eliminate duplication of the melody in octaves or unisons if not in the original, thin out the harmonic structure, re-balance the weight of the accompanying parts of unneeded sections or instruments that have been added; and change any mixture of timbres which do not maintain the contrast indicated in the original. All this should be accomplished in light of the band's instrumentation, strengths, weaknesses, and the performing capabilities of the students.[14]

One of the features in scoring practices in transcriptions noted in the "old band journal" editions and early 20th-century band arranging books is the theory of *parallelism*. By this is meant that each instrument in the band (or section of instruments) was assigned to a corresponding parallel instrument in the orchestra. There was so little deviation from this line of thinking that it seemed to be reduced to a mechanical procedure. For example, one of the favorite parallels used by proponents of this approach was that the clarinets were the "strings of the band." Justification for this was based on the fact that the clarinets are considered the "core" section of the band as the strings are of the orchestra. Considering the flexibility, intensity of tone, contrast in dynamics (especially "pp"), capacity for a sustained tone, and variety of devices available in the orchestral string section, this theory is lacking in practicability and usefulness if applied in each and every musical example. But the slavish rigidity that was apparent in this method likewise negated the possibilities of any contrast in timbre which the composer might have instilled into his original score.

The late, great composer-arranger Erik Leidzen had a personal method of transcribing from orchestral works that is refreshing and unique. He suggests two approaches to the problem. The first maintains that the instrumentation in a transcription must be identical or as close a copy of the original as is feasible, regardless of impracticality. The second, to which he subscribed, is that transcribing is a new art form, a new version of the original, scored as the composer might have had he composed the music for band.

There are certain devices composers incorporate in their scoring for the string section that are highly idiomatic, the effect of which can only be approximated (if at all) by wind instruments in a transcription. Some of these include *pizzicato*, repeated notes in rapid succession, *arpeggios*, tremolos, various bowing styles, and harmonics. Although arrangers have devised various techniques which serve as adequate, but usually awkward, substitutes for the original effect, they are not always easily playable even by experienced performers. These special effects are involved with the factor of difficulty and should be given primary consideration by the director in his selection of transcribed music for his library.

There is a certain amount of merit to the approach that the strings and clarinets are the basic choirs of their respective ensembles. For our purposes, however, this serves as a means of determining the level of difficulty of a transcription for one's band. In simple terms, the band director should carefully scrutinize the clarinet parts first of all when selecting this type of music for his library. Some musical idioms to look for are: arpeggiated figures, rapid rhythmic patterns with difficult articulations, awkward trills, and large intervallic skips within melodic or accompaniment passages.

Another section of the band's instrumentation which deserves special consideration is the bass, those instruments which are normally assigned the bass line in band scores. The band does not compare with the orchestra in the bass register in terms of agility and delicate nuances as well as the other typical string devices. The tubas (basses) are usually assigned the function of supporting both woodwind and brasses in band transcriptions. Aside from the range, the tuba cannot represent the orchestral contra-bass in all musical instances. This part must, therefore, be considered on the basis of the technical capabilities of the band's tuba players. The director who is blessed with a large section of contra-bass and contra-alto clarinets can edit the parts by deleting the tuba in passages where it supports the woodwinds.

The violoncello parts are frequently given to alto and bass clarinets, tenor and baritone saxophones, bassoons, and baritone. There is no question regarding the presence of the bass clarinet, saxophones, and baritone, but there is with alto clarinet and bassoons. The problem is that some arrangers seem to rely on these instruments to balance the upper string (violin, viola) parts which can be carried by Bb soprano clarinets, cornets, and flutes. In addition to their performing capacities, it comes down to a matter of actual numerical presence of these instruments in the band's instrumentation.

Leidzen felt that the most appropriate musical period for band transcriptions is the Classical, at least for symphonies. The melodic and harmonic structures are not too complex and the form is clearly outlined. Decisions for assignment of instruments are much easier to determine. The problem with many arrangers when transcribing music from this period is that they tend to double all parts beyond the composer's design. This simply destroys the balance of musical forces he had in mind when composing the work. These arrangers also tend to extend musical elements an octave higher or lower to accommodate certain instruments. The resultant effect is greater expansiveness but perhaps not in keeping with the stylistic characteristics of the period. There is the age-old argument of whether or not Beethoven would have written certain passages for flutes an octave higher had he the modern flute to consider in his scoring. The band director must employ the editing pencil, but judiciously.

Coda

Compared with transcriptions and arrangements from the early 20th century, present-day publications are more realistic in terms of source material and scoring practices. Source material is more varied so that there is not the great reliance solely on orchestral works. Orchestral material is selected on the basis of its adaptation to the band medium not only for the superior performing organizations but the average or weaker ones as well. Scoring techniques are based on contemporary concepts, such as larger flute sections, more reliance on and use of saxophones, and lower woodwind instruments such as the contra-alto and contra-bass clarinets. Scoring techniques are also more realistic in terms of expected results from individual instruments and sections. Present-day arrangers are attempting to make a band sound its best when utilizing music from another medium for their scores. Also, the younger or lower technical level bands are receiving greater attention concerning transcribed and arranged music. In the past, the arranger merely scored the music as he best knew how for his time and it was the band director's responsibility to "make it sound" or worry about suitability. There is also better quality literature used as original source material, especially for Class "C" and "D" bands.

Goldman thinks that as the number of good original band compositions increases, there will be less reliance on transcriptions and arrangements.[2] This may happen concerning transcriptions but perhaps not arrangements, at least not for this writer. Leonhard and House suggest that if the band director wishes to ". . . establish a program that is quite broad and truly forceful . . . he must keep things moving and progressing," and, ". . . he must promote a very wide and tasteful repertoire." They believe that this will help ". . . develop the initiative and responsibility of the players . . ." as well as building knowledge, discrimination, and judgment.[6] Falcone is perhaps the most forceful in his feelings on the matter. He states that ". . . a more compelling justification (for performing transcribed band music) is that our band students deserve the opportunity to study and perform the outstanding band literature and transcriptions of yesterday. It would be wrong to deny them the background and knowledge of these great works." [11]

Selected References

Books

1. Goldman, Richard Franko. *The Concert Band,* New York: Rinehart and Company, 1946.
2. Goldman, Richard Franko. *The Wind Band (Its Literature and Technique),* Boston: Allyn and Bacon, Inc., 1961.
3. Hind, Harold C. *The Brass Band,* London: Hawkes and Son, Ltd., 1934.
4. House, Robert W. *Instrumental Music for Today's Schools,* Englewood Cliffs, New Jersey: Prentice-Hall, Inc., 1965.
5. Kuhn, Wolfgang. *Instrumental Music: Principles and Methods of Instruction,* Boston: Allyn and Bacon, Inc., 1962.
6. Leonhard, Charles and Robert W. House. *Foundations and Principles of Music Education,* New York: McGraw-Hill, 1959.
7. Music Educators National Conference. *Perspectives in Music Education (Source Book III)* (Bonnie Kowal, ed.), Washington, D.C.: M.E.N.C., 1966.
8. Righter, Charles Boardman. *Success in Teaching School Orchestras and Bands,* Minneapolis: Schmitt, Hall, and McCreary Co., 1945.

Periodicals

9. Akers, Howard E. "The March Is Music Also," *The School Musician,* Vol. 35, No. 1, Aug.–Sept., 1963.

10. Bordo, Victor. "Music History Through Band Literature," *Music Journal*, Vol. XXVII, No. 10, Dec., 1969.
11. Falcone, Leonard. "Let Us Not Forget the Outstanding Band Literature of Yesterday," *The Instrumentalist*, Vol. XXI, No. 11, June, 1967.
12. McAllister, Forrest L. "What Has Happened?" *Music Journal*, Jan.–Feb., 1949.
13. Neilson, James. "The Aesthetics of Programming," *Journal of Band Research*, Vol. I, Autumn, 1964, No. 1.
14. Shepard, Wesley. "Interpreting Music of the Classical Period," *Journal of Band Research*, Vol. II, Spring, 1966, No. 1.
15. Wagner, Joseph. "Band Scoring Is Composition," *Music Journal*, Vol. XXVIII, No. 2, Feb., 1970.
16. Wagner, Joseph. "Dilemma of Concert Band Programs," *Music Journal*, Vol. XXVII, No. 1, Jan., 1969.

Monographs

17. Bachman, Harold B. *Program Building*, Chicago: Frederick Charles, Inc., 1962.

Unpublished Literature

18. Carter, Charles. "Panel Discussion on Band Literature," Proceedings of National Convention, College Band Directors National Association.
19. Cecil, Herbert M. *Fundamental Principles of the Organization, Management, and Teaching of the School Band*, unpublished dissertation, University of Rochester, 1953.
20. Desidero, Anthony R. *Teaching the History of Western Music Through Instrumental Performance in the Secondary School*, unpublished dissertation, University of Southern California, 1966.
21. Garner, Gary T. *Transcriptions for School Band of Selected Music Written Before 1800*, unpublished dissertation, University of Southern California, 1967.
22. Hindsley, Mark H. "Future Band Repertoire and Its Influence Upon Our College Bands," A Report for the 11th National Convention, College Band Directors National Association, Dec., 1960.
23. Lang, Philip J. "Band Repertoire," A Report for the 11th National Convention, College Band Directors National Association, Dec., 1960.

5

How to Locate and Acquire
New Band Literature

THE BAND DIRECTOR'S RESPONSIBILITY

We have suggested so far that the band director must be perceptive, careful, astute, and sensitive in the selection of music for his library. This requires a broad knowledge and experience with the literature and materials of the entire band field. If the director considers the band's library as its "course of study," he must plan as effectively as possible to provide for the different levels of pupil skills, the development of specific areas of technical facility and musicianship, and the various types of organization in his instrumental program.[11]

The search for and selection of repertoire which is ". . . interesting, fresh, (and) appropriate . . ." is a constant one, at least for the conscientious band director.[8] Occasionally, this process can be burdensome. The scope and responsibilities of a particular instrumental music program might limit the amount of time and physical stamina a director can devote to finding good music.[17] In the final analysis, it is the director's responsibility to select the very best possible materials that his band will study and perform.[17] One might ask why, or even, why bother? Would it not be easier, as some directors do, to play it safe and depend on familiar composers, arrangers, or types of music, and ". . . perform the same few pieces again and again . . . ?"[7] The major drawback to this approach is that it puts the band and its director in a *musical rut;* there would certainly be little opportunity for technical and musical development.

The failure or success of the instrumental music program depends, to a great extent, on the repertoire the director selects for his library. The director must, therefore, ". . . continually be on the search for new material which will fit his needs . . .", but be sure that he does not overlook standard and traditional literature as well. In this matter, Wareham quotes Wilson who states that if you "Examine the materials used by a school . . . you can pass fair judgment upon the value of the music program."[21]

Although the instrumental music program of this country underwent great strides in growth and development prior to 1940, the trend has been even more spectacular since then. The music publishing trade has responded to this growth by providing the necessary materials, at least in quantity if not always in quality. This means that publishers are constantly adding works to their catalogs which imposes a responsibility on the band director to keep up with new additions. New compositions at times indicate new trends, new ideas, new techniques, and progress or change in stylistic characteristics. Goldman warns, however, that ". . . a great deal of what is listed as 'new' is new in name only, but not in style or sound."[3]

Concerning the director's obligation for locating and acquiring new band literature, Fennell alludes to another factor which outwardly may seem subtle, but contains strong implications. He states that ". . . one can expand his daily excursions into the world of the band through the not always so simple desire for self-improvement."[12] The procedure for locating new literature is the key to this concept. Perusing scores, listening to recordings, attending live concerts, making choices, analyzing and studying the scores, and conducting the music in performance all add up to a creative process described as self-improvement. The possibility of the director falling into a musical rut thus may be avoided. It might also help guarantee the success of the instrumental program.

The renowned American composer Virgil Thomson feels that, when it comes to evaluating music for its value and worth, the professional musician is in a different position than the layman.

The layman need not exercise musical judgment, but the professional, especially a conductor, must do so to the incumbency he bears to his profession. He is, therefore, ". . . a music critic. He is obliged to make musical judgments and to act upon them." [14]

WHERE TO LOCATE NEW LITERATURE

Selective Music Lists

Although selective music lists *per se* soon become chronologically "dated," they are, nevertheless, one of the best means of reference sources for the band director. Unless one is totally familiar with, or has knowledge of every single band composition published during a single year, he must rely on such lists for information.

Music Teachers' Associations. Committees made up of experienced directors, either on a national, district, or area level, depending on the particular association, are formed to draw up selected music lists. These persons make an honest effort to select works which, in their estimation, represent quality, high standards, variety of type and style, and appropriate grading. On the point of grading, Arthur G. Harrell, Coordinator of the Music Selection Committee of N.I.M.A.C. (National Interscholastic Music Activities Commission), wrote in 1967 that the director should regard gradings only as a guide, since they are the subjective opinions of the Committees who prepared the lists.[21]

A few of the national associations which publish selective music lists are: *N.I.M.A.C.* (through the Music Educators National Conference); *C.B.D.N.A.* (College Band Directors National Association); *N.B.A.* (National Band Association); and *A.S.B.D.A.* (American School Band Directors Association). The N.B.A. publishes a list of band music which is intended to be comprehensive rather than selective. Its "Music List Committee" has included all of the titles brought to its attention and considered worthy of inclusion; the purpose is to suggest worthwhile and graded literature for use by college and school bands. Plans are to revise the list every three years. According to Al G. Wright, Chairman of the Music List Committee, the list is available to N.B.A. members at a reduced rate ($1.50 per copy) and to anyone else at $2.50 per copy.

The following excerpt from a letter to the author from Al Bohms, Coordinator of the A.S.B.D.A. Research Committee, explains that association's selective music list.

> The only list of high school band music which ASBDA has published, was presented in our 1969 Research Committee yearbook. This book is available only to our membership. The music is listed by sections, i.e.: Overtures, Concert Selections, Suites, Symphonies, Theme and Variations, Marches, and Solos with Band Accompaniment. It is not for sale but it may be acquired by any member for $1.00 postage and handling. This list was a result of polling the membership. No screening of the titles was done. The compositions listed were graded from easy to difficult but most of the numbers on the list range from medium to difficult.
>
> The 1970 yearbook will have a listing of compositions of junior high band material prepared by a committee of junior high band directors.

The 1969 list of publications published by the Music Educators National Conference includes "Selective Music Lists" containing graded band music as compiled by N.I.M.A.C. in 1968. The C.B.D.N.A. lists are devoted to a variety of items such as recently published band music, manuscript works, rental works, unpublished contemporary works, and solos with band accompaniment (published, unpublished, rental). These lists are available to the general membership as a part of the association's divisional and national conference proceedings.

State Bulletins or Guides. Most states, through their educational offices, publish selective music lists in their respective general school music handbooks, bulletins, or curriculum guides. These are intended as aids to the teacher for the technical and musical development of his students. There are many states which release special band lists compiled by their interscholastic activities committees via their official publications.

Some of the states which publish official selective music lists of graded band music are: Alabama, Southern California, Colorado, Connecticut, Florida, Maryland, Minnesota, Mississippi, New York, North Carolina, Ohio, Texas, and Virginia. The listings include title, composer and/or arranger, publisher, and grade of difficulty.[21] A partial table of contents in "The Official Manual and Selective Music Lists" of the Virginia Band and Orchestra Direc-

tors' Association (1967–1972) shows the following: Official
VBODA List of Band Music; Official VBODA Orchestra and
String List; Woodwind Solo and Ensemble List; Brass Solo and
Ensemble List; String Solo and Ensemble List; and Percussion
Solo and Ensemble List. The editors of the manual ". . . felt that
the purpose of this manual was to give as fine a selection as possible of the various publications for each category. However, this
work could not be intended to be a compilation of all published
materials now available."

Competition-Festivals. State music associations publish lists of
recommended or required music as a reference source to be used
in the selection of compositions to be performed by bands in competition-festivals. The compositions are graded according to level
of difficulty and, in some states, to conform with the particular
method of classifying schools in the respective state. Generally,
these lists contain new, recent, and older works. There is a diver-
gence in the number of grades of difficulty as well as the meaning
of these grades among these lists. For example, some states assign
a higher number for easy compositions and vice versa; there is
also lack of agreement between state lists on the level of difficulty
regarding the same piece of music.[21]

Clinics, Workshops, and Conventions. Perhaps one of the very
best means for locating new band music is the band clinic devoted
specifically to the performance of new literature. One type is the
"sight-reading" clinic in which one band plays through a large
number of compositions. Following each work, remarks are made
by the conductor regarding possible level of difficulty, interpretation, and rehearsal problems, in addition to other pertinent points.
Another type is the "materials" clinic which may feature more than
one band performing new publications, usually prepared in advance. The clinic host, assisted by the "reading band's" conductors,
prepares lists of the music to be performed. The host conductor
points out significant factors about individual compositions in this
type of clinic also. In both types, packets of scores provided by the
publishers are distributed to the attending directors for their
perusal during performances.

Workshops at the city, county, district, and state levels are
another source of band music lists. Many of these are held in
connection with conventions of music educators or band directors'

associations. Tauhert considers conventions to be ". . . one of the best means of determining current music educator needs." He strongly urges that directors avail themselves of the opportunity for talking to publishers' representatives at the individual display booths that ". . . are also sounding boards where we hear all manner of praise, advice, and criticism." [13]

Publishers usually provide attendees at these events with sample scores, catalogs, or thematic catalogs of their band publications. Sample scores are especially valuable if they represent works to be performed during one of these events. While at conventions, etc., the director should place his name on music publishers' mailing lists in order to receive scores, thematic catalogs, and/or notices of new releases. An alternative idea is to send all band music publishers a postcard giving one's name, school, school address, and the type(s) of musical ensemble(s) for which the director is responsible. Most publishers of band music are listed in "The Music Educator's Business Handbook" which is prepared and produced by the Music Industry Council. Several publishers issue a complete band catalog, including miniature scores, of their entire year's band output. If a director were to make up a file of such catalogs, he would eventually have a complete library of each publisher's scores.

Reviews and Listings in Periodicals. Two music periodicals devoted to subjects pertaining to school music are *The School Musician, Director, and Teacher,* and *The Instrumentalist;* each contains a listing and review of band publications as regular features. Ranges, keys, metric and rhythmic problems, solo passages, style and type of music, form, and possible level of difficulty or classification are among the many aspects described in these reviews. Because these columns are authored by experienced specialists, their advice is an invaluable aid to the director.

From time to time, lists and reviews of band music are printed in the official journal or publication of state music teachers' associations. These occasionally appear in the form of programs to be presented by all-district or all-state bands, or recommended band music in each classification for use in district and state competition-festivals.

The *Journal of Band Research,* official publication of the American Bandmasters Association, features complete analyses of selected compositions, usually original contemporary band music. The Volume II, No. 2, Summer-1966 issue of the Journal is a catalog of the current holdings to date of band music and recordings in the American Bandmasters Association Research Center. All of the music and recordings represented in the catalog have been donated by publishers, organizations, and individuals.

Attend Concerts and Retain Programs. Many directors are capable of distinguishing between good, fair, and poor music when they hear it, but not always when studying a score.[16] Therefore, one should have the experience of listening to many different works before making a comparison and evaluation.[4] The simplest means for accomplishing this is to attend concerts by other school groups in one's locality and competition-festivals. House suggests that the director ". . . keep a notebook listing every promising number brought to one's attention. Each work should be cataloged by composer, title, and publisher, and with some estimate of length and relative difficulty."[5] At reading clinics and conventions, the director should, when possible, procure copies of the scores for the works to be performed and have them in hand for the performance.

Recordings. A more recent means now being effectively utilized by many publishers to introduce their publications is by recordings; these are professionally produced but performed by school groups, mainly collegiate. In some cases, these recordings are available individually on a retail basis; in others, the director makes a purchase through yearly subscription or purchases sets of recordings.

Several publishers include a disc recording of excerpts from new releases along with miniature copies of the condensed scores; a few publishers issue recordings containing complete performances of new works, all free of charge. For the busy band director who may not be able to search through reference scores at conventions, etc., publishers' display booths have facilities for listening to tape or disc recordings of their music. This, in addition to "live" performances, are excellent for direct contact with new band literature. Regardless of the added production costs, some publishers consider recordings an important adjunct to their promotional methods, as well as a desire to be of educational service to the school band.

Colleagues and Experts. It would be a formidable task for any one director to be thoroughly familiar with the entire gamut of band literature, especially new compositions. Therefore, one must depend on the combined information suggested thus far. There is yet one more source of information for locating new band literature. The director should ultimately consult with his more experienced colleagues and experts who have established their reputations ". . . as teachers and their discrimination as program builders." [10] Many college and university band directors compile lists of selected band music for their instrumental methods courses (band administration, band literature, etc.), as well as lists of works performed by their respective organizations during the school year for distribution to interested persons in the band field. For example, the Eastman School of Music offers a selected listing of works for wind ensemble or chamber winds. The universities of Illinois and Michigan annually hold band clinics in which a considerable amount of new band music is analyzed and performed.

THE MUSIC PUBLISHER

We previously stated that there are about 50,000 school bands in the United States. This obviously places a great responsibility and demand upon band music publishers. Publishers have met the challenge with the production of a large volume of literature although there has been occasional criticism concerning its quality.[20] Arthur A. Hauser, speaking for the publishing industry in an address to members of C.B.D.N.A., stated that the publisher's ". . . responsibility is to encourage new worthwhile ideas in music; to encourage by publication the works of composers who wish to present their thoughts in contemporary musical idioms, and in general to help make music a vital expression of our cultural environment." [18]

Norman is highly complimentary of the music publisher when he says that they ". . . have been nothing if not ingenious in providing materials for the young . . . band. It would seem that there could arise no problem to which they, in some way or another, have not given consideration." Any fault for poor quality in literature must be borne equally by director and publisher. Fundamentally, the music publishing industry is a matter of cost and profit. The publisher is a businessman and the extent to which his company is financially successful is based on his and his editorial board's imagination and ability to satisfy customer demand. Rise in quality of the music offered by publishers is directly related to the desire for better music on the part of the director.[8]

Publishers' Services

On-approval Service. An aid to locating and acquiring new band music is the on-approval service offered by many publishers. Policies regarding this privilege vary from company to company so that the band director must apprise himself of a company's specific policy when requesting it. The director should consider on-approval service, whether from a publisher or local dealer, as a serious obligation of trust and abide by the conditions attending it in the same manner he would any other purchase for his instrumental program. It is simply a matter of professional ethics. Music publishing is a big, expensive trade with continually increasing costs of engraving, paper, and printing. To provide directors with free promotional materials, the publisher operates on a narrow margin of profit, especially concerning band compositions of large form or high quality. Some publishers recoup their losses, or near losses, by publication of lighter or "sure-fire" works that are certain to bring in more profitable income. Therefore, a director availing himself of an on-approval service should see to it that the portion of music not retained be returned in salable condition.

In its publication, *The Music Educator's Business Handbook,* The Music Industry Council recommends the following procedure for handling on-approval orders.[*]

1. On-approval order materials require the same definite and concise treatment as a purchase order, therefore, this privilege should be safeguarded by those to whom it is of service.
2. *Order carefully.* On-approval implies that the materials may not be exactly what is needed. To be of best help to directors,

---

[*] The Music Industry Council, an auxiliary of M.E.N.C., is a non-profit service organization which provides information on and understanding of the many business problems which confront the music educator. It serves as a liaison between the music educators of the United States and the manufacturing and publishing firms which supply the materials and equipment used in music education.

the publisher needs to know as much as possible about an individual director's interests and needs.

3. *Make your decision as soon as possible.* Materials are sent for a specified time only; be certain you understand the time limit so as not to delay the transaction.

4. *Materials on approval are charged to your account.* This is the publisher's, or dealer's only way of keeping track of the materials.

5. *After the approval period they become outright purchases.* If circumstances require it, a written request for an extension of the period will often be honored.[22]

A survey conducted of band music publishers regarding the subject matter of this chapter reveals a wide range of policies. Because the procedures are highly personal for each company, publishers shall remain nameless in the description of services offered.

Less than half the publishers do not offer on-approval service to individual directors. A large number of returns has proved it to be a rather costly service which the purchaser must ultimately absorb through an increase in publication costs. These companies find it no longer economically feasible to send out approval copies in light of the ample opportunities for directors to examine new works at local dealers, clinics, conventions, or through free reference scores, thematic catalogs, and recordings, Several of these publishers replace the on-approval service with free copies of scores, either full or miniature condensed copies. One or two companies limit on-approval copies to select institutions or to directors who place very large orders.

A few companies provide music on loan for use in selecting works to be placed on contest or competition-festival lists and will send it to the person or persons responsible for making the decisions. Many local and nationally-known dealers send out music on approval, especially large distributing houses which handle publications of all firms. The local dealer is normally better aware of the director's needs, interests, and problems and is able to give him more personal service in this matter.

Of those companies that *do* have an on-approval service, the following policy statements are indicative of the varying practices which they stipulate: (1) The director has a privilege of retaining the music for 10 days (nothing was stated about the amount of music he must purchase); (2) The director must purchase at least 50% of the music requested (no time limit given); (3) The director must purchase ⅓ of the music requested (again, no time limit mentioned); (4) The director must purchase *some* of the music requested (no time limit mentioned); (5) The director may retain the music for 30 days before deciding which works to purchase and which to return (no stipulation as to the amount he must purchase). In all these cases, the director must assume the responsibility of giving the music the same care he would any item borrowed, to collect the music after using it, to inventory the music and see that it is properly collated, to pay the return postage, to return the music to the publisher or dealer at the time specified and *in salable condition* (this was stressed as extremely important), and have the courtesy to include a "thank you" note for use of the music.

The director who requests on-approval material " . . . should describe as accurately as possible the needs which it must meet so that the firm will have at least a reasonable chance of sending material which will be retained and paid for." [1] Directors should bear in mind that publisher's costs for on-approval materials are based on several factors including postage, packing, and processing the request through the firm's various administrative channels.

Free Sets on Loan. Several publishers feel that it is a part of their function to send free of charge, on-loan, new band music to colleges or universities holding symposiums, workshops, music conferences, conventions, or clinics which feature music "reading sessions." In these situations, the music can be disseminated to a rather large audience of band directors at one time. These companies consider this phase of their promotional methods to be the most effective manner of introducing new music to a wide variety of band directors in the most economical way. One afterthought on this matter—this type of session usually requires a great many copies of music, very often on short notice; when the selections are made, publishers ask that they be notified immediately so that enough copies will be printed to take care of needs.[22]

One representative of the music publishing industry, in a talk to a convention of band directors, offered the following suggestions as an equitable solution to the problem of the burden of supplying music for clinics, conventions, etc. The music selected should be bought either with funds from the treasury of the group sponsoring the clinic, or from the sums collected as registration fees. The expenses of supplying the music would then be absorbed by many people in small sums rather than concentrated upon the overhead of the publisher. One state music teachers' association which follows this practice places the purchased convention music on sale a year later at a nominal charge.[19]

Coda

Fjeld quotes Williams who has several suggestions for aiding the band director in his quest for new band literature.

1. Maintain a current file of catalogs of various publishers of band music.
2. Maintain a current file of lists such as those published by M.E.N.C. and the National Music Camp at Interlochen, Michigan.
3. Keep on hand a number of books on the subject of selecting music for school bands.[3, 7, 17]
4. Maintain a file of programs of band music presented by contemporaries.
5. Cultivate the habit of studying current music magazines which bring to the attention of the band director many band compositions which are significant for some reason or other.
6. Make as extensive use as possible of band recordings as a means of becoming acquainted with better band music.
7. Do not overlook radio and television appearances of the better bands as a means of becoming acquainted with current band compositions.[17]

Selected References

Books

1. Davis, Ennis. *More Than a Pitchpipe,* Boston: C.C. Birchard and Company, 1941.
2. Goldman, Richard Franko. *The Concert Band,* New York: Rinehart and Company, 1946.

3. Goldman, Richard Franko. *The Wind-Band,* Boston: Allyn and Bacon, Inc., 1961.
4. Hoffer, Charles R. *Teaching Music in the Secondary Schools,* Belmont, California: Wadsworth Publishing Company, Inc., 1964.
5. House, Robert W. *Instrumental Music for Today's Schools,* Englewood Cliffs, New Jersey: Prentice-Hall, Inc., 1965.
6. Hovey, Nilo W. *The Administration of School Instrumental Music,* New York: Belwin, Inc., 1949.
7. Neidig, Kenneth I. *The Band Director's Guide,* Englewood Cliffs, New Jersey: Prentice-Hall, Inc., 1964.
8. Norman, Theodore. *Instrumental Music in the Public Schools,* Philadelphia: Ditson Company, 1941.
9. Prescott, Gerald R. and Lawrence W. Chidester. *Getting Results with School Bands,* New York: Carl Fischer, Inc., 1938.
10. Righter, Charles B. *Success in Teaching School Orchestras and Bands,* Minneapolis, Minn.: Schmitt, Hall, and McCreary Company, 1945.
11. Singleton, Ira C. *Music in Secondary Schools,* Boston: Allyn and Bacon, Inc., 1963.

Periodicals

12. Fennell, Frederick. "As I See It," *The School Musician,* Aug.–Sept., 1968, Vol. 40, No. 1.
13. Tauhert, Rudolph. "Publishers Cater to Needs," *Music Journal,* Sept., 1966, Vol. XXIV, No. 7.
14. Thomson, Virgil. "The Art of Judging Music," *The Music Educators Journal,* Nov.–Dec., 1964, Vol. 51, No. 2.
15. Wagner, Joseph. "Dilemma of Concert Band Programs," *Music Journal,* Jan., 1969, Vol. XXVII, No. 1.

Unpublished Literature

16. Cecil, Herbert M. *Fundamental Principles of the Organization, Management, and Teaching of the School Band,* unpublished dissertation, University of Rochester, 1953.
17. Fjeld, Marvin Wendell. *A Survey and Evaluation of Music Performed in Public Concert by Indiana High School Bands,* unpublished dissertation, Indiana University, 1959.
18. Hauser, Arthur A. An Address to Members of C.B.D.N.A., National Convention, 1952.

19. Hauser, Arthur A. "Musicianship and Good Performance," An Address to Members of C.B.D.N.A., National Convention, 1950.
20. Shaughnessy, Robert M. *Harmonic and Contrapuntal Elements in Selected School Concert Band Compositions,* unpublished dissertation, Boston University, 1963.
21. Wareham, Duane Emerson. *The Development and Evaluation of Objective Criteria for Grading Band Music Into Six Levels of Difficulty,* unpublished dissertation, The Penn State University, 1967.

Monograph

22. Music Industry Council. *The Music Educator's Business Handbook,* Washington, D.C., Music Industry Council, 1965.

6

Four Keys for Determining
Topnotch Training Literature

BUILDING A SOLID FOUNDATION
IS IMPORTANT

When the band director thinks about training literature, he reiterates the concept that the band library represents his program's "course of study." In this respect, training literature forms the foundation on which this course is based. But as Colwell notes, "Serving up good music is not like serving up food—there is no 'instant Beethoven' or 'Johann Sebastian Bach Mix.' Instruction books and teaching materials must be used for learning, and the teacher needs objectives to help him select the most satisfactory materials and instruction books. Objectives are a device to bring the fuzzy purpose of activities into the sharp focus of learning." [1]

Andrews and Leeder feel that the materials studied by the band have a great bearing on its success; these materials, whether for the beginning class or advanced band, ". . . should take into consideration the sociophysiological maturation of the students as well as their technical proficiency." [15] Many band directors experience a condition of an ever-changing status quo in their program, that is, qualitatively and quantitatively their programs are never exactly the same one year to the next. As in the case of music selected for performance, the director considers this factor in the choice of materials for his band library. This suggests that the truly sincere director has a knowledge of suitable and effective literature but also ". . . will keep abreast of the newly published materials and modern practices that pertain to their proper application." [12] Since the band director works for both immediate and long-range results, the selection of training literature which establishes a proper solid musical and technical foundation is tremendously important.

The director who has beginning instrument class instruction as a part of his teaching responsibilities soon realizes that he must have, or quickly achieve, a comprehensive understanding of wind and percussion instruments. Resource help may be found in that training literature which has a thorough, well-planned teacher's manual.[3] This factor is mentioned mainly to emphasize the importance of building a good foundation through a careful and analytical selection of training literature.

TYPES OF TRAINING LITERATURE

Since shortly before World War II, but most assuredly after it, the scope of training literature for bands has been astonishing regarding volume and variety of types. Today, the situation is more propitious for the director; he has available to him any number of method books that may be designed for or are suitable to his particular instrumental program. The main point he must realize is that ". . . no method book, regardless of its merit, can possibly adapt itself to every situation." [12] Therefore, the director must be quite certain that his selection is appropriate to his needs and objectives.

Elementary School

For many students the elementary school is their first contact and experience with formal instrumental music study. Instrumental music should provide the primary avenue to musicianship, the solid foundation to which we refer. Leonhard and House described students' experiences at this level as being ". . . largely investigative of all the aspects of music as it affects the individual. . . ." They also admonish the instrumental music in-

structor ". . . not to emphasize performance *per se* but to view
. . . playing as a means to developing broad musicianship." [5]

Earlier in this book, it was stated that the students' instrumental
experiences should be conceived as a continuous, on-going procedure from inception to the end of schooling. Materials for the
library should be selected to correlate with this approach. Mindful
of this fact, the director should choose beginning literature which
will establish the necessary fundamental knowledge and skills of
music in general and instrumental music in particular. Prescott
and Chidester enumerate knowledge and skills as consisting of
". . . such fundamentals as posture, tuning, breathing, time
evaluations, breath control, scale and interval fluency, articulation,
musical terms familiarity, solo playing, chamber music playing,
and other essentials." [7]

Junior High School

There are a number of schools throughout the United States in
which beginning instrumental instruction takes place at the junior
high school level and not before. In these cases, the recommendations made regarding elementary school training literature would
apply here.

If the junior high school represents the intermediate or second
level of the instrumental program, then its training literature must
be selected accordingly. At this stage, the band is tending more
toward a performance type of ensemble. In addition to a large
amount of concert music, the folders should contain technique
and/or drill books. Although some directors feel that the term
"drill" has a distasteful connotation, the idea of drill is a necessary facet of the students' total technical development.

Training material should be transitional, that is, an extension of
the knowledge, skills, and capabilities learned and developed during elementary school years; it is the next step within the continuity of the instrumental program's aggregate course of study.
For example, some directors use scales and arpeggios in a variety
of articulations and rhythmic patterns for the development of
"tonality feeling" as well as digital facility and velocity. There are
also exercises utilizing long tones and chords for developing good
tone and intonation control. Training literature might also include

short etude-type exercises for expression, dynamics, tempi, balance, etc. According to Cecil, another ". . . principle which is important in the training of good band members is that of sight reading." He continues, "Every class should devote a certain amount of time to reading material at sight." [13]

Senior High School

After high school, unless the student continues his instrumental experience in one of a variety of possible ways (college/university band, professional work of some form, municipal or civic band, etc.), this level may represent the consummation of his formal musical training and participation in a band. In his selection of training materials for senior high school bands, the director should think in terms of bringing his students to the highest level of musical refinement of which they are capable.

In contrast to the elementary and junior high schools, the students' technical and musical needs should have transcended from the general to the specific. In other words, at this school level the director must be aware of the fact that his band has particular weaknesses or is lacking in certain areas of musical knowledge or performing ability. He then has only to select the unique training literature to solve the isolated problem. There are a conglomerate of types of method books for just about every musical or technical problem confronting a band.

Again, there should be material which will help the student make a smooth transition from junior to senior high school. If the band as a whole may need more training in one or more of the musical elements (keys, meters, rhythm, balance, form, intonation, etc.), the director should include drill or technique studies as a definite part of the band's training literature. Some directors continue to stress good tone production and control through use of warm-up exercises, chorales, or chord progressions. Righter suggests that the library contain a certain amount of literature which has more value as training rather than program material, ". . . as a means of teaching specific skills." [8] This may be in the form of sight-reading music, or music too difficult for the band to perform in concert. Examples of training literature which may be used for various purposes are listed in the following section.

Resource Training Literature

Most beginning instrumental instruction books are designed to meet one or all of three categories: (1) class (homogeneous or heterogeneous); (2) full band or ensemble; and (3) individual (with or without piano).

An inspection of band music publishers' catalogs reveals a multitudinous differentiation in types of training books. As will be noted in the following list, the director has available to him training literature to meet such criteria as objectives, development of skills, knowledge, or solutions to unique problems.

Some types of method books are:

> Beginning instrumental instruction
> Tone quality development
> Scales and arpeggios
> Chords
> Rhythm and rest patterns
> Phrasing studies
> Articulation studies
> Musical style
> Intonation control
> Transition from instrument to instrument
> Musical fundamentals
> Ensemble experience
> Program materials
> Balance
> Rehearsal fundamentals
> Studies in various tempi
> Precision studies

Revelli, Prescott and Chidester agree that, with the number of books devoted to training beginning instrumentalists, each with their unique approach, principles and diversity of types of instructional material included in them, there is no need for additional publications on the market, it is already flooded to capacity.[7, 12] Sampson found that available method books generally reveal certain deficiencies, in spite of their scope, and there is still room for improvement, especially in light of current learning and teaching theories. These deficiencies will be noted later.

PROBLEMS, PROBLEMS!

Much of the training literature on the market is appropriate and useful for most of the school situations in the United States. Herendeen feels that ". . . many circumstances surround and dictate the efficacy of its (the individual method book) use in each individual school or system." [11] In his many articles for *The School Musician* magazine in which he has analyzed and reviewed a considerable number of method books, Herendeen describes the problems which publishers face with regard to this type of literature. He writes that the value of these books ". . . may well be contingent upon several factors effecting their usefulness. The teacher may variously desire the following:

1. Fast results for quick concertizing.
2. Slower beginner progress; no pressure for fast results and concertizing.
3. A beginner program in the 6th grade or above.
4. Less mature beginners at 4th grade level.
5. High school beginner classes.
6. Most efficient use of very little teacher time.
7. Supplementary material for advanced groups." [11]

From a practical viewpoint, it is difficult if not impossible for a publisher to meet each and every one of these demands in one single publication.

Sampson investigated deficiencies in past and current method books. He quotes Felmet who concluded the following factors concerning training literature:

1. Beginning instrumental method books do not make enough use of pictures.
2. Their instructions regarding the care of instruments are inadequate.
3. They tend to favor the B-flat instruments.
4. Only two out of five books evaluated contained testing material.
5. Most books did not include practice record charts.
6. Information about music literature was generally absent from method books.
7. Fingering charts were often difficult to understand. [14]

On the basis of applying an evaluative form, Sampson was able to arrive at the following list of deficiencies in method books generally:

1. Not enough special pages for individual instruments.
2. Insufficient use of chromatics.
3. Too little solo material.
4. Insufficient inclusion of trios and quartets.
5. Too few rounds and canons.
6. Not enough descants, *obligati*, etc.
7. Inadequate use of arrows to indicate new content material.
8. Insufficient inclusion of:  and pick-up notes.
9. Not enough syncopation.
10. Insufficient use of triplets.
11. Too little use of tetrachords (half scales) and complete scales.
12. Insufficient use of the key of "C".[14]

Sampson recommends that the instrumental teacher may be able to overcome these deficiencies by utilizing supplementary materials and, through experimentation, determine which combination of two or more method books would be effective for use in his program.

THE FOUR KEYS

Before describing the "keys" which will help open the door to selecting the very best possible training literature, it may be apropos to interpolate several categories under which training literature may be classified. Herendeen lists these as: "(1) All-Purpose Methods; (2) Supplemental Studies; (3) Interest Builders; (4) Enrichment Materials; and, (5) Special Area Texts." [11] Revelli analyzes some of the current training literature as ". . . torso or short-cut methods . . ." due to the fact that their ". . . objectives place emphasis upon (1) Motivation, (2) Mass production, (3) Public performance earlier than desirable." [12] He feels these are weak because they lack in sufficient training in technique and fundamentals.

An inspection of contemporary training literature and a survey of recommendations found in sources devoted to the subject of selecting this type of material suggest that the criteria may be grouped under four general headings: (1) Type or Purpose of the Literature; (2) Musical Criteria; (3) Educational Criteria; and (4) Physical Characteristics. These headings are not independent but vividly overlap and are, therefore, interdependent. For instance, the second and third headings contain individual factors which may apply equally well under either one.

Type or Purpose of the Literature

Is the literature intended for use by beginning instrumentalists, or for students at the intermediate or advanced levels? Beginning instruction methods are designed for use by individual instruments, class (homogeneous or heterogeneous), or full ensemble. There are more publications which are intended to serve all three purposes; however, the sections for individual use sometimes suffer due to lack of sufficient space to develop idiomatic technique and are written as a compromise method designed for varied usage.

A few publishers' catalogs include a wide range in types of training literature; because of this fact, they are able to limit the musical material within a single publication to specific areas or isolated musical problems (as noted in the list of types of method books). This is in contrast to the publisher whose training literature output is limited to one or very few publications; that company must, as much as possible, broaden the scope of the information offered in a single method book. When inspecting training literature the director must also determine whether the book is designed to emphasize fundamentals of music, the techniques required to play an instrument, or both. Literature at the intermediate and advanced levels emphasizes further development, knowledge, and skills in one or the other area (more technique or more musical knowledge).

The band director likewise must be concerned about the literature's "area of appeal." For example, the book may appeal to the slow learner or to the extra-achiever. With the amount of training literature on the market, one must also determine whether or not a publication has an original approach or if it is merely a rehash of other similar publications. The students' background must be considered when choosing training literature. Generally, there are three types: (1) students with no background in music; (2) students with some background in music; and (3) students with much background in music.[14]

A few author/composers feel that a book designed for training purposes should be usable by any combination of players; it should not be exclusively homogeneous. Others state that the main purpose of all instruction books is to present musical and technical fundamentals that any player must know about music and his own particular instrument at an express stage of development. In general, we may conclude that training literature should be selected to fit the type of class, group, or purpose for which it is intended. The director must be highly discriminative about his choice and arrive at a decision only after an exacting and lengthy analysis of all available materials.

Musical Criteria

Since we are involved with the development of musicianship, albeit the elementary level, perhaps the most important criteria in the selection of training literature is that it contains material of genuine musical quality and that it is suitable for the level for which it is meant to be used. The problem of providing musical material which would maintain a student's interest and foster his technical development at the same time begins with the author/composer and ends in the hands of the publisher. Norman analyzed the material found in the literature for training and instruction as varying between one of two extremes; ". . . from the traditional procedure of building a solid technical foundation before venturing into music to the complete abandonment of all attempts at a logical development of playing skill." [6] His recommendation is that an effective approach would be ". . . somewhere in between these extremes—a method so planned as to carry forward the interest of the child and at the same time provide the opportunity for attaining some degree of technical command." [6] Perhaps the most important point about musical criteria is that there should be as much variety as possible; as the students advance in knowledge, facility, and ability, the musical material should become more varied in style, keys, meters, rhythms, and articulation.

Melodic Approach.   Regardless of the approach, many experts feel that the fundamental orientation of beginning instructional material should be *melodic.* Generally, musical examples should consist of familiar melodies, folk songs, public domain music, art songs, and excerpts from "classical" sources. To provide a smooth transition from the general music class to the instrumental music class, tunes from general music book series are utilized in many method books. The use of such familiar music could serve as an ear-training aid in the detection of incorrect notes or carelessness regarding key signatures. Naturally, not all the musical material can consist of this type of literature. Author/composers tend to give original exercises or tunes "catch-name" titles for interest and appeal; this mode of presentation gives an attractiveness to lessons that could be deadly dull routine exercises for the student. Some author/composers of training literature are clever enough to develop technical studies from good, quality melodic sources.

Unison and Ensemble Studies.   There should be a balance between unison and ensemble material in the method book. Unison exercises are important for the use of comparison (by students with each other) and development of confidence on the part of the individual student. Unison material is likewise valuable for the intermediate and advanced player. Herendeen feels that "The beginner should have harmonized studies as soon as he is 'tone-sure' of himself." [11] Since a greater percentage of the player's future performing experiences will be in ensembles of various types and sizes, ensemble music in training literature is necessary, both from a musical and motivational point of view. Even beginning books should have several "program pieces" to provide students with a sense of feeling for playing in full band. Bilik, for one, strongly maintains that young players play too much ensemble or *tutti* style music; he claims that this brings about the ". . . problem of solo performance weakness. . . . By the 7th or 8th grade, a student should normally have enough confidence in his instrument to be able to leave the protective tonal confines of the ensemble, at least in a limited situation." [10] Although Bilik is referring to concert music, the concept may be applied to training literature as well.

Rhythm.   In addition to melodic interest, training literature should provide for solid rhythmic knowledge, comprehension, feeling, and correct performance. A parallel of rhythm (note values and duration) is rest or silence and representative symbols. The materials should include devices or exercises for proper development of counting rests. Method books vary in their approach to teaching rhythm; some use visual or sound symbols (up-and-down arrows, foot-tapping, hand-clapping) while others employ word associations.

After extensive experience with analyzing a wide range of training literature, Herendeen has some strong personal opinions and recommendations concerning the introduction of rhythm and note-value observance to beginning instrumentalists. First, he opines that ". . . following sufficient preparatory long tones, the beginning exercises should be compounded from the quarter note rather than the whole note. Since the quarter note may be considered basic to counting, it makes for quicker comprehension to start with the basic unit rather than the ultimate or resultant compound arrived at by adding." [11] Second, the most logical progression for learning dotted-note values is from large to smaller, such as a dotted-half note followed by a quarter, then a dotted-quarter note followed by an eighth-note, and lastly the dotted-eighth followed by a sixteenth-note. Third, a few books simplify the system of counting within a measure by basing the count of notes and compounds on their actual value and not on their ordinal beat in the measure. For example, "The notes and compounds are constructed of 'ones' . . . ," so, "A half note occurring on the third count would still be counted, 'one-two.' A dotted quarter is 'one-two-and' irrespective of its place within the measure." [11]

Miscellany. Naturally, the director will have to consider such specific items as key signatures, meter signatures, scales, dynamics, expression markings, note values, rhythm patterns, and form. Some experts recommend a limited amount of chromaticism in beginning training literature. Concerning the relative importance given to these within the broader framework of musical elements, the director must base his judgment on such factors as: the type of instrumental program he has in operation; the grade level he starts beginning students; whether the class is homogeneous or heterogeneous, etc.; the students' background (amount of prior study if any); the instrumentation of the beginning class; and the objectives and activities of the program.

Although one should not expect to find the same quantity of exercises as in a book especially designed for individual instruction, training literature should contain some special material for problems idiomatic to each instrument. Usually such exercises are in the form of supplementary studies for individual instrument problems. The book should contain sound and thorough fundamental concepts and training for each instrument in such factors as embouchure, position, articulation, tone production and control.

Related to the specific musical elements listed above would be a glossary of musical terms. Instrumental music should provide strong and positive instruction in the correct meaning and usage of musical terms. Some training literature includes musical terms and definitions within the context of separate lessons as the need and occasion arises. Further, whatever method is utilized in the book, there should be some provision for testing the students on musical terms.

Bilik writes, "The method book is a kind of hotbed for the growth and development of the six fundamentals upon which bands are judged at most state contests: balance, blend, intonation, tone production, fluency of technique, and musicianship." [10]

Educational Criteria

Logical Development.   Since the director should be concerned with the musical and technical maturation of his students, it follows then that one of the most important factors within this criteria is the logical, sequential development of the material in training literature. Norman defines logical development as ". . . the easy step-by-step progression of study material, one problem leading logically into another." [6] One of the shortcomings of some training literature is that the musical examples and technical exercises progress too rapidly. Very critical examination will reveal that ". . . too many new skills are introduced before others have had a chance to become established . . ." and causes ". . . the new learning (to) interfere with the old. . . ." [4] Kuhn calls this process *negative transfer of training.* As each new technique, problem, or unit is introduced, the student should be allowed a reasonable amount of time to absorb, assimilate, and master it before moving on to the next one. This can be accomplished through sufficient musical exercises to guarantee learning and development.

The director must bear in mind that the publisher who offers a limited amount of training literature in his catalog is most likely to include as much material for musical and technical achievement as is possible within the 25 to 35 total number of pages in the average method book. The publisher does this because his output in this instance would not include individual books on isolated instructional problems; also, publication costs (which determine retail sales costs) affect the scope and length of the book. A few publishers offer what might be regarded as a complete curriculum of course of study for band training from beginning to advanced studies via their training literature.

Unit-Lessons.   Several experts and author/composers each believe that all new elements introduced in the instruction book may be learned more effectively if applied to the musical content. Assimilation of knowledge and technique is more cogent if the book is divided into unit-lessons or topics. This method of structure tends to create ". . . a feeling of accomplishment within the child." [11] Brevity of the exercises is also a vital factor, especially at the beginning level. The major reason for this is the problem of endurance (embouchure fatigue, fingers, arms, breathing capacity, etc.). Another reason is that the young beginner is more likely to successfully complete a short exercise thereby allowing him the mental security of having done well.

Interest.   What has been described regarding logical development and the rate of speed at which new technique and information is introduced can affect interest. Previously, it was pointed out that, for various reasons, the instruction book should not progress too rapidly. The opposite effect could be equally detrimental; if the book moves too slowly, that is, too much space is alloted to each unit or topic, the students would not make good progress and possibly lose interest.

Norman describes the various devices which author/composers have used to produce an interesting and stimulating approach in their method books. "Some of the more common of these are: (1) the formation of the class into an ensemble so that the student immediately feels that he is actually doing the thing in which he is chiefly interested, i.e., participating in an orchestra or band; (2)

an abundance of material of sufficiently easy grade so that the pupil may advance rapidly in the instructional material; (3) a strong foundation laid in technical skill which will guarantee a steady growth upon the part of the pupil . . . (4) relating the instructional material to the music taught in the grade school classes thus insuring a continuous functioning unit of learning; (5) providing for the child's natural interest in music by furnishing him from the very beginning an abundance of fine melodies from which to draw technical studies as the need for them is felt by the student himself. . . ." [6]

Instrument Information. The method book should contain photographs of playing posture, holding position (hands, fingers, etc.), embouchure, etc., preferably posed by student-players of the same general age level as those using the book. Equally important are photographs or illustrations showing proper assembly of the instrument. These photographs can serve as a handy self-check system for the student when practicing at home. Directors and students would be less confused, and publishers could reduce their publication costs somewhat if the fingering charts in training literature were more closely related to the amount and type of technical material included in method books. For instance, there seems to be no practical reason for inserting a complete fingering chart, including alternate, chromatic, and trill fingerings, in a beginning instruction book. Those fingerings that are offered in the chart should be suitable to the requirements of the specific book. In intermediate and advanced level books, more complete charts would be mandatory. The director must acquire a complete set for all instruments for himself, and seek additional help from professionals. The text should indicate preferred fingerings in unusual or unique passages. Finally, instruction books should contain a thorough description of the proper care of each instrument, mouthpiece, reed (including selection and care), and what accessories should be purchased.

Miscellany. Revelli suggests that the instructional material should ". . . emphasize the development of the student's musical progress rather than his facility and technical aspects of performance." He offers the director one final factor when he recommends that the individual training literature book ". . . fulfill(s) its intended objectives and come(s) to a logical conclusion." [12]

Physical Characteristics

Reference to "physical characteristics," generally means such factors as editing, format, cost, durability, and overall attractiveness of the training literature. For purposes of clarification, physical characteristics will be discussed under two broad headings: *layout* and *physical appearance*.

Layout. First, one must consider whether or not the *format* shows good organization. Format includes the make-up of the book generally and the individual printed page specifically. To reduce publication costs, some publishing companies cram as much material into a limited amount of space as possible. The result is an overcrowded appearance to the page, thereby contributing to a difficulty in focusing one's view to specific items. Further, the musical staff, text, symbols (notes, accidentals, expression markings, etc.), are smaller than is practical, creating a diminishing in distinction, clarity, and legibility. The director must decide whether: the pages are clear and not crowded; if the notes, text, and symbols are clear, large, and easy to read; and the expression markings, articulations, and tempi indications are clearly and properly edited. The primary importance of format is that if it is properly set up, it should help the student learn more quickly and effectively.

Photographs, illustrations, and any diagrams should be well-designed, clear-cut, and accurate. This writer remembers one well-known beginning method book that contained a photograph of a clarinet player, but printed backwards! The fingering chart must be accurate and expressly designed for the age level to which the book is directed so that the student may easily comprehend it. The text, or explanatory material should be as complete as possible but at the same time concise. For out-of-class practice, the text must be grammatically stylized and structured to be interesting and understood by the student's school and age level without "writing down" to him. Although difficult to ascertain without a detailed inspection of all the part books, instructional literature should be free from typographical errors in the text and musical material. The type of musical terms included should be commensurate with the musical knowledge disseminated in the book.

Many band directors prefer to have a table of contents in the book, for one reason as a guide in making practice assignments. Other directors insist that training books, at least at the beginning levels, have practice, assignment, and progress charts for motivational purposes and to show the student his rate of accomplishment at any given point. The inclusion of a sheet (or sheets) of blank manuscript paper is helpful for the director who wishes to include some form of music theory lessons in his instruction. Music theory may include note names, key signatures, meter signatures, rhythm patterns, rest patterns, etc. As in other academic disciplines, the student should be able to symbolize his subject in addition to verbalizing it, or performing it. The director would find this approach useful in checking on the effectiveness of his teaching as well as an evaluative method of student learning.

Physical Appearance.   Although almost all training literature is printed on quarto size stock, a few publishers produce it in octavo or quick-step (march) size. There are band directors, especially in rural localities with many bus students, who prefer the latter simply because it fits into a small instrument case easily; with larger cases it does not matter. It is more important to be concerned about the size of the book as related to the amount of information or material that is contained therein. These two aspects must be taken into consideration by the band director in making his selection.

Is the physical make-up and appearance of the book appropriate to the type, purpose, and school level for which it is intended? Since the instruction book will undergo considerable usage, it must be able to withstand constant handling. Therefore, the cover should be durable, the binding strong, and of good quality. For the beginning student, the method book should be attractive and have an appealing design, especially regarding illustrations, photographs, and general layout. Publishing costs have been rising yearly. However, the cost of the individual book should be in keeping with its physical characteristics and the scope of the material included within it. It would seem unreasonable to pay a high price for a book that is limited or evokes negative reactions in each of the four keys described above. The cost also should be commensurate with the manner in which the book meets the musical, educational, and physical characteristics established as criteria by the band director.

THE TEACHER'S MANUAL

Many of the criteria which have been previously described as an aid in the selection of training literature may be applied to the teacher's manual. There are, however, several factors which are unique to a teacher's manual and must be considered separately.

First of all, it is questionable to give serious consideration to a particular method or instructional book unless the publisher has provided a manual to accompany it. Obviously, the manual for a beginning instrument class method will differ from that designed to develop a specific area of performance such as technique, intonation, precision, style, rhythm, etc. The manual must be more than a two-line, piano, or even condensed score. It is an indispensable tool for the instructor, particularly for a ". . . less experienced teacher who may be looking for suggestions on organization and teaching procedures." [4] For the experienced teacher who has chosen newly published training literature, the manual will serve as a means for aiding him to make the most effective use of it and obtain the objectives or results outlined in the material by the author/composer.

The following list suggests the ideal *minimum* number and types of features which *should* be included in a teacher's manual for a beginning instrument class method book.

1. Full conductor's score, with separate piano accompaniment, for all musical exercises, examples, etc.
2. Teaching suggestions, lesson plans, topics, units.
3. Explanation of problems and principles presented with each lesson plan, topic, or unit.
4. An index or table of contents which shows the instructor what and where to find the specific information in the manual and the corresponding page in the student's book.
5. Basic fingering charts, as required for the book, in a separate section for each instrument.

6. Description of tone production, breath control, embouchure, posture, holding position, assembly, and articulation for each instrument.
7. The same photograph for each instrument that appears in the individual instrument books.
8. An explanation of music theory if testing on this aspect is part of the approach in the book.[14]

Coda

Supplementary Literature

In the description of criteria which is applicable to the selection of training literature, the impression may have been given that somewhere there exists the "perfect" or "ideal" beginning method or instruction book. This is far from the truth because any one publication contains certain limitations. The director must recognize this situation and select the material which, according to his judgment, is most appropriate and suitable to his unique requirements. In addition, he must evaluate and select some form of supplementary literature not only to augment but to fill in the gaps in the basic book. Kuhn agrees with this but points out that the supplementary literature must be ". . . of the same quality and yet varied from the basic text. . . ."[4]

Some directors prefer to select a single book which will develop fundamental musicianship and technical facility on an instrument and supplement this with a separate book of simple pieces and program music. Supplementary literature is also necessary to provide musical experiences which will make up for individual differences among the students in the ensemble. Supplementary literature also may be chosen for additional studies which are characteristic for each instrument.

Suggestions

Regardless of the value, objectives, and intent of the training literature, it will not be any better than the director who uses it. Someone in the past said that music (performing, composing, teaching), is 90% perspiration and 10% inspiration. Concerning the selection and use of training literature, Herendeen reminds us that "The backbone of retention is learning-reinforcement-drill-relearning and further reinforcement." [11] At the beginning of this chapter it was stated that, unfortunately, conditions in most instrumental programs never remain exactly the same from year to year. This may mean that a technique or instruction book which worked one year may not achieve the same results the next. The director should avoid the pitfalls of complacency and be willing to try new techniques and new materials.

Evaluation of Training Literature

The following evaluative form is offered as a guide and an aid to the band director in his selection of training literature. The writer is indebted to his personal friend, Dr. Paul E. Steg, Music Department, Northern Illinois University, De Kalb, Illinois, who originally designed this form as a graduate course project and with whom he shared the class at Wichita State University. The form below is an adaptation of the original.

SOLO, CLASS, AND ENSEMBLE
METHOD BOOK EVALUATION FORM

Title: _____

Composer: _____ *Editor:* _____

Publisher: _____ *Copyright Date:* _____

Prices: (Teacher's Manual) _____ (Parts) _____

Classification: (Check where applicable)

____Band Method	____Band Techniques
____Solo Method	____Music Fundamentals
____W.W. Method	____Beginning Method
____Brass Method	____Intermediate Method
____Percussion Method	____Advanced Method

Instrumentation: (Mark the number of parts)

____Piccolo	____Alto Sax	____Baritone—B.C.
____Flute	____Tenor Sax	____Baritone—T.C.
____Oboe	____Baritone Sax	____Tuba
____E♭ Clarinet	____Cornets	____Tympani
____B♭ Clarinet	____Trumpets	____Percussion
____Alto Clarinet	____French Horns	____Full Score

_____Bass Clarinet   _____E♭ Horns   _____Conductor's Score
_____Bassoon   _____Trombones   _____Piano Score
                                               _____Teacher's Manual

Evaluation: (Check or comment briefly where applicable)
  1. Musical Features (sources, styles, desirability)

_____Folk songs   _____Musical comedy
_____Standard classics   _____Etudes
_____Modern music   _____Technical studies
_____Familiar music   _____Small ensembles
_____Rounds, canons   _____Full band
_____Original music   _____Quality of music
Representative titles: _____

_____

  2. Educational Features
_____Graded material   _____School level of book
_____Preparatory studies   _____Rate of development
_____Variety of style   _____All instruments parallel
_____Variety of technical in difficulty
problems   _____All instruments parallel
_____Theory material   in interest
_____Explanation of
instrument technique

  3. Special Features (physical make-up, editing, etc.)
_____Fingering chart   _____Lesson plans
_____Glossary of general   _____Instructions
terminology   _____Format
_____Glossary of musical   _____Editing
terms   _____Notation size
_____Photos—illustrations _____Practice chart
_____Care of instruments   _____Progress chart
_____Index   _____Assignment chart
_____Table of contents   _____Phrase markings
_____Work sheets   _____Dynamic markings
_____Blank manuscript   _____Metronome markings
_____Quality of paper   _____Piano score markings
_____Quality of printing   _____Cross cues in score
_____Motivational devices
_____Size of page (quarto,
octavo, march)

4. Difficulty

_____W.W. EZ Range
_____W.W. Medium Range
_____W.W. Difficult Range
_____W.W. EZ Technique
_____W.W. Medium Technique
_____W.W. Difficult Technique
_____Brass EZ range
_____Brass Medium Range
_____Brass Difficult Range
_____Brass EZ Technique
_____Brass Medium Technique
_____Brass Difficult Technique

_____Percussion Reading
_____Percussion Rudiments
_____Percussion Reading—
Rudiments
_____Frequency of chromatics
_____Frequency of key change
_____Frequency of meter change
_____Frequency of tempo change
_____Difficult rhythms

Use the reverse side for further comments.

Selected References

Books

1. Colwell, Richard J. *The Teaching of Instrumental Music,* New York: Appleton-Century-Crofts, 1969.
2. Hoffer, Charles R. *Teaching Music in the Secondary Schools,* Belmont, California: Wadsworth Publishing Company, Inc., 1964.
3. House, Robert W. *Instrumental Music for Today's Schools,* Englewood Cliffs, New Jersey: Prentice-Hall, Inc., 1965.
4. Kuhn, Wolfgang. *Instrumental Music: Principles and Methods of Instruction,* Boston: Allyn and Bacon, 1962.
5. Leonhard, Charles and Robert W. House. *Foundations and Principles of Music Education,* New York: McGraw-Hill Book Company, 1959.
6. Norman, Theodore. *Instrumental Music in the Public Schools,* Philadelphia: Ditson Company, 1941.
7. Prescott, Gerald R. and Lawrence W. Chidster. *Getting Results with School Bands,* New York: Carl Fischer, Inc., 1938.
8. Righter, Charles B. *Success in Teaching School Orchestras and Bands,* Minneapolis, Minn.: Schmitt, Hall, and McCreary Co., 1945.
9. Singleton, Ira C. *Music in Secondary Schools,* Boston: Allyn and Bacon, 1963.

Periodicals

10. Bilik, Jerry H. "A Missing Ingredient in Music Education," *The School Musician,* Vol. 35, No. 8, April, 1964.

11. Herendeen, James F. "Let's Look at Methods" (A Clinical Column), *The School Musician*, beginning September, 1960.
12. Revelli, William D. "The Selection and Evaluation of Teaching Materials," *Etude*, Nov., 1954.

Unpublished Literature

13. Cecil, Herbert M. *Fundamental Principles of the Organization, Management, and Teaching of the School Band,* unpublished dissertation, University of Rochester, 1953.
14. Sampson, Ulysses Thomas. *An Identification of Deficiencies in Past and Current Method Book for Beginning Heterogeneous Wind-Percussion Class Instrumental Music Instruction,* unpublished dissertation, Indiana University, 1968.
15. Wareham, Duane Emerson. *The Development and Evaluation of Objective Criteria for Grading Band Music into Six Levels of Difficulty,* unpublished dissertation, The Pennsylvania State University, 1967.

7

A Proven Method for
Systematic Acquisitions

THE LIBRARY AND EXPENDITURES

Long-Range Planning Is a Must

If the band director wishes his instrumental music program to steadily progress, improve, and function effectively, then he must see to it that the various ensembles within the program have an adequate supply of appropriate music. The library must be regularly supplemented not so much from week to week or month to month, but rather on a long-range basis.[9] Since, as we have stated before, conditions for some bands change from year to year, many directors plan their acquisitions annually. Singleton, however, feels that the library should be ". . . developed over a period of years, partly to avoid the need for large expenditures in any one year and partly to permit purchase of new music as it is published."[10] Whatever approach the director favors, acquisitions should be made in terms of the objectives he has determined for his particular program. Additions to the library must provide the students with musical experiences which are necessary in attaining those objectives. This, then is what is meant by long-range planning; as the director selects each piece of music, whether for performance or training, he must consider it as building toward specific end results.

Judicious Use of the Budget

The acquisition of new literature is not the only major concern of the band director regarding the expansion of materials in his library. He must also consider the replenishment factor. Directors are prone to use certain compositions from one year to the next; parts become worn out due to frequent use and must, therefore, be replaced. There is also the situation of parts which have been lost and must be replaced. When purchased as part of a "set" (the total instrumentation), these individual parts are not too expensive, but when purchased as extra parts they can add up to a surprisingly large financial output (i.e., 15¢ to 20¢ per part in the "set" compared to about 75¢ to $1.25 as extra parts). The matter of ordering complete instrumentation and extra parts will be discussed later in this chapter.

Oddly enough, band directors generally have a reputation for lacking proper, efficient, and business-like management of the administrative aspects of their programs. Too often this seems to be the popular opinion among school administrators, publishers, and to a certain extent, also music dealers. We refer to the planning, use, and management of the budget or funds allocated for instrumental programs. Concerning acquisitions to the band library, Norman feels that "There is no department of instrumental organization where money invested can so quickly disappear as in inefficient management of the library." [8] A prerequisite for the band director in the supervision of his band program is careful planning of literature to be acquired, the budget, and the judicious use of available funds all in a business-like manner. The casual, haphazard approach indeed has no place in this function of instrumental music.

The writer has urged that the band director select only the very best or highest quality literature available according to the performing level, technical abilities, instrumentation, scope and function of his particular band. Norman warns the director of the possibility of "starving" his band musically due to a lack of music which fulfills the above factors and exemplifies ". . . the cheap clap-trap that floods the market." He continues, "The best is none too good. One saves nothing by economizing too rigidly in this department." [8] This statement hits home if one bears in mind that music of lower quality usually has limited value or use; it does little else than take up space in the library and stagnate there.

In addition to acquisition of new concert literature and replacement of worn or missing parts, Prescott and Chidester remind the director that he also has the duty of ". . . adding solo and chamber music literature, method books, standard texts, phonograph records, miniature scores, etc. . . ." to the library.[9]

BUDGETING AND ACQUISITIONS

Naturally, if the band director is to administer the band library efficiently, then a specific amount of money from the band's yearly budget should be allocated for this purpose. School boards and other administrative units vary in the manner in which they provide operational funds for the band or instrumental program. Some schools allocate a lump sum to be used for all expenditures incurred by the band while others break the funds down into individual areas such as music, equipment, uniforms, maintenance-repair, and miscellaneous (office supplies, accessories, etc.). Whatever the case, the band director must determine the amount of money his band library annually requires to meet the program's responsibilities and objectives.

Kuhn points out that "Some school systems insist on planning ahead and handing in purchase requests for all the materials needed for the school year. . . ."[6] If the director hopes to realize progress and steady improvement in his students, he has no other recourse than to make certain that he is not wasting precious monies on trivial or ineffective music. Since the director must operate within the framework of his school's business procedures, careful, advance planning of acquisitions to the library is a necessity.[6]

Be Systematic

The amount of money the director apportions for the library from his overall budget will depend upon such factors as: the number of performing organizations in the program; the instrumentations of the various organizations; the types of activities and performances for which his program is responsible. This implies that the director must establish ". . . a library budget made up of separate categories to show the types of music to be purchased," and assign a relative value of importance to each of these various categories.[10] Singleton goes so far as to recommend that the director give the individual categories a percentage weight as a method for determining the amount of music within each type he should acquire during the school year. He cautions that the percentages should be ". . . adjusted as needed to build a new or maintain an established library, or to supply the needs of large or smaller performing groups."[10] According to Singleton the percentages are:

Heavy concert music	30%
Light concert music	20%
Marches	5%
Novelties	3%
Chorales	3%
Solos with full accompaniment	3%
Ensemble drill and tuning exercises	3% [10]

By subdividing the library budget in this manner, the director would be able to use it as a guide for purchasing music as well as building a comprehensive and balanced library in all classifications.

Another breakdown of music by types would be the following: concert, marching, training, sight-reading, and entertainment. Many directors are cautious of overbuying the "quick-hit" popular tunes since they are a "one-shot" seasonal item. As an adjudicator and clinician, the writer has had the privilege of meeting and discussing the matter of band literature with many persons who have earned the reputation of being successful instrumental music teachers. In practically all instances, these men strongly advocated the inclusion and regular use of sight-reading materials in the band library. Ivory offers a broader, more general division of band music as an approach to alloting percentages for budgetary purposes. They are:

I. *Serious*	II. *Characteristics*
Suites, etc. originally written for band	Concert marches
Transcription of standard-symphonic overtures	Standard marches
Chorales	Operetta, musical comedy selections
	Potpourris, medleys, fantasies

  III. Light   *IV. Miscellaneous*

Novelties
Modern American rhythms
Popular hits
Spanish, Latin-American rhythms and marches
Program-type concerts overtures, etc.
Themes from or improvisations on standard
  symphonic works [14]

Prescott and Chidester warn against ". . . leaning too heavily toward any one type; (because) the library needs to be a balanced one." [9]

Distribution of the Budget

In 1938, Prescott and Chidester recommended the following amounts for band music allotments: ". . . $700 a year for a complete band—$500 a year for an average band—$400 a year for a small band." [9] In 1949, Jones listed these figures for expenditures of band funds for the library: small school—$250; average school—$500; large school—$950.[5] The rising costs in the publishing of band music is reflected in current retail prices which have increased at least 100% since the 1930s and '40s. So, if one were to use the amounts suggested above as guidelines, he should revise them accordingly.

Based on the $700 figure, Prescott and Chidester break the distribution of the budget down into three main headings and apportion sums to each ". . . to show the relative proportions of the three main elements and their component parts. . . (1) Administration and Upkeep on the Present Library—$50.00; (2) New Music—$450.00; (3) Other Band Literature—$200.00." [9]

A few of the country's major music dealer houses recommend that if the band director's school business policy allows it, he should place a blanket purchase order with his local dealer and make purchases against it. The dealer would assume the major bookkeeping responsibilities and periodically advise the director as to the status of his account. To these dealers, this seems to be the most business-like manner of handling this segment of the band budget. It certainly would save the director and the school purchasing agent considerable time and effort in making out separate purchase orders each time the director needed to make an acquisition. This method also might avoid any possible administrative errors or tie-ups in requisitioning music for the band library. There are band directors who prefer to place orders directly with the publishers; perhaps the local dealer (especially a small local dealer) may be out of stock on certain items due to a limited inventory. These persons want to be able to procure the music when needed. The solution is to anticipate one's needs far enough in advance for the dealer to have the item on hand when necessary.

A PROVEN METHOD

Your Local Music Dealer

The director should use the facilities of the complete educational music store. If the director is fortunate enough to have a music dealer in his town or nearby locale, it would be both ethical and practical to place orders for music directly with him. Music dealers feel that the director should consider buying music for his band in the same way he does the instruments and other equipment. One does not normally deal with the manufacturer of instruments as far as purchase orders are concerned.

Several music publishers likewise recommend that the band director patronize the local dealer. There are several advantages to this procedure. The dealer is in a good position to offer the director personalized service. Most of them are quite well informed about the musical and technical capabilities, needs, and requirements of the school bands in their area. He is, therefore, vitally interested and concerned about the director and his band. Many dealers suggest that the director leave his instrumentation with them so that when the director places an order for music, the dealer will fill it in the most economical way. It is the dealer who has information about new releases and can advise the director about them and their appropriateness to his band. Directors may keep the number of accounts at a minimum by ordering their music from one source.[4] Due to matters of economy, many publishers are discontinuing the policy of making extra parts readily available. The dealer, however, can provide extra parts as a part of his service to bands and their directors.

Kurtz is surprised to learn that many directors are unaware of the number and types of services offered them by music dealers. He enumerates them as: "(1) Music on approval. The dealer will 'loan' you music . . . for examination as to its suitability for your group. This music can be titles of your choice, or if you prefer, the Educational Director will assemble your music for you. . . (2) Pre-paid order forms, both first class and air mail, are available for the asking.(3) Free filing envelopes and indexing cards, per title, are furnished by some of the music sources. (4) Prompt, efficient, one day service is available from many of the larger dealers who carry a complete stock of all publishers. (5) Periodic listings of new materials are offered to those who take the trouble to get their name on the mailing list. (6) Several of the dealers, publishers, and instrument manufacturers will assist in making available as clinician-conductors, their educational directors, heads of departments, composers, and outstanding well-known music personalities." [15]

Instrumentation

The band director who has projected an ultimate instrumenta-tion for his band, based on the objectives for his program, should order music according to that instrumentation, even though he has not realized it at the time.[9] While building the program, some of his library will include unused parts, but it is a point of economy to purchase music in this manner rather than pay for expensive extra parts at a later date. In other words, if the band's in-strumentation is not firmly established but has possibilities for increasing, the director ". . . should be sure to choose an arrange-ment large enough to provide for the future development of the band." [17]

Until recently, publishers issued band works in different sets which varied in number of parts and instrumentation. For ex-ample, some publishers offered sets designated as "Small Band," "Full Band," and "Symphonic Band," while another labeled his "Small Band," "Concert Band," and "Full Band." This meant that a director could purchase a band composition which, although scored for a full instrumentation, was available without such parts as 2nd flute, 2nd oboe, 2nd bassoon, alto or bass clarinets, and 3rd and 4th horn. These parts were scored as "doubling" instruments and, while their inclusion might enhance the performance of a particular piece, they were not absolutely vital. It is true that such situations were limited to "easy" and Class C and D works. Most of the major works were published only in a full or symphonic band instrumentation with extra parts available to fill out larger bands.

Grasso states that these conditions posed some confusion for band directors and publishing and financial problems for the music publishing industry. In 1964, as chairman of the Band Instrument Committee of the Music Publishers' Association, he gave a report to the Fourth Annual Meeting of the North American Band Directors' Coordinating Committee in Chicago. Mr. Grasso described the publishing industry's pride of its share and contribution to the development of the present-day band. Periodically, however, it becomes necessary to get down to the "nit" and "grit" (profit and loss) of publishing. He informed the committee that "Publishing music is a business. To survive in business one must make profits. To make a profit one must *sell* his product. To *sell* his product one must find a market." [12] At that time, publishers were faced with a serious dilemma due to the fact that the band as a single-unit concept as it was once known no longer existed. Now it is ". . . an organization known by a myriad of titles, such as: Concert Band, Symphonic Band, Symphony Band, Wind Ensemble, Marching Band, Gridiron Band, Basketball Band, Pep Band, Military Band, etc., *ad infinitum*." [12] The major concern to the publishers was "What actually is this organization with its many descriptive titles? What should its instrumentation be? For practical musical purposes, how large a musical complement should the band be?" [12]

To find a solution to the problems, representatives of the music publishing industry began a series of meetings with a committee made up of members of the American School Band Directors' Association (A.S.B.D.A.). After many subsequent meetings and correspondence via questionnaires with members of the A.S.B.D.A., definite recommendations were agreed upon. The result of that action was the following Music Publishers' Association Recommended Instrumentation for a band: [12]

Full Score
Condensed Score
C Piccolo
1st Flute—2
2nd Flute—2
1st Oboe
2nd Oboe (if scored)
1st Bassoon
2nd Bassoon
    Contra-Bassoon (if scored)
E♭ Clarinet
1st B♭ Clarinet—3
2nd B♭ Clarinet—3
3rd B♭ Clarinet—3
E♭ Alto Clarinet
B♭ Bass Clarinet
Contra-Bass Clarinet E♭ and
    BB♭ back to back (if scored)
1st E♭ Alto Sax
2nd E♭ Alto Sax
B♭ Tenor Sax
E♭ Baritone Sax
1st B♭ Cornet—2
2nd B♭ Cornet—2
3rd B♭ Cornet—2
1st B♭ Trumpet (if scored)
2nd B♭ Trumpet (if scored)
E♭—F Horns back to back
1st Trombone
2nd Trombone
3rd Trombone
Baritone Treble Clef
Euphonium Bass Clef
Basses—4
String Bass
Tympani
Percussion—4 (if scored)

Symphonic Band

Full Band plus the following additional:
Flutes—2
B♭ Clarinets—1 each

E♭ Alto Clarinet—1
B♭ Bass Clarinet—1
B♭ Cornets—1 each
Euphonium—1
Basses—2

That was in 1964. To ascertain present-day policies, a survey of band music publishers was made regarding sets and extra parts as related to the most economical way for directors to order music. A compendium of the most common responses from that survey follows. A difference of opinion still exists as to the most feasible policy for providing an adequate set of parts to the director. According to their estimation, the trend is to the "Complete Band" set in place of the old "Full" and "Symphonic" sets; on the basis of information from both band directors and dealers, companies have turned to the "Complete" set almost 100%. A few publishers have retained publications in full and symphonic band sets (consisting of the older catalog items copyrighted before the adoption of the newer set), and their newer issues in the "Complete" or "Symphonic" set as some of them refer to it. The change was brought about by an analysis of opinions among band directors that it is cheaper to buy the new set than the old full band set plus extra parts. One company in particular reported that it publishes more parts in the new set than is recommended by the Music Publishers' Association instrumentation. More important is the fact that items are published in their new sets because they are so scored by the composer rather than any stipulation by the company editorial policy.

One respondee felt that one reason why most publishers offer a single set is because there has been so much duplication of extra parts, even in violation of the Copyright Law! Although extra parts are available with the new "Complete" set, it includes sufficient parts for 100 or more performers (about 65 to 70 parts) at least for serious or major works. Some publishers continue to print two editions, full and symphonic, for their "easier" or Class C and D band publications and the new set for more difficult compositions.

From a purely technical angle of the publishing business, one publisher attributed the trend to the new set to automation and the realization of full employment. This company continued to print full and symphonic sets for every band composition feeling that it could better serve the interests and needs of the band director. Print quotations for both full and symphonic print runs and the complete set alone brought this company to the conclusion that the single set is more economical. While the director of a small band may consider it a waste of money to receive more parts than he can use, the publisher can make the larger set of parts available to all band directors at a lesser figure than he must ask for the old full set if he is to print both full and symphonic sets. It is, therefore, more frugal for the director to order the complete (or symphonic) set. It is more expensive to buy extra parts individually than it is to buy the complete set and have extra parts on hand.

The publisher's plight may be seen in the fact that it costs him a minimum average of $5.00 to process each order received. The problem becomes obvious, for example, when he receives an order for three extra parts retailing from 50¢ to $1.25 each. As a result, he sells only complete sets so that extra parts may not be necessary. The actual cost per part when it is included in a complete set is much lower than the price for extra parts individually.

A compilation was made of the instrumentation and number of parts available in the new "Complete" set offered by band music publishers in their latest issues (1969–70). The instrumentation and average number of parts (not including the scores) may be noted in the table.

The major exceptions to the table figures were publications for the "very young band" (elementary and junior high school) in which cases the "Complete" set was printed out but with a modified or limited instrumentation and fewer number of parts for each instrument. One composition contained a total of 47 individual parts plus scores. Several scores indicated combined parts printed on one page, such as: 1st and 2nd flutes, 1st and 2nd E♭ Alto Sax, E♭ Alto Clarinet and E♭ Contra-Bass Clarinet, B♭ Bass Clarinet and BB♭ Contra-Bass Clarinet, E♭ Alto Clarinet and E♭ Baritone Sax, B♭ Bass Clarinet and B♭ Bass Sax, Contra-Bassoon with String Bass, and F and E♭ Horns back to back. Other differences in the instrumentation of individual works was due to unique scoring ideas of the composer rather than company policy. Band instrumentation has not changed radically since the late '30s. The number of parts included in the new set is an indication of the

COMPLETE OR SYMPHONIC SET

Piccolo	1
1st Flute	3
2nd Flute	3
1st Oboe	1
2nd Oboe	1
English Horn (if scored)	1
1st Bassoon	1
2nd Bassoon	1
Contra-Bassoon (if scored)	1
E♭ Clarinet (if scored)	1
1st B♭ Clarinet	3–4
2nd B♭ Clarinet	3–4
3rd B♭ Clarinet	3–4
E♭ Alto Clarinet	2
B♭ Bass Clarinet	2
E♭ Contra-Bass Clarinet (if scored)	1
BB♭ Contra-Bass Clarinet (if scored)	1
1st E♭ Alto Sax	1–2
2nd E♭ Alto Sax	1–2
B♭ Tenor Sax	1
E♭ Baritone Sax	1
B♭ Bass Sax	1
1st B♭ Cornet	2–3
2nd B♭ Cornet	2–3
3rd B♭ Cornet	2–3
1st B♭ Trumpet (if scored)	1
2nd B♭ Trumpet (if scored)	1
1st F Horn (with E♭ Horn)	1
2nd F Horn (with E♭ Horn)	1
3rd F Horn (with E♭ Horn)	1
4th F Horn (with E♭ Horn)	1
1st Trombone	1–2
2nd Trombone	1–2
3rd Trombone	1–2
Baritone (treble clef)	1
Baritone (bass clef)	2
Basses	6
String Bass (if scored)	1
Tympani	1
Percussion	4

Total = 64–75 parts

emphasis on other than traditional sections, while the addition of certain instruments (not generally included prior to the '50s) has been commensurate with the evolution of the style and type of band music.

Akers pleads with us not to think of the publisher as a crusader; although he will be pleased to cooperate in helping directors with problems, the solutions must be worked out by the directors as a body. The publisher, mindful of customer needs, wishes, taste, and trends, will do all he can to provide the very best materials at a fair price.[11] This brings us to an important matter. Regardless of current highly sophisticated and very efficient reproduction equipment, the band director has a legal and moral responsibility to himself, his students, the publisher, and his profession to purchase needed extra parts and scores in the usual purchasing procedures rather than make illegal copies. Last-minute desperation measures are no excuse. The proper approach is to plan and anticipate one's needs far enough in advance in order that the source of supply is able to procure all materials in plenty of time for the band's rehearsals and performance.

Considerable description has been devoted to the new "Complete" set; also, there are deviations to this instrumentation according to the character of the music and the musical and technical level of the band for whom the music is intended. Most publishers and dealer houses still advocate that a practical system for acquisitions is for the director to supply his source with the band's instrumentation and request that orders be filled in the most economical way.

Full Versus Condensed Scores

The band score has had almost as significant a development as the band itself. The score has evolved through a variety of types beginning with the single-line "lead sheet" when the conductor was also a performer in the band (usually solo cornetist). From the single-line, the score evolved into a two-line piano-conductor score then into a three- (with two treble and one bass line) and-four-line (two treble and two bass lines) condensed score and finally the full score. A compromise type of score, between the full and condensed versions, is the 8-line score for compositions of limited instrumentation, and simple melodic, rhythmic, and harmonic structure.

When the full score began to be included as a regular part of the printed sets with each new publication, there arose a difference of opinion among band directors regarding the inherent values of the full versus the condensed score. That the full score was included with many selections at all was due to an increasing demand for it by directors throughout the country. Cecil feels that ". . . the full score facilitates rehearsing and is well worth the extra money it costs." [17] Kuhn agrees with him and adds that a full score may be used ". . . as a tool for careful analysis, study, and teaching. . . ." [6] Goldman presents two viewpoints. He states, "It is obvious that a conductor cannot be expected to give an understanding performance of a work if he does not know what notes each instrument is supposed to play and if he does not clearly perceive the relation of the parts to the whole. Such knowledge can be derived only from a complete score which shows him exactly what the composer or arranger has written. A well-made condensed score can often be adequate, if the instrumental cues are clearly indicated and if the conductor takes the trouble to supplement his study of the conductor's score by an examination of the individual parts. But this is a roundabout and clumsy way of doing things, involving considerable waste of time." [2]

Opponents of the full score claim that their daily teaching schedule leaves little time for thorough and complete score study. Others state that their bands do not contain an instrumentation worthy of the purchase cost of a full score. A few directors argue that their performance schedule is so "tight" (few rehearsals between performances), that a full score is not needed and would only hamper the director's rehearsal routine. One statement which keeps "popping up" whenever this subject is discussed is that the director must constantly turn pages which interferes with his conducting technique and concentration process. Critics of the condensed score claim that orchestral conductors rarely, if ever, resort to use of condensed scores. One must remember, however, that orchestras tend to perform a more standard repertoire than do bands and their conductors more often than not conduct these works from memory. The best that a "plain ole' E-flat band director" can do to match this feat is usually when he conducts a standard march, the more talented band director notwithstanding. Goldman describes the ideal conditions in which a condensed score may be used; "Working with a band which has practically unlimited time to prepare for an occasional concert, a bandmaster can afford to take the necessary time during rehearsal to find out, if necessary, just what is written for each instrument." [2]

The policy, or approach, followed and advocated by the writer and a great number of band directors with whom he has discussed the matter, is that both full and condensed scores are purchased with the set if they are available. The full score is utilized for study, preparation, and use during rehearsals while the condensed score is used during the actual performance of the music. By the time of the performance, the music is known to the conductor and performers so there is no need for the full score; the condensed score also eliminates the time-consuming action of turning pages and allows the conductor to concentrate on the music itself. Many band directors prefer to use a condensed score when "reading through" pieces, while selecting music for performance, or during the sight-reading portion of the rehearsal. A detailed knowledge of the score is not absolutely required under such circumstances.

What are publishers' policies concerning the full and condensed score? One publisher offers full scores for traditional and serious original publications but only condensed scores for music theatre (musical comedy), movie, and television music. Another publisher's policy is to supply a full score for A and B level publications or other complicated work or works that are intended for festival or concert use; light programmatic works of easier levels do not require full scores. A few publishers produce both condensed and full scores of everything from the junior level on up; elementary school band material is printed with an 6-, 8-, or 9-line score. Several publishers limit the publication of full and condensed scores to compositions for high school level and higher while the "easier music" publications (for junior and elementary school bands) contain only condensed scores. For "smaller band numbers" the full score is too expensive to engrave and produce.

For one publisher, the decision to publish full or condensed scores is based on two factors, first, the economic factor and second, the complexity of the score itself. A highly complex work cannot be fully realized in a condensed version and most complex works have a full score in the set as a matter of policy. If a full score does not really serve much more purpose than a condensed one, a condensed score is published. If the score is felt to have the merits in both versions, a full and condensed score is published. For economic reasons, it is quite obvious that condensed scores are cheaper to produce than full scores. A few publishers print condensed scores only. One publisher substantiates a point of view propounded shortly before in this chapter. The company conducted a survey among band directors to determine their preference and use of full and/or condensed scores. The results indicated a preference for a full score in rehearsal and a condensed score for performance. Based on these findings, the company's policy is to publish both full and condensed scores except for easy works in which case a three-or-four-line score is apparently sufficient.

One company publishes full and condensed scores on almost its entire band output except for marches and "novelties"; another prints full and condensed scores for 80% to 90% of their band publications. In 1969 one publisher quoted a cost of $15.00 per page for setting up a full score. Other exceptions to the above policies are in the case of one company which publishes only condensed scores for most works except for an occasional full score, and another which usually does not produce both full and condensed scores in the same arrangement.

Recommended Procedures for Ordering

When placing an order for music, no matter from what source, it is vitally important that the band director give complete information. Many publications, especially arrangements and transcriptions for band of music from other media, are available in more than one edition and marketed by more than one publisher.[4] The director should specify some or all of the following items, depending upon the nature and type of music: (1) title; (2) composer; (3) arranger—if necessary; (4) the publisher; (5) the publisher's catalog number—if necessary; (6) what set—if necessary; and, (7) the school's purchase order or requisition number. At first glance, this process may seem somewhat elementary, especially to the experienced band director. Yet, publishers and dealers continue to be amazed at the amount of orders they are unable to fill and must return requests simply due to the fact that the director neglected to include an important fact such as the title, instrumentation, etc. The director should be certain to give complete information pertaining to each selection he wishes to purchase especially if the order is to be handled by the school, city, or county purchasing office.

One point concerning ordering music which publishers and dealers wish to strongly emphasize is that the band director should plan his program and music needs in ample time to allow for ordering and receiving the music; if at all possible, avoid last minute telephone calls either to the dealer or publisher, which particularly in the busy seasons are difficult enough to comply with and service. Delays in servicing orders are caused by other factors as well. For example, one publisher states that often they receive orders from an instrument house manager who happens to be a friend of the director and usually may not even have an account with a music publisher. Therefore, such an order runs into difficulties and delay in service, etc. Because of the rise in cost for processing orders, some publishers are now requesting dealers to consolidate orders for extra parts with other orders. The effect of this policy is to delay receipt of parts to the schools since the dealer must wait for the consolidation. A major problem, especially for dealers and publishers, is that concerned with the necessity for extra scores at contest time. Too many band directors wait until the last possible moment before selecting their contest pieces; then they order three scores from the dealer who probably does not have them in stock and must get a rush order from the publisher, often special delivery. Publishers have discussed the possibility of providing three extra scores with each set, but either the cost would be prohibitive or many band directors would resent having to pay for material they did not need nor intend to use. To reiterate, until another solution is found, the director must make his selection in sufficient time to get the extra scores he needs.

Samuel Kurtz (Lt. Col., USAF, Ret.), now "on the other side of the counter," cites a few examples of circumstances in which dealers were unable to fill orders because of insufficient information.

One example is the director who requests a rush order for "Pomp and Circumstance" by Elgar but neglected to inform the dealer of which arrangement he preferred and the dealer has seven different arrangements on his shelf. Another director, presumably in haste, ordered march books and attached an instrumentation to his letter but forgot to include the title of the book! Occasionally, dealers are amused at letters from beginning instrumental music students such as the following: "Enclosed is my father's check for $1.00, please send at once—Easy Steps to the Band." The dealer has no other recourse than to inform the student that he/she forgot to designate the instrument. The reply from the student reads, "Please rush my book. I already have my instrument—it's a new (NEVERFLUB)." [15]

The problem of requisitions for music which are processed through an office other than the director's can be a difficult and frustrating one for dealer and director. Kurtz describes the band director who picks up about $100.00 worth of musical materials at the store and requests the dealer to defer billing until he receives a purchase order from the director's school. The purchase order arrives but is not marked "Confirmation." In a large retail outlet where memos may not get transmitted between departments in time or not at all, the purchase order is now processed as a new order and the irritated band director has a duplicate set of materials on his hands! [15] Kurtz does admit, however, that these examples represent a small minority (less than 1%) of the band directors who patronize his company.

Coda

There is a popular opinion, without substantive basis however, that band directors are notoriously weak in efficient, proper, and business-like management of their instrumental programs. Regardless of the verity of this impression, the band director would greatly enhance the administrative aspect of his position if he were to avail himself of *The Music Educator's Business Handbook* which is prepared and produced by The Music Industry Council.*

---

* A copy of this handbook is available from: *The Music Industry Council*, 1201 Sixteenth St., N.W., Washington, D.C.

The following suggestions from this handbook pertain both specifically and generally to the matter of obtaining the best possible service when purchasing music for the band library.[16]

The Band Director's Business Correspondence

Those letters which are legible, concise, and well-organized quite obviously receive immediate attention. Any other type is pigeonholed for possible unscrambling and/or further correspondence with the writer. The recommendations below may be of value in avoiding service delays and errors.

Type It When You Can.   Typewritten letters, even those with erasures, etc., provide fewer errors in reading. If one must resort to handwritten letters, it is best to print titles, proper names and street addresses. If numbers are involved in the order, be sure they are legible.

Use Professional Letterhead Stationery.   A printed letterhead, giving name, position, and address is perhaps the most useful item in business and professional correspondence. Whether or not one uses a letterhead, three facts must be included in all letters: (1) your full address (street number, town, state, zip code); (2) your full name and initials plainly written; and (3) your official position.

Avoid the Multi-Purpose Letter.   Even though your correspondence is directed to one company, do not include several unrelated items of business on one letter, for example: an order for music, a payment on account, and a request for sample materials. Each of these is handled by separate departments within the company and the letter will have to remain in each until the request or business is transacted. It is best to write three individual memoranda, each addressed to the proper department, and insert them in one envelope to one company.

General Suggestions on Ordering

As described before, insufficient, incomplete, and unclear orders cause delays and errors. The following ideas may help avoid them.

Use the Publisher's Current Catalog.   Each band director

should maintain a file of the most recent, current, catalog or book of thematics from all publishers of band music. When ordering music, it should be specifically identified by complete name (title, composer, arranger), description (edition and set), and, if one is given, the stock number by the publisher or supplier.

Coordinate with the Purchasing Department. The dealer and/or publisher must be notified if the band director's school or school system has a purchasing department or specifically requires administrative approval of orders. Business houses are obliged to observe whatever purchasing procedures are established by the school or school system. The band director must supply his own administrative department, or central purchasing agency office, with complete and accurate information to avoid confusion and errors in requisitions.

Give Explicit Shipping Instructions. State clearly to whom the order is to be sent, to whom it is to be charged, and how shipment should be made (parcel post, express, etc.).

Keep Charge Accounts Clear and Separate. In some cases, instrumental music teachers are responsible for more than one organization which requires the establishment of more than one account, and a personal account in addition. Do not allow transactions which belong to your personal account to become entangled with accounts of the organization or school you represent. There are a great number of instances in which school officials or purchasing agents receive invoices and statements for materials which should have been charged to the director's personal account, and the director finds himself charged with items purchased for his organization and belong to that account. Transactions involving separate accounts should be *kept* separate.

An Order Form for Band Music

To insure a clear understanding of the director's orders, the Music Industry Council recommends that a form be used. They have found it to be useful because it can be adapted easily to one's own needs and instrumentation. The example given next is a modification of the form in the handbook. (See also the order form used by the University of Illinois Bands on page 206.)

(SAMPLE ORDER FORM)
BOARD OF EDUCATION

City, State, Zip Code

Date: _____

Requisition Number: _____

To: _____

Please send to: _____

Charge to the account of: _____

Title _____

Composer _____ Arranger _____

Publisher _____ Catalog number _____

Copies

_____Full Score	_____2nd Bassoon
_____Condensed Score	_____Contra-Bassoon
_____Piccolo	_____1st Cornet in B♭
_____1st Flute	_____2nd Cornet in B♭
_____2nd Flute	_____3rd Cornet in B♭
_____3rd Flute	_____1st Trumpet in B♭
_____1st Oboe	_____2nd Trumpet in B♭
_____2nd Oboe	_____1st and 2nd Flügelhorns
_____English Horn	_____1st Horn in F
_____E♭ Clarinet	_____2nd Horn in F
_____1st B♭ Clarinet	_____3rd Horn in F
_____2nd B♭ Clarinet	_____4th Horn in F
_____3rd B♭ Clarinet	_____1st Horn in E♭
_____E♭ Alto Clarinet	_____2nd Horn in E♭
_____B♭ Bass Clarinet	_____3rd Horn in E♭
_____E♭ Contra-Bass	_____4th Horn in E♭
Clarinet	_____1st Trombone
_____BB♭ Contra-Bass	_____2nd Trombone
Clarinet	_____3rd Trombone
_____Soprano Saxophone	_____Baritone (bass clef)
_____1st E♭ Alto Saxophone	_____Baritone (treble clef)
_____2nd E♭ Alto Saxophone	_____String Bass
_____B♭ Tenor Saxophone	_____Basses
_____E♭ Baritone Saxophone	_____Tympani
_____B♭ Bass Saxophone	_____Drums
_____1st Bassoon	_____Harp

Ordered by _____

Position _____

Selected References

Books

1. Bradley, Carol June (ed.). *Manual of Music Librarianship*, Ann Arbor, Michigan: Music Library Association, 1966.
2. Goldman, Richard Franko. *The Concert Band*, New York: Rinehart and Company, 1946.
3. Green, Elizabeth A.H. *The Modern Conductor*, Englewood Cliffs, New Jersey: Prentice-Hall, Inc., 1961.
4. House, Robert W. *Instrumental Music for Today's Schools*, Englewood Cliffs, New Jersey: Prentice-Hall, Inc., 1965.
5. Jones, Bruce L. *Building the Instrumental Music Department*, New York: Carl Fischer, Inc., 1949.
6. Kuhn, Wolfgang. *Instrumental Music: Principles and Methods of Instruction*, Boston: Allyn and Bacon, 1962.
7. Leonhard, Charles and Robert W. House. *Foundations and Principles of Music Education*, New York: McGraw-Hill, 1959.
8. Norman, Theodore. *Instrumental Music in the Public Schools*, Philadelphia: Ditson Company, 1941.
9. Prescott, Gerald R. and Lawrence W. Chidester. *Getting Results with School Bands*, New York: Carl Fischer, Inc., 1938.
10. Singleton, Ira C. *Music in Secondary Schools*, Boston: Allyn and Bacon, 1963.

Periodicals

11. Akers, Howard E. "The Publisher—Friend of the Music Educator," *The School Musician*, Vol. 35, No. 2, Oct., 1963.
12. Grasso, Benjamin V. "The Music Publishers' Association," *The School Musician*, Vol. 35, No. 9, May, 1964.
13. Hauser, Arthur A. "The Band and the Publisher," *The School Musician*, Jan.—Feb., 1949.
14. Ivory, Paul S. "Band Programs in Minnesota," *Journal of Research in Music Education*, Spring, 1953.
15. Kurtz, Samuel. "On the Other Side of the Counter," *The School Musician*, Vol. 39, No. 7, March, 1968.

Monographs

16. The Music Industry Council. *The Music Educator's Business Handbook*, Washington, D.C.: The Music Industry Council, 1965.

Unpublished Literature

17. Cecil, Herbert M. *Fundamental Principles of the Organization, Management, and Teaching of the School Band,* unpublished dissertation, University of Rochester, 1953.

8

Twenty-Six Aids for
Cataloging, Filing, and
Indexing the Band Library

ORGANIZE IT!

Equally important to the problem of selecting music for the band is the director's responsibility for the organization and management of the library. Regardless of the size of the instrumental program, the library will undoubtedly consist of hundreds of separate musical compositions. This represents a considerable financial investment. Therefore, the organization, care, and maintenance of the library cannot be left to casual, haphazard, unsystematic management.[7] The director must design and utilize library procedures which are systematic, efficient, and time-saving; they must help accomplish whatever is necessary both effectively and quickly. These procedures are a prerequisite to the proper cataloging, filing, indexing, storage, distribution, and handling of the library; they may save countless hours during the course of a school year for the director and his library staff. There is an economic factor involved too. Consider the number of individual parts, folios, or method books which are needlessly lost or not turned in and the money which must be spent for replacements.

Also, there is no greater disruptive element, or interference with the band's *espirit de corps* during a rehearsal, than poor library management.

Base the System on the Size of the Library

The system which the band director designs for his library encompasses several broad areas. The matter of purchasing music has been discussed; storage, distribution, and handling will be described in subsequent chapters. Therefore, this chapter will be limited to recommendations and suggestions concerning the cataloging (classification), indexing, and filing of band music.

The operating system for the band library often is a good yardstick for measuring ". . . the efficiency with which a director manages his department." [5] Band directors throughout the country employ quite a number of systems ranging from the simplest to the very complex and elaborate. Whichever system the director adopts, he must base it on the needs of his particular program. This decision might include such factors as: the number of current entries in the library, allowing for future acquisitions; the present and projected size of the band and its instrumentation; the scope of the instrumental program, that is, the number and type of organizations which one library must service; and the band's general function and activities. The system must be adequate enough to meet all these needs and remain efficient at the same time. The director should guard against developing procedures which could become excessively complex thereby negating any possibility for smooth operation and time-saving efforts because the system is hopelessly entangled in and mired down by unnecessary detail or "red tape."

Separate Libraries

Many directors are responsible for more than one band in a school system, i.e., elementary and junior high school, junior and senior high schools, or possibly all three levels. If the bands are housed in separate buildings, there is no problem in maintaining separate libraries. Any number of situations exist in which two bands must use the same rehearsal room and other facilities. If the program's economic structure will support it, the bands should have separate libraries for storage, filing, indexing, and distribution operations.[16] This requires more administrative effort on the director's part, but it would tend to eliminate possible confusion (such as entire compositions or parts ending up in the wrong folios, etc.). If this is not feasible, the minimum facility for separation of libraries is distribution (storage of folios and envelopes or music in current use). With separate libraries, the director must employ the same basic system for each one and also whatever minute modifications are necessary.

THE SYSTEM AND TWENTY-SIX AIDS *

Cataloging

The administrative task of organizing and managing the band library includes the use of forms and records. Leonhard and House warn the director that ". . . the overmeticulous handling of forms and records (might interfere) with instruction . . ." while the adherence to an antiquated system could result in their loss of value and effectiveness.[9] They suggest that the type of records and forms employed and their mode of application are valuable only to the extent that they assist the persons using them in efficient organization and operation.

First, the band library should be cataloged, that is, each selection or item must be classified according to type. There are many ideas regarding cataloging; it is virtually impossible to recommend any one ". . . system of classification which would be suitable for all conditions. . . ."[5] The director might find one among the following as adequate and suitable to the needs of his particular program.

Singleton suggests several general classifications which ". . . might include chorales, marches, novelties, overtures, popular selections, sacred music, solos with full accompaniment, suites, symphonic excerpts, and so forth."[13]   (1)

Ivory recommends three broad categories with sub-classifications within each: [14]   (2)

---

* "*Aids*" will appear in the right-hand margin as a circled number: (1)

   A. *Serious Band Music*
       Suites, etc. originally written for band by movements
       Transcriptions of standard symphonic overtures
       Transcriptions of other symphonic works
       Chorales (often used as warm-up numbers)
   B. *Characteristic Band Music*
       Concert marches
       Standard marches
       Operetta, musical comedy selections
       Potpourris, medleys, fantasies
   C. *Light Band Music*
       Novelties
       Modern American rhythms
       Popular hits
       Spanish, Latin-American rhythms and marches
       Program-type concert overtures, etc.
       Themes from, or improvisations on standard symphonic works

Hovey feels that the following classification divisions ". . . will be adequate for most grade and high school organizations: A—Street marches (band only); B—Concert marches; C—Standard overtures; D—Symphonic excerpts; E—Light overtures; F—Suites; G—Miscellaneous concert selections; H—Musical comedies, operettas; J—Popular numbers; K—Descriptive compositions, novelties; L—Sacred music, including Christmas; M—Instrumental solos, duos, etc. with band or orchestra accompaniment; P—Patriotic music." [5]

The Southern Music Company of San Antonio, Texas, in its brief monograph, suggests the following classification guide: [15]

Concert Music	Sacred Music
Galops	Marches
Marches	Selections
2/4 Marches	Overtures
6/8 Marches	Easter
4/4 Marches	Christmas
Concert Marches	Hymns
Funeral Marches	Selections and Fantasies
Sacred Marches	Concert
With Trumpet and	Operatic
Drum Corps	Musical Comedy
Wedding Marches	Solos with Band Accomp.

National Music
  America
  Australia (and all
    other countries)
Novelties (etc.)
Overtures
  Easy
  Concert
  Dramatic
  Operatic
Patrols
Polkas
Popular

(Duets, Trios, Quartets)
  Altos
  Basses
  Cornets
  Clarinets, etc.
Suites
Symphonies and Symphonic
  Movements
Tangos
Trombone Novelties
Waltzes
  Easy
  Concert
  Dramatic
  Etc.

A discussion with Mark Hindsley (Emeritus Director of Bands, University of Illinois) revealed that he had readjusted his ideas concerning musical classifications and developed an entirely new listing. He recommends that the director list each number under its primary classification, or under a combination of classifications.

SUGGESTED MUSICAL CLASSIFICATIONS   ⑤

(Mark Hindsley)

Ballet
Choral (numbers with chorus or optional chorus)
Concert March (all marches except of military or quick-step variety)
Concerto
Dance (do not nessarily include here ballet, waltz, or national dances)
Descriptive (picture, story)
Fanfare
Galop
Holidays (vacations, outings, rather than religious or patriotic)
March (military, quick-step)
Medley (primarily medleys of songs, such as selections and overtures from musical shows, some operas)
Military (land, sea, and air)
National (indicate name of country, group of countries, or region)

Nautical (pertaining to the sea, other waterways)
Novelty (primarily entertaining, humorous)
Opera (any excerpt, except possible selections, medleys of songs)
Oratorio
Overture (suggest omission here of overtures to operas, shows)
Patriotic (apply only to U.S.A.; other patriotic music under National)
Rhapsody (if in title; include also Fantasy)
Sacred (or religious)
Solo (include also duet, trio, etc., indicating instruments)
Song (suggest primarily single, "art" songs here, omitting choral, medley, national opera, oratorio, patriotic, sacred, solo, etc.)
Suite
Symphonic (such as symphonic poems)
Symphony (anything from a symphony)
Uncl. ("Unclassified"; a catch-all for everything else)
Waltz

One may develop a personal classification by selecting the best features from the foregoing sources. The following suggested list is an amalgamation of those features:

1. *Marches*—street and field
2. *Marches*—concert
3. *Popular Music*—singles, not including stage band
4. *Light Overtures*—original band music
5. *Standard Overtures*—transcribed or arranged from symphonic literature
6. *Light Concert Music*—original, arranged, or transcribed, one-movement works
7. *Concert Music*—arranged, transcribed, one-movement works (fugues, excerpts from symphonies, toccatas, fantasias, etc.
8. *Symphonies*—original band music, multiple form
9. *Suites*—original band music, multiple form
10. *Suites*—arranged or transcribed, multiple form
11. *Dance Forms*—original, arranged, or transcribed, including Ballet
12. *Sacred Music*—including religious
13. *Grand and Light Opera*—selections, excerpts

14. *Music Theatre, Musical Comedy, Film Music, Television Background Music*—selections and excerpts
15. *National Music*—original and arranged, folk and patriotic
16. *Combined Band and Choral Works*
17. *Stage Band Music*
18. *Instrumental Solos, Duets, etc.*—with band accompaniment
19. *Solos, Duets, etc.*—with piano accompaniment
20. *Ensembles*—woodwind
21. *Ensembles*—brass
22. *Ensembles*—percussion
23. *Ensembles*—mixed
24. *Band Collections*
25. *Ensemble Instruction Material*
26. *Individual Instruction Material*

Note that this classification system makes a distinction between: original band music, single movement; arranged or transcribed band music, single movement; original band music, multiple form (two or more movements, related); and, arranged or transcribed band music, multiple form. The longer, single-movement compositions, such as operatic selections and excerpts, or music theater selections and excerpts, are classified separately.

Quite naturally, a small band library would require fewer classification categories than listed above, while a larger, more extensive and detailed library would necessitate most or all of them. The director should base his system on the size of the library he expects to have.[5]

Indexing

Within the total band music library system, the band director must develop a card index file for all the materials included in the library. An index is vitally important for several reasons. First, it serves as a means for inventorying the musical holdings of one's instrumental department; second, it aids the filing of materials in the library when making decisions regarding classification and filing; third, there are many instances when the director needs to use the index as a ". . . quick reference when planning programs. . . ."[7] For example, "The teacher may not always know just what compositions he wants but may have only a set of stipulations in his mind rather than the name of a piece."[2] Occasionally the director may be planning his programs for the entire school year; the index facilitates his "browsing" through the cards. Fourth, periodically the director must assess what musical materials he has on hand for replacement of missing or worn parts. Perhaps the director may want to use a particular piece of music and he must know whether or not all parts are on file. The index would provide him with instant information.

There exist varying opinions regarding the index card file concerning the number of cards for each composition (one card or cross-indexed), the information to be included on each card, and even the mode of filing the cards in the drawer.

Kuhn, Prescott and Chidester, and the J. W. Pepper Company, feel that it is not necessary to have more than one card per work. In the case of a small instrumental library Kuhn thinks that the cards should be indexed ". . . according to titles." Later, "As the library grows and becomes more complex, a cross-reference index according to composers must be added. The director may then wish to establish various classifications of music which he finds useful in his planning."[7] Prescott and Chidester suggest that the card include the following information: ". . . File Number, Date Acquired, Title, Character, Composer, Publisher, Arranger." Further, the cards are to be filed alphabetically by composer.[11] Cecil recommends only two types of cards: title and classification.[16] The main difference of opinion seems to be which card is to be considered the "main" one, composer, title, or classification. The important thing is that any work should be located quickly and easily.

The method this writer has used and recommends, consists of a three-way cross-reference card index file; the cards (not smaller than $3'' \times 5''$) are designated "Title Index," "Composer Index," and "Classification Index." Each card is of a different color: the title card is blue; the composer card is white; and the classification card may be salmon, pink, or yellow. The cards each include the same basic information: (1) classification; (2) title; (3) composer; (4) arranger (if necessary); (5) file number; (6) publisher; (7) copyright date; (8) accession date; and (9) performance time. Many directors who use this same system have the above information printed on one card only, usually the "Composer

Index" or "Title Index." In addition, the instrumentation for each individual work is entered on the back of the composer card and dates/places of performances on the back of the title card. The system provides the band director with all the pertinent information he may need at any one particular time. Illustration 8-1 shows sample cards as described above. Illustration 8-2 shows information to be included on the back of the composer and title cards.

COMPOSER Schuman, William FILE NO:_____

TITLE When Jesus Wept_____

PUBLISHER Merion Music, Inc. ARRANGER_____

CLASSIFICATION Sacred_____

COPYRIGHT DATE 1959 PERFORMANCE TIME_____

ACCESSION DATE Jan. 13, 1960_____

(Instrumentation on reverse side)

Illustration 8-1
Composer Card (front)
Title Card (front)
Classification Card

TITLE Introduction and Scherzo

COMPOSER Weed, Maurice   FILE NO:_____

PUBLISHER Neil A Kjos Music Co ARRANGER_____

CLASSIFICATION Miscellaneous Concert

COPYRIGHT DATE 1959   PERFORMANCE TIME_____

ACCESSION DATE Jan. 12, 1960

(Dates and places of performance on reverse side)

Illustration 8-1

CLASSIFICATION   Sacred

TITLE When Jesus Wept

COMPOSER Shuman, William   FILE NO:_____

PUBLISHER Merion Music, Inc ARRANGER_____

COPYRIGHT DATE 1959   PERFORMANCE TIME_____

ACCESSION DATE Jan. 13, 1960

(See Composer Index for Instrumentation)
(See Title Index for Performance Dates)

Illustration 8-1

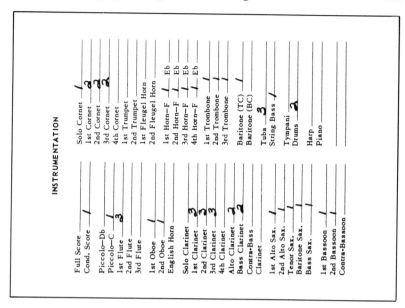

Illustration 8-2
Composer Card (back)

Date	Played by at:

Illustration 8-2
Title Card (back)

The University of Illinois and Southern Illinois University bands use similar cards for their indexing systems. The system consists of a three-way card file with varying colors for each one. However, only the "Composer Index" card contains the main information including: composer, file number, title, publisher, arranger, classification, copyright date, and performance time. Although "other information" may be written or typed on the reverse side of the cards, they are left blank. Illustration 8–3 shows a set of index cards from the University of Illinois Bands Library.

Composer.. File No.......................

Title...

Publisher.. Arranger............................

Classification.. Copy Date.............................

Library: UI............. Harding............ Sousa............ Clarke............ ....

Performance Time................................

(Other information on reverse side............)

UNIVERSITY OF ILLINOIS BANDS
COMPOSER INDEX

5M—7-57—63492

Title...

Composer.. File No.......................

(See Composer Index for other information)

UNIVERSITY OF ILLINOIS BANDS
TITLE INDEX

5M—7-57—63493

Illustration 8-3

Composer...

Title...

Classification.........   .... File No..........................

(See Composer Index for other information)

UNIVERSITY OF ILLINOIS BANDS
Classification Index

Illustration 8-3

An elementary school band director informed the writer of yet (11) a fourth index card which serves as a *location* card. The main entry on it is a file and drawer identification and the particular composition listed under that entry (title and composer). The cards are filed according to the method of enumerating the files and drawers of the band library. The fourth card also serves as the library inventory card.

Foster recommends a separate card file for marching band music (12) and materials used for football game appearances. The information is more specialized and includes ". . . composer, title, maneuver, dance, precision drill, and concert." [3]

If the band library is extensive enough, that is, it contains a (13) large amount of holdings, there should be separate filing trays, drawers, or boxes for the title, composer, and classification cards. A smaller library will not require separation, but three-way cards should be separated just the same. The title cards should be arranged alphabetically by title. Articles such as "The" and "A" should be disregarded and placed at the end of the title. For example, "The Showman March" would appear on the title card as "Showman March, The." Composer's cards are arranged alphabetically by the composer's last name. Dividers with tabs bearing the classification division names should be used with the "Classification Index" and the cards arranged alphabetically by title within each division.

The director in charge of a small band with a small library will probably decide to use one card for his indexing system. In this case, the card should contain the information listed in Aid 9 and arranged in the card file tray or box by classification and alphabetically by title in each category.[13]

The indexing system developed and proposed by the Southern Music Company includes a card file method which may be adapted to any of the foregoing systems. It includes three cards: "Title Card," (white); "Composer's Card," (blue); and "Classification Card," (salmon). As may be noted in Illustration 8-4, each card contains the same information in addition to instrumentation. The flexibility of these cards is that they may be used for band and/or orchestra and adapted either to a one-card, two-card, or three-card cross-reference system since each card is printed up the same way (except for the top heading). An added feature on these cards, which may be of value to the school band director, is the item referring to "Grade" level.

FORM 1   **TITLE CARD**

NAME OF COMPOSITION   COMPOSER

PUBLISHER   PUBLISHER'S NO.   CLASSIFICATION

GRADE   PERFORMANCE TIME   LIBRARY NO.

INSTRUMENTATION

____Full Score	___ 2nd Oboe	____3rd Bb Cornet	____Baritone T. C.
____Conductor	____English Horn	____4th Bb Cornet	____Baritone B. C.
____1st Flute	____1st Bassoon	____1st & 2nd Bb Fluegelhorns	____ String Bass
____2nd Flute	____2nd Bassoon	____1st & 2nd Bb Trumpets	____Basses (Tuba)
____3rd Flute & Piccolo in C	____Contra Bassoon	____1st Horn in Eb	____Drums
____Db Piccolo	____1st Eb Alto Saxophone	____2nd Horn in Eb	____Timpani
____Eb Clarinet	____2nd Eb Alto Saxophone	____3rd Horn in Eb	____1st Violin
____Solo Bb Clarinet	____Bb Tenor Saxophone	____4th Horn in Eb	____1st Violin A
____1st Bb Clarinet	____Eb Baritone Saxophone	____1st Horn in F	____1st Violin B
____2nd Bb Clarinet	___ Bb Bass Saxophone	____2nd Horn in F	____1st Violin C
____3rd Bb Clarinet	____Soprano Saxophone	____3rd Horn in F	____2nd Violin
____4th Bb Clarinet	____C Mel. Saxophone	____4th Horn in F	____Viola
____Eb Alto Clarinet	____Solo Bb Cornet	____1st Trombone B. C.	____Cello
____Bb Bass Clarinet	____1st Bb Cornet	____2nd Trombone B. C.	____String Bass (Orch.)
____1st Oboe	____2nd Bb Cornet	____3rd Trombone B. C.	____Piano
			____Harp

SOUTHERN MUSIC COMPANY
BOX 329 — SAN ANTONIO 6, TEXAS

Illustration 8-4

FORM 2   **COMPOSERS CARD**

NAME OF COMPOSITION   COMPOSER

PUBLISHER   PUBLISHER'S NO.   CLASSIFICATION

GRADE   PERFORMANCE TIME   LIBRARY NO.

INSTRUMENTATION

Full Score	2nd Oboe	3rd Bb Cornet	Baritone T. C.
Conductor	English Horn	4th Bb Cornet	Baritone B. C.
1st Flute	1st Bassoon	1st & 2nd Bb Fluegelhorns	String Bass
2nd Flute	2nd Bassoon	1st & 2nd Bb Trumpets	Basses (Tuba)
3rd Flute & Piccolo in C	Contra Bassoon	1st Horn in Eb	Drums
Db Piccolo	1st Eb Alto Saxophone	2nd Horn in Eb	Timpani
Eb Clarinet	2nd Eb Alto Saxophone	3rd Horn in Eb	1st Violin
Solo Bb Clarinet	Bb Tenor Saxophone	4th Horn in Eb	1st Violin A
1st Bb Clarinet	Eb Baritone Saxophone	1st Horn in F	1st Violin B
2nd Bb Clarinet	Bb Bass Saxophone	2nd Horn in F	1st Violin C
3rd Bb Clarinet	Soprano Saxophone	3rd Horn in F	2nd Violin
4th Bb Clarinet	C Mel. Saxophone	4th Horn in F	Viola
Eb Alto Clarinet	Solo Bb Cornet	1st Trombone B. C.	Cello
Bb Bass Clarinet	1st Bb Cornet	2nd Trombone B. C.	String Bass (Orch.)
1st Oboe	2nd Bb Cornet	3rd Trombone B. C.	Piano
			Harp

SOUTHERN MUSIC COMPANY
BOX 329 — SAN ANTONIO 6, TEXAS

Illustration 8-4

FORM 3   **CLASSIFICATION CARD**

NAME OF COMPOSITION   COMPOSER

PUBLISHER   PUBLISHER'S NO.   CLASSIFICATION

GRADE   PERFORMANCE TIME   LIBRARY NO.

INSTRUMENTATION

Full Score	2nd Oboe	3rd Bb Cornet	Baritone T. C.
Conductor	English Horn	4th Bb Cornet	Baritone B. C.
1st Flute	1st Bassoon	1st & 2nd Bb Fluegelhorns	String Bass
2nd Flute	2nd Bassoon	1st & 2nd Bb Trumpets	Basses (Tuba)
3rd Flute & Piccolo in C	Contra Bassoon	1st Horn in Eb	Drums
Db Piccolo	1st Eb Alto Saxophone	2nd Horn in Eb	Timpani
Eb Clarinet	2nd Eb Alto Saxophone	3rd Horn in Eb	1st Violin
Solo Bb Clarinet	Bb Tenor Saxophone	4th Horn in Eb	1st Violin A
1st Bb Clarinet	Eb Baritone Saxophone	1st Horn in F	1st Violin B
2nd Bb Clarinet	Bb Bass Saxophone	2nd Horn in F	1st Violin C
3rd Bb Clarinet	Soprano Saxophone	3rd Horn in F	2nd Violin
4th Bb Clarinet	C Mel. Saxophone	4th Horn in F	Viola
Eb Alto Clarinet	Solo Bb Cornet	1st Trombone B. C.	Cello
Bb Bass Clarinet	1st Bb Cornet	2nd Trombone B. C.	String Bass (Orch.)
1st Oboe	2nd Bb Cornet	3rd Trombone B. C.	Piano
			Harp

SOUTHERN MUSIC COMPANY
BOX 329 — SAN ANTONIO 6, TEXAS

Illustration 8-4

It has been suggested in Aid 6 that the band director include solos and ensembles as a facet of his total band music library system. An index card file should likewise be made of the holdings of the instrumental music program in this classification also. Illustration 8–5 shows sample cards for indexing solo and ensemble music. The only minor drawback to the features appearing on the card is with reference to grade level. There are but three levels listed on the cards; most state instrumental music activities associations require as many as five grade levels for evaluating music. The director should make whatever modifications are necessary in this case; he should file these cards separately from the band music.

*D - DIFFICULT M - MEDIUM E - EASY	TITLE CARD	** EXACT INSTRUMENTA- TION SHOULD BE WRIT- TEN IN UNDER GENERAL HEADING OF ENSEMBLES

NAME OF COMPOSITION   COMPOSER AND/OR ARRANGER

_____   _____   _____ ___I OR D___II OR M___III OR E _____
PUBLISHER   PUB. NO. PERFORMANCE TIME   CLASS OR GRADE*   LIBRARY NO.

TYPE OF SOLO OR ENSEMBLE**

____ Db Piccolo	___Cornet	____Woodwind Duet	. Brass Quintet
____C Piccolo	___Eb Alto or Melophone		____Brass Sextet
____C Flute	____French Horn	____Woodwind Trio	
____Eb Clarinet	____Trombone		____Larger Brass Ensemble
____Oboe	____Baritone ...B.C.____T.C.	____Woodwind Quartet	
____English Horn	____Tuba	____Woodwind Quintet	____Drum Ensemble
____Bassoon	____Snare Drum		
____Bb Clarinet	____Xylophone or Marimba	____Woodwind Sextet	____String Duet
____Alto Clarinet	____Vibra Harp or Celeste		
____Bass Clarinet	___Violin	____Larger Woodwind Ensembles	____String Trio
____Alto Saxophone	____Viola	____Saxophone Quartet	___String Quartet
____Tenor Saxophone	____Violoncello		
	____String Bass	____Saxophone Sextet	____Piano Quartet (Violin,
____Baritone Saxophone	___Piano		Viola, Cello & Piano)
____Bass Saxophone	____Harp	____Brass Duet	
			__Larger String Ensemble
		____Brass Trio	
____Any other (write in)	____Any other (write in)		____Any other (write in)
		.. Brass Quartet	
___ Any other (write in)	____Any other (write in)		____Any other (write in)

P. O. Box 329   SOUTHERN MUSIC COMPANY   San Antonio 6, Texas
FORM 30

Illustration 8-5

°D - DIFFICULT
M - MEDIUM
E - EASY

COMPOSER'S CARD

** EXACT INSTRUMENTA-
TION SHOULD BE WRIT-
TEN IN UNDER GENERAL
HEADING OF ENSEMBLES.

NAME OF COMPOSITION

COMPOSER AND/OR ARRANGER

_____I OR D ___II OR M ___III OR E _____

PUBLISHER   PUB. NO.   PERFORMANCE TIME   CLASS OR GRADE°   LIBRARY NO.

TYPE OF SOLO OR ENSEMBLE**

____Db Piccolo	___Cornet	____Woodwind Duet	____Brass Quintet
____C Piccolo	____Eb Alto or Melophone		
____C Flute	____French Horn	____Woodwind Trio	____Brass Sextet
____Eb Clarinet	____Trombone		
____Oboe	____Baritone B.C. ___ T.C.	____Woodwind Quartet	____Larger Brass Ensemble
____English Horn	____Tuba	____Woodwind Quintet	____Drum Ensemble
____Bassoon	____Snare Drum		
____Bb Clarinet	____Xylophone or Marimba	____Woodwind Sextet	____String Duet
____Alto Clarinet	____Vibra Harp or Celeste		
____Bass Clarinet	____Violin	____Larger Woodwind Ensembles	____String Trio
____Alto Saxophone	____Viola	____Saxophone Quartet	____String Quartet
____Tenor Saxophone	____Violoncello		
____Baritone Saxophone	____String Bass	____Saxophone Sextet	____Piano Quartet (Violin, Viola, Cello & Piano)
____Bass Saxophone	____Piano	____Brass Duet	
	____Harp		____Larger String Ensemble
____Any other (write in)	____Any other (write in)	____Brass Trio	____Any other (write in)
____Any other (write in)	____Any other (write in)	____Brass Quartet	____Any other (write in)

Order All Music and Supplies from:

P. O. Box 329   **SOUTHERN MUSIC COMPANY**   San Antonio 6, Texas

FORM 31

Illustration 8-5

°D - DIFFICULT
M - MEDIUM
E - EASY

CLASSIFICATION CARD

** EXACT INSTRUMENTA-
TION SHOULD BE WRIT-
TEN IN UNDER GENERAL
HEADING OF ENSEMBLES.

NAME OF COMPOSITION

COMPOSER AND/OR ARRANGER

_____I OR D ___II OR M ___III OR E _____

PUBLISHER   PUB. NO.   PERFORMANCE TIME   CLASS OR GRADE°   LIBRARY NO.

TYPE OF SOLO OR ENSEMBLE** -

____Db Piccolo	____Cornet	____Woodwind Duet	____Brass Quintet
____C Piccolo	____Eb Alto or Melophone		
____C Flute	____French Horn	____Woodwind Trio	____Brass Sextet
____Eb Clarinet	____Trombone		
____Oboe	____Baritone____B.C.____T.C.	____Woodwind Quartet	____Larger Brass Ensemble
____English Horn	____Tuba	____Woodwind Quintet	____Drum Ensemble
____Bassoon	____Snare Drum		
____Bb Clarinet	____Xylophone or Marimba	____Woodwind Sextet	____String Duet
____Alto Clarinet	____Vibra Harp or Celeste		
____Bass Clarinet	____Violin	____Larger Woodwind Ensembles	____String Trio
____Alto Saxophone	____Viola	____Saxophone Quartet	____String Quartet
____Tenor Saxophone	____Violoncello		
____Baritone Saxophone	____String Bass	____Saxophone Sextet	____Piano Quartet (Violin, Viola, Cello & Piano)
____Bass Saxophone	____Piano	____Brass Duet	
	____Harp		____Larger String Ensemble
____Any other (write in)	____Any other (write in)	____Brass Trio	____Any other (write in)
____Any other (write in)	____Any other (write in)	____Brass Quartet	____Any other (write in)

Order All Music and Supplies from:

P. O. Box 329   **SOUTHERN MUSIC COMPANY**   San Antonio 6, Texas

FORM 32

Illustration 8-5

The J. W. Pepper Company, in its brochure, "Music Library System," recommends the use of one card, the "Title Card." This card provides such information as type of music, playing time, special problems, performance dates, specific parts. Instrumentation is indicated on the back of the card. The Pepper Company feels that their system is a flexible one, suitable for libraries of all sizes and types. A small band may need only one set of such cards; supplementary cards may be made out as cross-reference cards according to the needs and library size of the band. Illustration 8–6 shows the front and back of the Pepper file card.

WOODWINDS

Fl: I_____ II_____ III_____ Pic: Db_____ C _____ Ob: I_____ II _____ Engl. Hn._____

Eb Clar._____ Bb Clar: Solo (I)_____ (II) _____ (III) _____ (IV)_____ Alto Clar. _____

Bass Clar._____ Other: _____ Sax: Eb Alto: (I)_____ (II) _____Bb Tenor_____

Eb Bari. _____ Bb Bass _____ Other: _____ Bsn: I _____ II _____Contra _____

BRASS

Horns: I_____II_____ III _____ IV_____ Cornets: I _____ II _____III _____ IV_____

Trpts: I____ II____ III ___ IV_____ Fluegelhorn ____Trombones: I ____ II ___ III_____

Bari. (Euph) B.C. _____ Bari. T.C. _____ Tuba: Eb_____ BBb _____

PERCUSSION

S.D. _____ B.D. _____Tymp. _____ Cym. _____ Bells _____ Chimes_____

Other: _____

STRINGS

Vln: I_____ II_____ III _____ Vla: _____ Cello: _____ Bass:_____

MISCELLANEOUS

Harp __ _____ Piano _____ Celeste_____ Organ _____Other: _____

Illustration 8-6
(front)

```
                                                    Library
Title_____  Number _____
                                    ☐ Band  ☐ Orchestra  ☐ Ensemble
_____ ☐ Quickstep ☐ Octavo ☐ Concert

Composer and/or Arranger _____
Type of Number_____(Classification Guide)_____
Publisher_____ Original Cost_____ Date Added_____
Playing Time:_____ Condensed Score _____ Full Score _____
                    (List performance dates below.)
_____




PEPPER LIBRARY SYSTEM CARD #10-1        J. W. PEPPER & SON, INC.        [jwp]
© 1965, J. W. PEPPER & SON, INC.        PHILADELPHIA · ATLANTA · DETROIT
```

Illustration 8-6
(back)

Filing

The flexibility which may be applied in setting up a band music library filing system is succinctly described by Colwell. He writes, "As any librarian can tell you, there is practically no limit to what can be done in a library routine. Besides listing the music by composer, a cross-filing system by titles is useful, and this can be expanded to cross-filing by type of composition, by the filing numbers, by the size of the playing group demanded, by date of publication, by instrumentation, and on and on." [2]

Some of the factors which determine the method of filing the music by the director and his library staff are: (1) the scope and type of cataloging (classification) system; (2) the indexing method; (3) the number, size, and type of filing or storage cabinets for the music; (4) the number of separate organizations within the instrumental program which the library must service; (5) the size of the library; and (6) the variety or number of different types of musical material housed in the library. Obviously, a great number or wide variety within each of these factors means a more sophisticated, detailed, or elaborate filing system.

Logically, there are at least five ways of filing band music. They are: (1) filing only by size and accession within each size, regardless of title, composer, or classification; (2) filing by size, then alphabetically by composer; (3) filing by size and then by classification; (4) filing by size and then alphabetically by title; and (5) filing strictly by acquisition or accession regardless of size. While some directors utilize one of these ways, others employ a combination method of filing music.

The Southern Music Company, Prescott and Chidester recommend that the first step is to divide the music by size, namely: *March* or *Quick-Step; Medium* or *Octavo;* and *Concert* or *Quarto.* Southern Music Company points out that there may be a fourth size, the *European* or *Extra Large Size;* Prescott and Chidester call it the *Foreign Size* and advise that definite provision should be made for it. Prescott and Chidester designate each file size with a Roman numeral: *I*—march size; *II*—octavo; *III*—American; and *IV*—Foreign. The Southern Music Company designates each size with a letter: *A*—march size; *B*—octavo; *C*—concert; and, if a larger size, *D*—European. In Prescott and Chidester's method, the next step is to file the compositions alphabetically by composer according to size. One must assume that since there may be several drawers of music in each size, there will be a further method of indicating the location of each composition in the file index. These authors do not mention any other designation. Southern Music Company's method numbers all compositions in each size group in accordance with the size of the music; i.e., march size—A-1, A-2, A-3, etc., octavo size—B-1, B-2, B-3, etc., and concert size—C-1, C-2, C-3, etc. Their brochure does not describe in what particular order the music is to be placed before numbering it, that is, whether by title, composer, or accession.[11–15] When filing by size, filing alphabetically either by title or composer within the size group would be suitable.

Hoffer writes that the band director can file by title, composer, ⑰
type of music, ". . . or whatever classification the teacher finds
useful." He goes on to say, however, that "The system of filing
alphabetically by composer is generally not recommended for
school . . . instrumental works, because much of the music is
derived from folk origins and has been adapted by arrangers
whose names are not readily familiar. An alphabetical placement
by title is preferable." [4] He recommends filing first by size, then
by title within that size. Hoffer feels this system makes the most
efficient use of space.

In the J. W. Pepper system for filing music, each new selection ⑱
is given a library or accession number on receipt of the music, and
before it is cataloged and filed. This number appears on the
Master Index (an inventory or acquisition book), Title card, the
scores and individual parts, filing box, and file cabinets. The music
is then filed according to the *library* or *accession* number rather
than by classification, composer/arranger, size, etc.[17]

Cecil offers two ideas for filing band music. The first is to place ⑲
music in file cabinets according to the director's classification
system and to arrange the cards in the index file according to this
same classification, or alphabetically by title. The second idea is
to arrange all the music alphabetically by title. He warns that this
latter idea does not consider the fact that band music is printed
on sheets of varying sizes which would make filing somewhat
awkward. "Whatever system is used," Cecil writes, "the main
requirement is ease of locating a selection; the director should be
able to locate a filing in the card catalog and from this card should
be able to find quickly the number he wants." [16]

Hovey advocates ". . . numbering, cataloging, and filing in- ⑳
strumental compositions according to *type of selection*, i.e., with
all marches together, all suites together, etc." He feels that there
are many advantages to this system.[5] Singleton's method is to file
all selections of each type together and have drawers of the
particular size for the music provided especially for it. Then,
". . . each category (is) identified by a file-number prefix and
each selection by the prefix plus the file number. Chorales, for
example, would be numbered C-1, C-2, and so on." [13]

Two related, but slightly varying systems in use are the following. In the first, the index cards play a highly important part as the classification is carefully noted on them. The music is separated by size and placed in the file drawers according to the classification on the cards, but placed *chronologically according to acquisition.* The individual selections are numbered consecutively in each drawer; the drawer identification and envelope number are also noted on the index cards.

For the second of these systems, the music is separated by size and then filed *strictly by chronological acquisition or accession;* no attempt is made to arrange the music by classification or alphabetically by title or composer. It is thought unnecessary to file by classification as it involves wasted space. This method eliminates the problem of constantly rearranging the music in the file drawers to accommodate new acquisitions. The classification system is made on the index cards. File drawers are identified by a letter-number prefix and the individual compositions numbered consecutively in each drawer. Since these systems are based on filing by chronological acquisition, they would seem to be quite suitable for a very small library or one which does not include the variety of classifications listed under "Cataloging" in this chapter. With growth in quantity and variety of selections in the library, the band director may wish to retain this system; he need only add more file drawers of the proper size. Newly acquired compositions would be given the next number in a drawer without disturbing the old ones.

Jones describes a slightly more complex library filing system for the band with a large and varied collection of band music. In his breakdown of sizes, Jones uses "B" for band (in case the orchestra music is filed in the same storage area), "a" for march size, "b" for octavo size, and "c" for concert or quarto size. He employs a three-way cross-index card file system. Based on Jones' classification, a file drawer identification marking appearing as "$\frac{B2c}{W}$" is interpreted as follows: B = band music, 2 = an overture, c = quarto size, and W = the title of the work which begins with that letter.

Jones also recommends a fourth ". . . permanent record card

for each number on cards 5 inches by 7 inches, giving the following information:

(1) Title
(2) Composer
(3) Opus number
(4) Arranger
(5) Classification (musical)
(6) National classification (grade of difficulty) *
(7) Library number
(8) Accession number
(9) Number of parts
(10) Check instrumentation (on printed list)
(11) Time of performance_____minutes. Conductor
(12) Remarks
(13) Evaluation [6]

In Jones' system, the music is filed according to classification, and then arranged alphabetically within each category.

College and university bands have a feature in their organizational structure not normally found in junior and senior high school instrumental programs. Many colleges and universities have more than one concert band in order to provide enough performing organizations for the number and varying technical levels of students who wish to participate in them. This means that the band library must contain enough music to service these bands and that the quality must be commensurate with the functions and capabilities of each one.

The University of Illinois Bands have three basic concert organizations within their departmental structure, but with subdivisions the total is actually five. The bands are: the *Concert Band* (large and small), the *First Regimental Band,* and the *Second Regimental Band* (two sections). The library is so organized that the music is evaluated and filed according to its appropriateness for each band. In the library system, the quality of the music is evaluated first; the Director of Bands is responsible for this judgment. Its present library, and all new acquisitions, is evaluated and filed according to specific divisions (designated by

---

* The manual originally listed in Jones' book has changed titles and sources. One may substitute a state classification or grade of difficulty in place of the national.

code letters) as described below. The following quotation from the University of Illinois Bands *Library Science* guide will give a clear picture of the evaluative method and divisions.*

1. "A" indicates excellent music which has adequate instrumentation for the Concert Band or can be brought up to that point by the addition of but a few parts.
2. "B" indicates excellent music which does not have enough parts for Concert Band use. In addition, there is no plan for the Concert Band to use it in the foreseeable future. Generally, however, there are enough parts for the First and Second Regimental Band use, or there would be if but a few parts were added.
3. "C" indicates music which is good, but is not as good as that in "A" or "B". This is music worthy of school band use. Most generally there are enough parts for the Second Regimental Band instrumentation.
4. "D" indicates music of little worth which has been assigned to the 'outer limbo.'
5. "F" indicates foreign editions of band literature.
6. Size suffixes are added to the above letters of evaluation.
   a. "L" indicates large size (quarto) music.
   b. "O" indicates octavo music.
   c. "M" indicates march size music.
7. Additional music categories.
   a. "L" when used alone refers to large size old editions.
      i. Good music
      ii. Not usable by the Illinois Bands because of outdated arrangements and inadequate instrumentation.
      iii. Source material for "rearranging."
   b. "O" when used alone, refers to octavo music of the same caliber as "L".

Of these divisions, #7 requires further commentary. This group has been relegated to the "Reserve" section of the band library. Music in 7-a-L is still performed on occasion and still appears as a file number on the index cards; the others are presumably considered obsolete.

Enumerating Selections and File Drawers. There seems to be as much variation in the method of enumerating individual selections and file drawers as in all previous steps of the library system.

---

* *Band Library Science at the University of Illinois,* a mimeographed guide.

The sources which advocate filing by classification recommend marking the files and drawers according to the individual categories in the classification system. Hovey, Leeder and Haynie, and Singleton use capital letters while Hoffer suggests Arabic numerals. Prescott and Chidester the Roman numerals. Applying Hovey's classification and enumerating method, file(s) "A" would contain *Street Marches* and their index cards would show the entry "A-1", "A-2", "A-3", etc., since there would be more than one file of "A" classification. The director has one of two possibilities for numbering the individual compositions, either sequentially from "1" to the end of that particular classification, or sequentially from "1" to the end within each individual drawer. ㉔

One assumes that in the Prescott and Chidester method an Arabic numeral is given to each selection within the various sizes. For example, march size works would have file numbers "I-1", "I-2", "I-3", etc., and octavo size the "II-1", "II-2", "II-3", etc., identification markings.

The classification system compiled from the best features of the sources described in the "Cataloging" section of this chapter has 26 categories in it. This would lend itself nicely to assigning one letter of the alphabet to each category for filing purposes. In the case of the small band library, with few file cabinets, which may be filed by accession, it would simply be a matter of numbering the file drawers sequentially from "1" on, either to the end of the drawer or to the last accession in the last drawer. For the system which contains a large number of holdings and has the music filed by chronological acquisition within each size, it would be best to use a combination of capital letters and numbers. For example, march size works would be filed under "A-1", "A-2", "A-3", etc., with the individual selections numbered consecutively for each separate file drawer. Another example would be a quarto size work listed on the index card as "C-3-20", meaning: quarto file, drawer 3, selection #20.

The University of Illinois Bands' music is filed according to the evaluative divisions previously described. An entry on an index card reading "AL 1 A" would be interpreted as: ㉕

1. First capital letter indicates the general section of cabinets to which the music has been assigned, in this case "A" quality.

2. The second capital letter indicates the size within that section, in this case "L" means large or quarto size.

3. The number which follows indicates the filing cabinet number within that section, in this case "1" means the first file cabinet in section "A".

4. The capital letter which follows the number indicates the drawer in that filing cabinet, in this case drawer "A" of file cabinet "1".

The file cabinets in each section are arranged in the following manner:

AL 1 A	AL 2 A	AL 3 A	AL 4 A	
AL 1 B	AL 2 B	AL 3 B	AL 4 B	Etc.
AL 1 C	AL 2 C	AL 3 C	AL 4 C	
AL 1 D	AL 2 D	AL 3 D	AL 4 D	

According to John Cranford, Head Librarian, the University of Illinois Bands, all marches are filed in one section, exclusive of concert marches. Quality evaluation is not assigned to street marches. The file cabinets are arranged and designated in the following manner:

M7A	M7B	M8A	M8B	
M7C	M7D	M8C	M8D	Etc.
M7E	M7F	M8E	M8F	
M7G	M7H	M8G	M8H	

There are two rows of marches filed in each drawer, the reason for the second capital letter following the number. The music is placed in the drawer in a position similar to that when reading the music on the stand or from a march folio. Arranged or manuscript music used by the *Football Band* during the fall season is filed in the "Reserve" section of the library (#7, "Additional music categories" of the evaluation code system). The present system for filing their music in each file drawer is by *chronological acquisition*. With such a tremendously great number of holdings and with so many yearly acquisitions, Cranford stated that chronological filing is by far the most practical procedure.

In addition to enumerating file cabinets and drawers (each designation which should be indicated on the filing envelope, folder, or box), there is the matter of enumerating the individual parts of each composition, including the scores. Some directors think it unnecessary to number the separate parts; the instrumentation indicated on the proper index card or on the outer side of the filing envelope (folder or box) is sufficient for checking parts. However, other directors feel that numbering individual parts is not only a time-saving procedure, but also a valuable aid to the band librarian in keeping a correct inventory, especially when re-filing the music after it has been performed by the band and taken out of the folders. Directors of very large concert bands, with many players and folders to a part, prefer to designate each part with a "desk number" (usually Roman numerals) corresponding to the folder number for that part, rather than number the parts consecutively. For example, "1st Clarinet—IV" is the fourth desk folder for that specific part. Regardless of the system the the director selects, if the filing envelope, folder, or box does not have an instrumentation printed on its outer cover, then the director should use a form of inventory sheet to check parts, etc. The order form sent to the music dealer or publisher for purchasing new music, as described in Chapter 7, may also serve as an inventory form simply by attaching it to the filing envelope. The University of Illinois Bands "Library Filing Record and Parts Inventory" sheet which follows can be taped in the filing jacket by the librarian; because these jackets are made from jute stock, the sheet is taped to the inside cover. It eliminates the necessity of having to refer to the index card file each time the librarian wants to inventory the parts.

UNIVERSITY OF ILLINOIS BANDS

Library Filing Record and Parts Inventory

Composer _____ File No. _____

Title _____

Publisher _____ Arranger _____

Classification _____ Copyright Date_____

Library: UI____Harding____Sousa____Clarke____Hindsley____

Full Score			Solo Cornet		
Condensed Score			1st Cornet		
D♭ Piccolo			2nd Cornet		
C Piccolo			3rd Cornet		
1st Flute			1st Trumpet		
2nd Flute			2nd Trumpet		
3rd Flute			1st Flügelhorn		
1st Oboe			2nd Flügelhorn		
2nd Oboe			1st Horn—F		
English Horn			2nd Horn—F		
1st Bassoon			3rd Horn—F		
2nd Bassoon			4th Horn—F		
Contrabassoon			1st Horn —E♭		
E♭ Clarinet			2nd Horn—E♭		
Solo Clarinet			3rd Horn—E♭		
1st Clarinet			4th Horn—E♭		
2nd Clarinet			1st Trombone		
3rd Clarinet			2nd Trombone		
4th Clarinet			3rd Trombone		
Alto Clarinet			4th Trombone		
Bass Clarinet			Euphonium (BC)		
E♭ CB Clarinet			Baritone (TC)		
B♭ CB Clarinet			Tubas (Basses)		
String Bass			Timpani		
1st Alto Saxophone			Bass Drum, Cymbals		
2nd Alto Saxophone			Snare Drum		
Tenor Saxophone					
Baritone Saxophone			Harp		
Bass Saxophone			Piano, Celeste		

Coda

What About Filing Scores?

For some directors, the question arises as to whether conductor's scores should be filed separately or with the individual parts of the instrumentation. Part of the solution may be found in the necessity for the scores to be readily available to the director for quick or frequent periodic reference. The director whose band performs at many and widely varying events during the school year is continually "browsing" through card files or scores selecting music for these programs. It might be a bit more convenient for him to have scores filed in his office or with the main band library but in separate cabinets. Again, in the case of a small band library, it is not too awkward for the director to have to thumb through envelopes to pull scores.

Directors who are opposed to filing scores separately are of the opinion that this is one of the easiest ways to lose or misplace scores. According to these persons, separating the score from the parts is similar to detaching the head from the body! Also, many directors simply do not have the extra file space available.

The music curriculum in the majority of colleges and universities includes at least one course devoted to school band organization and administration; there is also at least one course devoted to scoring for the band. The study and examination of music for school bands is usually an integral part of the course outline in one or both instances. College and university band directors, who are likely to be the instructors in these courses, find it more functional if the scores of the music used in connection with such courses were filed apart from the instrumentation.

The recommended procedure in the above case is to either order an extra score, or if a full and condensed score are included in the set of parts, then the condensed score is filed in the score file. A separate score file card is made and filed in the same manner as the main index file; the same file number for the main index card is placed on the score card. Filing the scores in the cabinet should follow the same method as that for the set of parts. The main index card and inventory sheet should indicate that a score is filed separately. Some form of check-out system should be employed for scores filed separately.

What to Do with Old Music

Practically every band library contains a number of selections which are no longer performed. This condition may be due to the music's lack of suitability (old, obsolete, limited performance value), or perhaps there are many missing or mutilated parts and the director considers it economically impractical to replace them. Righter describes the situation of the director who takes over an instrumental program and finds the band library in a run-down, neglected condition. His first objective, therefore, is to organize and rehabilitate the library as quickly as possible. Righter says that the "Neglect of school music libraries over the years, by different teachers with different ideas and standards, has left an unending trail of incomplete sets, torn parts, and much musical material that should have been discarded years before." [12] The director should divide his library into two units, one the "active library" and the other the "stored or inactive library." The "active" library should contain only those works which have been recorded on cards, parts replaced, worn parts repaired, and the instrumentation brought up to strength. The "stored" library will contain any other music the director feels is not useful, poor musically, or of which he has incomplete sets. Righter suggests that the director not discard the music in the "stored" library too soon because ". . . it may be necessary to use some of this material during the period of re-organization." [12] Eventually, some of it must be discarded and some used with smaller ensembles or for special performances.

Cecil feels that music considered to be obsolete belongs in the inactive file; this way it will not occupy valuable file cabinet space and can be relegated to boxes and kept in a storage room. The index file cards on this music should be pulled and placed in a separate tabbed section in the index card file noting that it is inactive. [16]

Summary

1. The system for filing the music in the band library depends upon the size of the library, the scope and variety of the music

contained in it, and the number of performing ensembles the library music services. The systems will range from the simplest to the very elaborately detailed.

2. Whatever system is put into practice by the director, it should be efficient, systematic (well-organized), and time-saving (ease in locating materials and in management).

3. The first step in setting up a system is to classify all the music by *type*. Several methods are in vogue; the method used should be based on the size of the band library as well as the variety of types of materials included in it.

4. A three-way cross-filing index system is strongly recommended for most libraries. Cards should be indexed for individual selections by the composer, title, and classification with provisions for indicating instrumentation and dates of performances on them. Composer and title cards may be arranged alphabetically by name, but classification cards should be arranged alphabetically either by composer or title; the latter is recommended.

5. The method for filing music in the file cabinets also depends on the size of the library and the amount of storage equipment on hand.

6. Music may be filed regardless of size, and then alphabetically either by title or composer.

7. Music may be filed alphabetically by title or by size.

8. Music may be filed alphabetically by composer according to size.

9. Music may be filed according to type or classification, first grouping it by size and then arranging it alphabetically either by title or composer within each type category.

10. Music may be filed by strict chronological accession but first grouped according to size. This is perhaps the most popular procedure utilized by band directors; it is the easiest to use because it eliminates the problem of reshuffling the music from drawer to drawer to make room for new acquisitions, or rearranging the envelopes for the same reason.

11. File cabinets and individual drawers should be enumerated for efficient, systematic filing methods. These indications should, of course, appear on the index card for each selection. The enumerating system may be correlated with the classification of the music.

12. The separate categories in the classification system may be given either capital letters and/or numbers. If the music is filed by classification, the file drawers are identified by these letters or numbers and the individual selections numbered sequentially in each drawer. Since there will be several drawers for each category, a combination letter-number for each one is necessary.

13. Conductor's scores may be filed with the individual parts of the set or in a separate file cabinet depending on the director's preference or the necessity for quick or frequent reference of the scores by him.

14. Old, obsolete works, or those with incomplete sets of parts, should be filed in separate cabinets, boxes, or discarded completely.*

Selected References

Books

1. Bradley, Carol June (ed.). *Manual of Music Librarianship,* Ann Arbor, Michigan: Music Library Association, 1966.
2. Colwell, Richard J. *The Teaching of Instrumental Music,* New York: Appleton-Century-Crofts, 1969.
3. Foster, William Patrick. *Band Pageantry,* Winona, Minnesota: Hal Leonard Music, Inc., 1968.
4. Hoffer, Charles R. *Teaching Music in the Secondary Schools,* Belmont, California: Wadsworth Publishing Company, Inc., 1964.
5. Hovey, Nilo W. *The Administration of School Instrumental Music,* New York: Belwin, Inc., 1949.
6. Jones, Bruce L. *Building the Instrumental Music Department,* New York: Carl Fischer, Inc., 1949.
7. Kuhn, Wolfgang. *Instrumental Music: Principles and Methods of Instruction,* Boston: Allyn and Bacon, 1962.
8. Leeder, Joseph A. and William S. Haynie. *Music Education in the High School,* Englewood Cliffs, New Jersey: Prentice-Hall, Inc., 1958.

---

* The author is indebted to Mr. John Cranford, Head Librarian, University of Illinois Bands, for his warm cooperation and willingness to describe their library science system, offer advice and pertinent materials pursuant to their system. Our heartfelt thanks.

9. Leonhard, Charles and Robert W. House. *Foundations and Principles of Music Education*, New York: McGraw-Hill, 1959.
10. Music Library Association. *Code for Cataloguing Music*, Washington, D.C.: Music Library Association, 1941–42.
11. Prescott, Gerald R. and Lawrence W. Chidester. *Getting Results with School Bands*, New York: Carl Fischer, Inc. and Minneapolis, Minnesota: Schmitt, Hall, and McCreary, 1938.
12. Righter, Charles Boardman. *Teaching Instrumental Music*, New York: Carl Fischer, Inc., 1959.
13. Singleton, Ira C. *Music in Secondary Schools*, Boston: Allyn and Bacon, 1963.

Periodicals

14. Ivory, Paul S. "Band Programs in Minnesota," *Journal of Band Research*, Spring, 1953.

Monograph

15. Southern Music Company. "How to Index Your Band or Orchestra Music Library," San Antonio, Texas: Southern Music Company, 1945.

Unpublished Literature

16. Cecil, Herbert M. *Fundamental Principles of the Organization, Management, and Teaching of the School Band,* unpublished dissertation, University of Rochester, 1953.

Addenda

17. Pepper, J. W. and Son, "How to File and Find Music," Philadelphia: J. W. Pepper and Son, Inc., 1966.

9

How to Effectively Use
Student Helpers in Managing and
Maintaining the Band Library

THE DIRECTOR NEEDS A LIBRARY STAFF

The band library may consist of hundreds or thousands of single works each containing many separate parts for the conductor and individual instruments. Considering the probable inventory already on hand plus the many new annual acquisitions, a great amount of attention must be given to keeping account of all this material. "The instrumental director must, therefore, devise adequate means of keeping the many thousands of items in order. For this purpose he needs a staff that will be instructed to carry out the details of the library system." [4] A well-trained library staff will conserve the band director's energies, thoughts, and time which he can better apply to his musical and other administrative responsibilities. For example, concerning the time factor, the director has enough to do studying scores, selecting music for concerts, planning rehearsals, teaching beginning instrument classes, and the other myriad details of his position.

Prescott and Chidester claim that "A great deal of time and money can be saved if the band library is used systematically." [5] Time probably refers to the proper distribution of music to the players, collecting the music after it has been performed, quickly locating compositions or individual parts, and generally contributing to an efficient rehearsal procedure. The economic factor involves: keeping an accurate inventory; preventing the loss of single parts; and the repair of worn parts, music folios, and filing envelopes (boxes or folders).

A large instrumental music program, with its attendant voluminous, complex library, requires a library staff for more efficient administration of the band library. Once the director has established his library system, he needs a staff to keep it in good operational condition and order. The various categories within the management of the library are generally similar regardless of the library's size; the mode of operation, however, will vary with the amount of detail designed for each category.

After the director has devised and set into operation a library system, ". . . it can normally be maintained by student assistants, with a minimum of supervision from the teacher." [2] The number of student workers depends, of course, on the size of the library, the complexity of the system, the number of organizations involved in the instrumental program, and if the students must do additional duties (such as serving as uniform or instrument managers). In a small school system, the director usually manages the library with the help of at least one student worker.

At the high school level, most directors are able to make up a library staff from student volunteers. One high school band director recruits student librarians from the staff of "band officers" elected by the band members. The elected librarian(s) serve(s) a tenure of one school year, unless re-elected. Jones firmly believes in the value derived from student participation in the government of instrumental music. His approach is to appoint the librarian ". . . upon application and acceptance of qualifications; usually is (the) promotion of the outstanding assistant librarian of the preceding year." [3] In contrast, college/university bands normally have funds allocated or available to them for hiring student workers to manage the various facets of the band program. The amount of funds determine whether or not it is necessary to assign the same student(s) or different students to various tasks (music library, uniforms, instruments, office).

Bands which experience a rapid turnover in student helpers might adopt a policy followed by several large university bands. This consists of a notebook describing the entire library system and routine. In addition to a detailed description of the library operation, the notebook contains sample copies of all forms used in connection with the system and its procedures along with remarks for their usage. Through the notebook, students can train themselves in the library routine. The director, however, should initially explain it to the librarians. Such a notebook helps keep the library system intact; any changes in procedures may be made as needed.

LIBRARY ROUTINE

Each director must establish his own routine for managing and maintaining the band library. Logically, it can and should be divided into successive steps or divisions ranging from a few simple steps to a complex, numerous, detailed routine. For Prescott and Chidester, the steps ". . . correspond to the journey a composition takes from the time it is ordered until it has been used in the band room and replaced in the files." They include: "1. Ordering; 2. Cataloging; 3. Filing; 4. Distributing; 5. Signing out for overnight practice; and 6. Replacing in files."[5] An added step might be a general inventory at the end of the school year.

A Routine for Entering New Acquisitions

Entering new acquisitions into the band library represents one of the more important aspects of the library routine in terms of the amount of time it occupies during each school year. This phase of the routine includes the procedure for cataloging, filing, and indexing the music. A variety of procedures may be employed.

Prescott and Chidester suggest that after the music arrives, the first step is to check the parts against the instrumentation. Then each page of every part is rubber-stamped with the name of the school band; loose middle pages must be stamped and titled as well to prevent misplacement. After these steps, the music is placed in its folio.[5] Cecil describes the same routine but adds that after the music is placed in a folder, it is cataloged and indexed before it is filed.[8]

Kuhn is more detailed in his description of the steps the librarian must follow.

Directions to Librarian for Filing a New Number [4]

1. Make out appropriate inventory sheet and check the kinds and number of parts.

2. Fill out Instrumental Music Library Card.

3. Assign library number (acquisition number) and drawer or shelf number, indicating these numbers on the inventory sheet and library card.

4. Separate parts and trim to appropriate size.

5. Stamp name of school and organization on each part.

6. Arrange parts in order of conductor's score and place them in filing envelope.

7. Label filing envelope with library number, shelf or drawer number, composer, title.

8. Place parts and score in filing cabinet, inventory sheet in inventory file (loose leaf folder or binder), library card in card index.

Jones is even more detailed in his "Step-by-step outline of cataloging music." [3]

    a. List in accession book, giving the following information:

        (1) Accession number

        (2) Date

        (3) Title

        (4) Composer

        (5) Arranger

        (6) Edition

        (7) Publisher

        (8) From whom purchased

        (9) Order number

      (10) Invoice number

      (11) Cost of arrangement

      (12) Cost of extra parts

      (13) Total cost

      (14) Librarian's initial

    b. Put accession number on music; always in the same place on all numbers.

   c. Trim music; if march size, cut to 5 inches by 7 inches.
   d. Stamp with band, orchestra, or school stamp.
   e. Put parts in order according to (instrumentation) list.
   f. Number music . . .
   g. Classify for filing (*according to list given in Chapter 8*) . . .
   h. Prepare folders of heavy, durable paper . . .
   i. Put classification number, title, composer, on back of folder; stand it up like a book.
   j. Make catalog cards; use regulation library catalog cards and cataloging procedure.
   k. Fill out permanent record card for each number (*described in Chapter 8*) . . .
   l. File music in proper order in bin
      (1) File according to classification
      (2) Arrange alphabetically within each classification [3]

The J. W. Pepper system for filing music begins with the *Master Index* sheet; this is a numerical and statistical record of the contents of the music library. As each piece of music is acquired, the following information is entered about it on the *Master Index:* (1) *Library Number;* (2) *Title;* (3) *Composer* and/or *Arranger;* (4) *Number of Parts and Cost.* The *Library Number* indicates the physical location of the music in the library. After the selection is entered in the *Master Index*, the *Title* card is filled in with all necessary information and is filed alphabetically in a file box. If supplementary cards are used, Pepper suggests one set made and filed by classification and a possible third set filed by composer-arranger.

The Pepper File-Finder Boxes, which contain the scores and parts, have the same basic information printed on them as the *Title* card. If more than one box is required for a single composition, each has the same identical information filled in.

Marking the Parts

Marking the score and separate instrumental parts may be thought of as preventative maintenance because it helps put and keep the music in order, aids the inventory procedure, and deters the loss or misplacement of parts. The score and parts should be marked in some manner before they are placed in the file cabinets.

Kownatsky recommends that the "Music should have marked on the separate parts the file number, the marks of possession, and the number indicating that part's order in the instrumentation for easy filing and counting purposes."[1] Prescott and Chidester propose that the parts be arranged in order of the band's instrumentation and then each part numbered consecutively. This becomes the distribution order for the parts used by the band; they do not mention what to do with extra parts.[5]

For very large high school and college/university bands, with several players to each part, marking the parts by "desks" would be quite suitable; it allows for the later addition of extra parts and does not require the formulation of an elaborate digital system. The librarian may use either Arabic or Roman numerals. Therefore, parts are designated as: *1st Flute, Desk I* (or *1*); *1st Flute, Desk II* (or *2*); *1st Flute, Desk III* (or *3*); etc.

Jones recommends numbering the music by one of two plans: "(1) Number each part consecutively, or (2) Give each part a letter, then number the several parts, e.g., conductor's scores are given the letter *A*; if there is more than one score, they should be numbered *A-1, A-2, A-3*, etc."[3] Assuming that the Piccolo part would follow the conductor's scores, it would be marked "*B-1*", the 1st Flute parts as "*C-1*", "*C-2*", "*C-3*", and the 2nd Flute parts as "*D-1*", "*D-2*", "*D-3*", etc.

Inventory Sheets

Commercial band music filing envelopes or boxes have an instrumentation printed on the outside cover. This convenience may serve the librarian as an inventory device for checking the parts of a new order against the instrumentation, or checking for worn or missing parts after the music is collected. Band directors who make their own folders out of heavy-weight paper or jute stock, should make up an inventory sheet (mimeographed or printed) indicating the band's instrumentation order; these sheets should be glued to the inside upper cover (not the outside where it may be torn off). The following "Extra Parts Order Form" used by the University of Illinois Bands, could be adapted and used as an inventory sheet.

UNIVERSITY OF ILLINOIS BANDS

Extra Parts Order Form

To _____ Date _____

Please furnish band parts to numbers as indicated below:

1 _____   6 _____
2 _____   7 _____
3 _____   8 _____
4 _____   9 _____
5 _____   10 _____

	1	2	3	4	5	6	7	8	9	10	Additional Notations
Full Score											
Condensed Score											
C Piccolo											
1st Flute											
2nd Flute											
3rd Flute											
1st Oboe											
2nd Oboe											
English Horn											
1st Bassoon											
2nd Bassoon											
Solo Clarinet											
1st Clarinet											
2nd Clarinet											
3rd Clarinet											
4th Clarinet											
Alto Clarinet											
Bass Clarinet											
String Bass											
1st Alto Saxophone											
2nd Alto Saxophone											
Tenor Saxophone											

Baritone Saxophone										
Solo Cornet										
1st Cornet										
2nd Cornet										
3rd Cornet										
1st Trumpet										
2nd Trumpet										
1st Horn (F)										
2nd Horn (F)										
3rd Horn (F)										
4th Horn (F)										
1st Trombone										
2nd Trombone										
3rd Trombone										
Euphonium (BC)										
Baritone (TC)										
Basses (Tubas)										
Timpani										
Percussion										
Harp										

Ordered by: _____

Righter calls the inventory list the "Master Chart of Instrumentation for Band," and suggests that it be posted in the library. He further recommends that "Continuous checks should be made against these master lists and no set of parts should ever be placed in, or returned to, the active file unless it conforms to the master list. The advantage of this system is that it assures the conductor that *every number* in the active file can be used at any time, without a precheck of parts. This is a great satisfaction and it will save time and lost motion. . . ." [6] An inventory of individual selections should be kept up-to-date so that the director need not be placed in the frustrating position of lacking a sufficient number of parts for a selection he wishes to include at the next rehearsal. A sample inventory form as used in the University of Illinois Bands library follows. It serves mainly as a chronological accession form.

INVENTORY FORM

File No.	Composer	Title	Classification	Published	Lib.	File Date

An added feature in the band library routine is the "Check Sheet," a type of work order form on which may be indicated those parts which need repair, replacement due to wear, or are missing. Torn parts may be repaired with commercial tape, but 3-M "Invisible Mending Tape" is better for this purpose rather than the heavier cellulose variety which hardens, becomes brittle, and yellows with age. For parts with several single inside pages, or conductor's scores, hinged tape (with varying numbers of leaves) allows for easier handling and longer wear. Edging tape, applied with a special edging machine, is one of the best means of repairing the creases between pages.

Coda

Although the organization, care, and maintenance of the band library is the direct responsibility of the director, trained student personnel should execute as much of the daily library operation, procedure, and routine as possible. The band director must train student workers in systematic procedures of cataloging, indexing, and filing; in this case, a "Library Routine" notebook is a handy device.

A broad, general routine would include: (1) Checking the parts of new music against the score or band instrumentation for completeness; (2) Cataloging (classifying) the music according to type; (3) Marking or numbering the score and parts (a marking system which allows for additional or extra parts is recommended);

(4) Rubber-stamping the score and parts with the school and organizational name; (5) Giving the music an acquisition (inventory), file, and drawer number; (6) Filling out library index cards for each selection; (7) Making up a filing envelope, box, or folder with the instrumentation and file number indicated on it; (8) Making up an Inventory Sheet for the "Acquisition Ledger" and for the folder (if a non-commercial folder is used) giving the instrumentation and other pertinent information on it; (9) Filing the music in its proper cabinet, drawer, or shelf; and (10) Making a continuous, periodic inventory for completeness of instrumentation, missing parts, worn or torn parts, as a method for keeping the library up-to-date.

Selected References

Books

1. Bradley, Carol June (ed.). *Manual of Music Librarianship.* Ann Arbor, Michigan: Music Library Association, 1966.
2. Hoffer, Charles R. *Teaching Music in the Secondary Schools,* Belmont, California: Wadsworth Publishing Company, Inc., 1964.
3. Jones, Bruce L. *Building the Instrumental Music Department,* New York: Carl Fischer, Inc., 1949.
4. Kuhn, Wolfgang. *Instrumental Music: Principles and Methods of Instruction,* Boston: Allyn and Bacon, 1962.
5. Prescott, Gerald R. and Lawrence W. Chidester. *Getting Results with School Bands,* New York: Carl Fischer, Inc., 1938.
6. Righter, Charles B. *Teaching Instrumental Music,* New York: Carl Fischer, Inc., 1959.
7. Singleton, Ira C. *Music in Secondary Schools,* Boston: Allyn and Bacon, 1963.

Unpublished Literature

8. Cecil, Herbert M. *Fundamental Principles of the Organization, Management, and Teaching of the School Band,* unpublished dissertation, University of Rochester, 1953.
9. University Bands, *Band Library Science at the University of Illinois,* mimeographed brochure.

Monographs

10. Pepper, J. W. and Son, Inc. (Don H. Razey, ed.). *How to File and Find Music,* Philadelphia: J. W. Pepper and Son, Inc., 1966.

10

How to Teach Proper Care
and Control of the
Library and the Literature

Now that the band director has developed criteria for selecting literature, learned how to locate and systematically acquire new music, has designed and established a management routine for cataloging, filing, and indexing the music, his next administrative task is to develop techniques for care and control of the band library. Efficient management of the band library requires the use of several different types of records and a set of categories for an orderly care and control routine. The most important ingredient, however, is a diligent, industrious librarian (not forgetting a conscientious band director, of course).

Although filing systems vary, the following record items are necessary for the *minimum* in good management and control: (1) Library index file cards; (2) File envelopes, boxes, or folders; (3) Concert band folders; (4) Marching band folders and flipfolios; (5) Sign-out cards for concert and marching bands; (6) Music order blanks; and (7) Inventory sheets. A minimum number of categories for care and control of the library include: (1) Filing the music; (2) Sorting the music; (3) Distributing the music for rehearsal and concert; (4) Collecting the music for collating and re-filing; (5) Control of sign-out music; (6) Care of storage facilities; (7) Periodic inventory; and (8) Maintenance and repair of the music, folios, folders, etc.

"To maintain an efficient, usable library, the director must organize the care and storage of the music in a manner that will require a minimum of his time." [4] Entire compositions or individual parts must be located quickly; sorting, distribution, and collecting must be accurate and handled with dispatch. In addition to time, other factors involving efficient administration of the library are economy and aid to the rehearsal routine. For proper management of his library, the director should not stint on quantity or quality of types of record items, storage, and other equipment units. On the other hand, it would not be practical for him to have this material in quantities beyond that which he actually needs for care and control. A few aids to rehearsal routine include distribution of music or folders, collecting the folders, and providing the individual folders with missing or repaired parts. It was mentioned before that there is nothing more frustrating during or detracting from a rehearsal than to have to stop because single parts or even an entire selection are missing. As it concerns library management, much of the responsibility for a good rehearsal routine is the director's. While some directors do not mind asking the librarian to distribute a selection during the rehearsal, this procedure is somewhat distracting. The director should plan his rehearsals well in advance regarding specific music he wants in the folders and relay this information to the librarian.

MAINTENANCE AND UPKEEP

Torn, worn, or mutilated parts should be repaired immediately. The director must, of course, keep adequate and proper supplies on hand for this purpose. It was recommended in Chapter 9 that the librarian use thin, "invisible" type mending tape (such as 3-M) as well as edging and hinged tape. Other supplies for the library might include a typewriter, scissors, paper cutter, paste, glue, masking tape, marking pencils, felt-tip pens, manuscript fountain pens, manuscript paper in assorted sizes, and other necessary maintenance or repair items.

Folios and Folders

One form of preventative maintenance is the use of some type of heavy, durable folio for filing concert and march music. There are three basic types: (1) envelope; (2) box; and (3) folders made from manila paper or jute stock. Kownatsky feels that ". . . music can best be protected in a box. Boxes, for most efficient use of space, should be made in two stable dimensions and increments of ¼″ increasing thickness, ranging from ½″ to about 6″. The two stable dimensions, 12½″ front to back and 14½″ wide, will accommodate all but large folio scores." [1] He offers two alternative types of filing materials. The first ". . . is a protective cover of stiff binder's board fitted with tapes which can be tied to hold the set together." Kownatsky goes on to say that if

---

No. or Title

EMBUR FILING ENVELOPE NO. 14

INSTRUMENTATION	NO.	CASE NO.	SHELF NO.

Conductor
Piccolo
Flutes
Oboes
Bassoons
Eb Clarinet
1st Bb Clarinet   TITLE (A)
2nd Bb Clarinet   (B)
3rd Bb Clarinet
Alto Clarinet
Bass Clarinet
1st Alto Saxophone   CHARACTER (A)
2nd Alto Saxophone   (B)
Tenor Saxophone
Baritone Saxophone
1st (Solo) Cornet   COMPOSER (A)
2nd Bb Cornet   (B)
3rd Bb Cornet
Trumpets
1st Horn
2nd Horn
3rd Horn
4th Horn   PROPERTY OF
Baritone T. C.
Baritone B. C.
1st Trombone
2nd Trombone
3rd Trombone
Basses
Drums
Tympani

EDUCATIONAL MUSIC BUREAU INC. 434 S. WABASH AVENUE, CHICAGO, ILL. 60605

Illustration 10-1
March Size

boxes and boards ". . . are too expensive, one may resort to red-rope expanding envelopes, large enough to accommodate the music and strong enough to withstand wear." [1] The J. W. Pepper Company of Philadelphia is an example of one firm which supplies the heavy-weight paper boxes for filing purposes.

There are several inexpensive types of commercially-printed envelopes available. One type has an open end for inserting the music; another has a flap over the opening with a clasp for closure; a third type also has a flap over the cover but uses strong binding string to fasten the opening. All three, and the commercial boxes, have one feature in common, the outside cover has all the necessary information about the work, including the instrumentation, printed on it for inventory purposes. Illustrations 10-1, 10-2, and 10-3 are examples of filing envelopes in march, octavo, and quarto size respectively; this type has an open end.

No. 12

No. or Title

FILING **EMB** ENVELOPE

INSTRUMENTATION		NO.　CASE NO.　SHELF NO.

✦ ORCHESTRA ✦	✦ BAND ✦
Conductor Score	Conductor Score
Flutes & Piccolo	1st Flute
1st Oboe	2nd Flute
2nd Oboe	Piccolo
English Horn	1st Oboe
1st Clarinet	2nd Oboe
2nd Clarinet	English Horn
1st Bassoon	1st Bassoon
2nd Bassoon	2nd Bassoon
Saxophones	Eb Clarinet
1st Horn	1st Bb Clarinet
2nd Horn	2nd Bb Clarinet
3rd Horn	3rd Bb Clarinet
4th Horn	4th Bb Clarinet
1st Trumpet	Alto Clarinet
2nd Trumpet	Bass Clarinet
3rd Trumpet	1st Alto Saxophone
1st Trombone	2nd Alto Saxophone
2nd Trombone	Tenor Saxophone
3rd Trombone	Baritone Saxophone
Tuba	1st (Solo) Cornet
Tympani	1st Cornet
Drums, etc.	2nd Bb Cornet
Piano	3rd Bb Cornet
Harp	Trumpets
1st Violin	1st & 2nd Eb Horns
2nd Violin	3rd & 4th Eb Horns
3rd Violin	1st & 2nd F Horns
Viola	3rd & 4th F Horns
Cello	1st & 2nd Trombones (BC)
Bass	3rd Trombone (BC)
	Baritone (TC)
	Baritone (BC)
	Basses
	String Bass
	Tympani
	Drums
	Bell Lyra
	Harp

TITLE $\frac{(A)}{(B)}$

CHARACTER $\frac{(A)}{(B)}$

COMPOSER $\frac{(A)}{(B)}$

PROPERTY OF

ORDER FROM EDUCATIONAL MUSIC BUREAU, INC., 434 S. Wabash Ave., Chicago, Ill.　60605

Illustration 10-2
Octavo Size

FILING EMB ENVELOPE
No. 16

No. or Title

INSTRUMENTATION

ORCHESTRA
Conductor Score
Flutes & Piccolo
1st Oboe
2nd Oboe
English Horn
1st Clarinet
2nd Clarinet
1st Bassoon
2nd Bassoon
Saxophones
1st Horn
2nd Horn
3rd Horn
4th Horn
1st Trumpet
2nd Trumpet
3rd Trumpet
1st Trombone
2nd Trombone
3rd Trombone
Tuba
Tympani
Drums, etc.
Piano
Harp
1st Violin
2nd Violin
3rd Violin
Viola
Cello
Bass

BAND
Conductor Score
1st Flute
2nd Flute
Piccolo
1st Oboe
2nd Oboe
English Horn
1st Bassoon
2nd Bassoon
Eb Clarinet
1st Bb Clarinet
2nd Bb Clarinet
3rd Bb Clarinet
4th Bb Clarinet
Alto Clarinet
Bass Clarinet
1st Alto Saxophone
2nd Alto Saxophone
Tenor Saxophone
Baritone Saxophone
1st (Solo) Cornet
2nd Bb Cornet
3rd Bb Cornet
Trumpets
1st & 2nd Eb Horns
3rd & 4th Eb Horns
1st & 2nd F Horns
3rd & 4th F Horns
1st & 2nd Trombones (BC)
3rd Trombone (BC)
Baritone (TC)
Baritone (BC)
Basses
String Bass
Tympani
Drums
Bell Lyra
Harp

NO.   CASE NO.   SHELF NO.

TITLE (A) (B)

CHARACTER (A) (B)

COMPOSER (A) (B)

PROPERTY OF

EDUCATIONAL MUSIC BUREAU, Inc., 310 W. Polk Street Chicago, Ill. 60607

Illustration 10-3
Quarto Size

Righter objects to the expansion-type envelope because he feels that the ". . . expansion device will wear and tear the edges of the music. . . ." The chief objection to the use of a clasp envelope is the difficulty of inserting the parts into the envelope and also the danger of tearing the edges of the music in the process.[9] He and several other sources prefer a folio made of fairly stiff material such as manila paper or jute stock. These persons, however, differ in specifications for dimensions and other minor details. Righter, for example, describes his folio as follows: (See Illustration 10-4)

A–A′, B–B′, C–C′, D–D′: folds (height of music or slightly higher)

B–C, B′–C′: width of music

A–B, A′–B′, C–D, C′–D′: thickness of music [9]

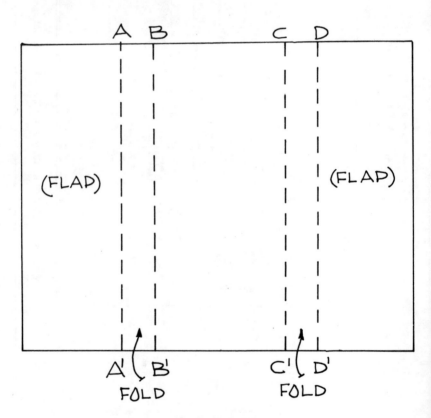

Illustration 10-4
Righter's Folio

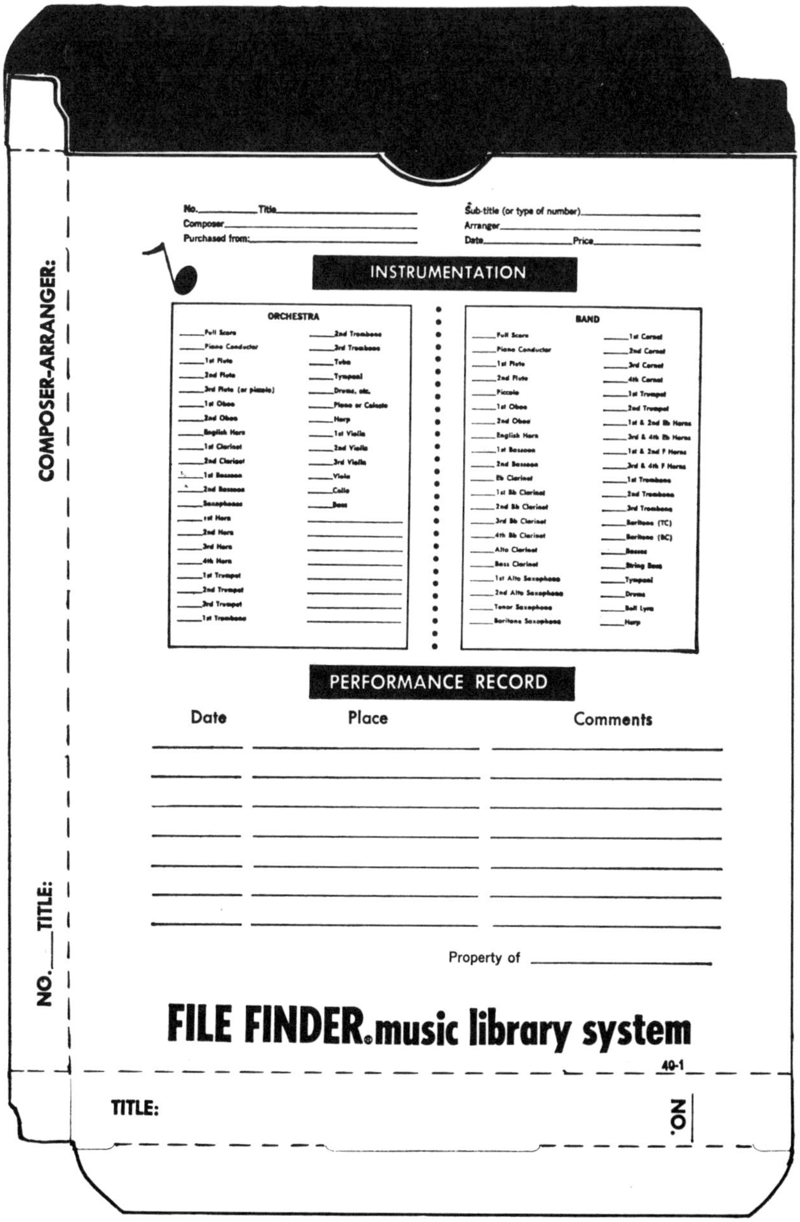

Illustration 10-5
J. W. Pepper File Finder

Illustration 10-5 shows the J. W. Pepper "File Finder" music filing and storage box. Printed designations provide sufficient space for information regarding cataloging (classification), filing, and indexing. The boxes will allow the director and his library staff to use them for inventory purposes without having to resort to the index card file. The design of these boxes will assist the director who wishes to keep the number of index cards per individual composition to a minimum.

Music Storage

The band director must consider two basic types of music storage, one for filing his music and the other for storage of his rehearsal folders. Metal cabinets with roll-out drawers are recommended for filing music because they are more accessible and offer better protection. The library will need two sizes: letter and legal.[2] A storage cabinet for rehearsal folders is a great convenience for prompt and efficient rehearsal. The style preferred by many directors is the horizontal pigeon-hole type; it must contain enough compartments to accommodate all the folders. If possible, the library should have separate cabinets for concert folders and march folios. The march cabinet, also a horizontal pigeon-hole type, should be portable, with casters, so that it can be transported to and from the field or street. A space-saving style of concert folder cabinet, commercially available, is one which combines the conductor's desk (or stand) and folder storage cabinet.

Sorting Racks

An important necessity for the working area of the library are sorting racks; they provide librarians with a place to sort and distribute music. The director may also use them as a means for studying individual parts of the music in the folders. These may be built into the wall or roll-away on casters. For the director who wishes to construct his own racks, M.E.N.C. suggests the following structural features:

> A sorting rack should consist of four or five slanting shelves, one inch by 15 inches by 75 inches (or longer), with one inch by two inch strips at the bottom of each shelf

to hold the music in place. The size of the largest folios used in schools is about 12 inches by 15 inches. Each shelf of the sorting rack should be made to hold the desired number of these folders, allowing two inches between folios for over-lapping of music, or 14 inches width per folio. Two or more racks should be placed against the wall or walls of the music library, rehearsal room, or office, preferably at the corner, so that the person or persons using the racks may do so with a minimum of walking. Sufficient shelf space should be pro-vided for the greatest number of folios used by any one musical organization.[7]

If the band budget cannot absorb the cost of separate concert folder storage cabinets, M.E.N.C. recommends built-in shelves for stacking folders. This may be done in one of two ways: (1) shelves for individual folios; or (2) shelves for each section of the band. If one shelf is assigned each section, the section leader dis-tributes and collects the folios at the rehearsals. Directors con-sider this a time-saving procedure and less confusing than requiring individual players to be responsible for their folders.[7]

Regarding sorting racks, one must keep in mind that for ease of viewing and working, the shelf slant increases from the top to the bottom shelf so that the bottom shelf appears to be almost horizontal.

The ideal situation, of course, is to have separate sorting racks for each organization, one for concert and one for marching. If only one sorting rack is used, it should be clearly labeled for each part, each section, and each organization.

Shelf Identification Systems. For the band library with but one sorting rack, each part may be identified with colored plastic stick-on labels, the type made by a labeling tape writer machine. For example, concert folder parts may be of a contrasting color from the march folios. The shelves of the pigeon-hole cabinets are similarly identified. March flip-folios may be placed in each sec-tion of the sorting rack in a vertical position thereby making it possible to put two march folios in each section. Instrumental music programs that have more than one concert organization should use contrasting color labels for each organization.

The sections on the sorting racks and the shelves in the pigeon-hole cabinets, for concert music, are labeled in score order and identified by the name of the instrument; if there is more than one copy for a part, it is further identified by stand or part number (whichever method the director uses in his marking system for filing purposes). The concert folders are marked according to the identification system on the racks and cabinets. For march music, the racks and cabinets (if separate) are marked according to the identification system the director employs in his band's marching formation. The positions in the band formation should be placed on the envelopes and flip-folios.

To save wear and tear on the music, and flip-folios, it is strongly urged that the director issue a march-size music envelope during marching season. The music to be performed for a particular field or street event may be taken from the envelope and inserted into the flip-folio as required rather than stuffing all the music in the flip-folios. These envelopes should be marked similarly to the flip-folios. Foster uses and recommends three sets of folios for marching bands. One set is to be used for music to be performed on parade or in the stands. The other two are for holding the music performed for field pageantry. "One set issued at the beginning of the week for a new pageant, while the other, with the past week's pageant, is turned in. The librarians will then have one week to remove one pageant and refill the folio with another." [2] Presumably, the first folio (parade and stand) contains music performed each week and remains in the student's possession until the end of the marching season.

LIBRARY ORDER ROUTINE

As in the other aspects of the library system, the routine will vary with the size of the library, the number and type of records used, and the type of storage and sorting equipment maintained in it.

Sorting, Distributing, and Collecting

Prescott and Chidester simply state that "The process of distributing music involves two essential steps: placing the parts in the band folios, and placing the folios in the pigeon-hole cabinets where the band members obtain them before rehearsal. No music is passed out during the band rehearsal."(!) [8] Cecil recommends the same procedure but specifically mentions that *each player* takes the folder from the cabinet and returns it at the end of the rehearsal.[11] The following excerpts are from Jones' step-by-step outline for sorting and distributing music.[5]

   a. Putting music in the folios:
     (1) Fill out repertoire slip (similar to an inventory sheet)
     (2) Put music in folios according to prescribed procedure
       (a) Mark folios with stickers showing name of the organization . . .
       (c) Arrange folios . . . on the sorting racks in order by instrumentation list
       (d) Lay parts from filing envelope or folder on the correct folios; since music is in same order as folios, this is in same order as folios, this is quickly done . . .
       (f) Place march music in manila envelopes marked to correspond with each march folio . . . march folios are checked out to individual pupils, and each is responsible for his own folio and for the music it contains
       (g) Check carefully to see that all folios are covered, and missing parts noted . . .
       (h) Put each part inside its folio, and return folios to their usual place

Kuhn offers a set of directions to librarians for distributing and collecting music.

When placing music in the rehearsal folders:
1. Place folders in sorting rack in order of the score. . . . Make certain that stand numbers are in correct order.
2. Sort music in each appropriate folder, placing each piece in front of the folder. After all pieces have been sorted out in this way, double-check to make sure that each piece is placed with its correct folder. Then place music inside of pocket of each folder, collect folders in order of score and parts from the sorting rack and return them to storage cabinet.
3. Extra parts are kept in the filing envelope and are stored in a designated cabinet set aside for this purpose.

When taking music out of folders:

1. Place folders in sorting rack in order of score, as before.
2. Take music out of each folder, placing it in front of each folder on the sorting rack.
3. Collect each selection in order of score and number of parts.
4. Combine collected music with extra parts from the filing cabinets.
5. Check condition of each part; mend and erase wherever necessary.
6. Check parts against inventory sheet. Note any missing parts.
7. When everything is in order, place all parts into their designated filing envelope and return to file.[6]

Here are a few helpful suggestions for band librarians from the J. W. Pepper monograph: (1) Librarians must post a list of folio contents; revise it daily if necessary; (2) Keep a red or black pencil in each folio for quick marking of music—*never use ink in marking music!*; (3) Librarians should post notices on the bulletin board and players should automatically check the board for all routine announcements; (4) Players must report to the librarian, not the conductor, shortages, mistakes, or problems concerning folio contents; (5) It may become necessary to substitute parts —if so, the librarian must consult the conductor on his wishes (since this is a musical judgment); (6) Paper clip new music to any active Sign-Out Cards—at the same time, librarians may leave a note indicating removal and return of any music which may have been recalled when the folio was taken out; (7) the conductor advises librarians which titles are to be removed and when —Librarians then announce on the bulletin board when folios may *not* be taken home on a given day—If players can be instructed to place those titles on top of all the music in the folio before returning them to the folio rack, a lot of the librarian's time can be saved.[12]

The "Library Order Routine" for the University of Illinois Bands is one of checks, counter-checks, and controls all the way down the administrative line. The binding ingredient and controlling element is the "Library Order" form (a sort of routing slip) which is used to initiate action and provide pertinent information. (See Illustration 10-6.)

UNIVERSITY OF ILLINOIS BANDS
LIBRARY ORDER

Composer_____ File No._____
Title_____
Publisher_____ Arranger_____
Band_____ ☐ Concert Folios ☐ March Folios ☐ Special_____

_____
_____
_____
_____

In_____ _____ _____ _____ _____
Out_____ _____ _____ _____ _____

Conductor   Librarian
3M—8-61—74802

Illustration 10-6

Check-Out Procedures

In checking out music for practice at home, in the band practice rooms, etc., the player should sign out for the entire folder of music rather than one, two, or a few pieces of music. In the first place, the folder itself serves as a means of protecting the music against wear or mutilation as the music probably will be carried in the instrument case. Also, there is a greater possibility of losing parts when not carried in a folder. To facilitate checking out music, a card is placed in the concert or march folder for this purpose; the player signs the card with his name and date, and leaves it in place of the folder. The individual student is personally responsible for the folder and its contents when he checks it out.

Forms. Illustrations 10-7 and 10-8 show sample check-out cards for march folios. Illustration 10-9 is an example of a concert folder check-out card. Illustration 10-10 is also a concert folder check-out card except that it is constructed in the form of a folio with the information printed on all four sides. The purpose for this is that, if any new music is added to the folders, it is placed inside this check-out card.

FOLIO NO._____

MARCH FOLIO SIGN-OUT CARD

Name_____

Address_____

Phone_____

Home Room_____

Your signature on the reverse side constitutes an agreement to be responsible for the return of the above folio (valued at $_____), and its' contents, as of the date signed out. Lost or damaged parts will be charged to the signee, at the rate of   cents   per part.

PEPPER LIBRARY SYSTEM CARD #10-5   **J. W. PEPPER & SON, INC.**
© 1965, J. W. PEPPER & SON, INC.   231 North Third Street, Philadelphia, Penna., 19106

Illustration 10-7
(front)

Illustration 10-7
(back)

Illustration 10-8

CHECK OUT CARD FOR BAND FOLIO

BAND_____ FOLIO_____ STAND NO._____
      (Name or Number)   (Where More Than One is in Use)   (Or Name of Instrument)

You may check out this Folio of music by signing your name, date, and number of parts withdrawn in the spaces provided below. Place this card in music cabinet instead of Folio, or file with Librarian or Director, according to method used. Upon the return of the Folio have your Librarian or Director sign in space opposite your withdrawal signature, thereby receipting its satisfactory return. THIS FOLIO MUST BE RETURNED BEFORE THE NEXT REHEARSAL WHICH REQUIRES ITS USE.

SIGNATURE OF BANDSMAN OR STUDENT	OUT DATE	PARTS OUT	SIGNATURE OF LIBRARIAN OR DIRECTOR	IN DATE	PARTS IN

ORDER ALL MUSIC AND SUPPLIES FROM

SOUTHERN MUSIC CO.

1100 BROADWAY   SAN ANTONIO 6, TEXAS

Illustration 10-9

FOLIO CARD

UNIVERSITY OF ILLINOIS BANDS

FOLIO _____   BAND _____

IMPORTANT: THIS CARD MUST NOT BE TAKEN FROM THE BAND BUILDING OR OTHER REHEARSAL OR PERFORMANCE AREA.

This card will normally be kept in the *back pocket* of the concert folio. When taking the folio for individual practice, the band member will date and sign below, and leave this card on the music stand or with the librarian.

SINGLE PIECES OF MUSIC MAY NOT BE TAKEN FROM THE FOLIO.

The member who takes a folio will understand that he assumes responsibility for the proper care and safe return of it and its contents at the next rehearsal or performance of the organization. When returning the concert folio, the band member will again date this card and will transfer to the folio any new music which has been placed inside the card.

DATE TAKEN	SIGNATURE	DATE RETURNED	DATE TAKEN	SIGNATURE	DATE RETURNED

(64906)

Illustration 10-10

Coda

Plate 1: A type of card index file cabinet. Courtesy of University of Illinois Bands, John Cranford, Head Librarian.

Plate 2: A type of music filing cabinet, with drawers for single selections. Courtesy of the Lyons Band Instrument Company, Elmhurst, Illinois.

Plate 3: The Norren sorting rack, roll-away type with casters. Lyons Band Instrument Company.

Plate 4: Built-in sorting rack for concert folios. University of Illinois Bands.

Plate 5: Built-in sorting rack for concert or march folios, showing march folios placed two to a section and various identification markings. University of Illinois Bands.

Plate 6: March folio cabinet with door in horizontal position as work table; can be removed from frame and used as a roll-away unit. Courtesy of Wenger Corporation, Owatonna, Minnesota.

Plate 7: March distribution and folio storage cabinet. Lyons Band Instrument Company.

Plate 8: Roll-away concert folio storage cabinet, with doors. Wenger Corporation.

Plate 9: Roll-away concert folio storage cabinet. Lyons Band Instrument Company.

Plate 10: Roll-away conductor's desk, adjustable for height, can be used also for conductor's storage cabinet, or concert folio storage cabinet. Wenger Corporation.

Plate 11: The Wenger conductor's desk shown as a combined conductor-desk-folio storage cabinet.

Plate 12: Band library work area, showing cabinets for materials and supplies, working table and distribution area. University of Illinois Bands.

Plate 1: Card Index File Cabinet

Plate 2: Music Filing Cabinet

Plate 3: Norren Sorting Rack

Plate 4: Built-in Concert Folder Sorting Rack

Plate 5: Built-in Sorting Rack for Concert and Marching Folders

Plate 6: March Folio Cabinet with Door for Work Table

Plate 7: March Distribution and Folio Storage Cabinet

Plate 8: Roll-away Concert Folio Storage Cabinet

Plate 9: Roll-away Concert Folio Storage Cabinet

Plate 10: Roll-away Conductor's Desk

Plate 11: Roll-away Conductor's Desk; adapted as
Concert Folio Storage Cabinet

Plate 12: Band Library Work Area

Selected References

Books

1. Bradley, Carol June (ed.). *Manual of Music Librarianship*, Ann Arbor, Michigan: Music Library Association, 1966.
2. Foster, William P. *Band Pageantry*, Winona, Minnesota: Hal Leonard Music, Inc., 1968.
3. Hoffer, Charles R. *Teaching Music in the Secondary Schools*, Belmont, California: Wadsworth Publishing Company, Inc., 1964.
4. Jones, Archie (ed.). *Music Education in Action*, Boston: Allyn and Bacon, 1960.
5. Jones, Bruce L. *Building the Instrumental Music Department*, New York: Carl Fischer, Inc., 1949.
6. Kuhn, Wolfgang. *Instrumental Music: Principles and Methods of Instruction*, Boston: Allyn and Bacon, 1962.
7. Music Educators National Conference. *Music Buildings, Rooms, and Equipment*, Washington, D.C.: Music Educators National Conference, 1966.
8. Prescott, Gerald R. and Lawrence W. Chidester, *Getting Results with School Bands*, New York: Carl Fischer, Inc., 1938.
9. Righter, Charles B. *Teaching Instrumental Music*, New York: Carl Fischer, Inc., 1959.
10. Singleton, Ira C. *Music in Secondary Schools*, Boston: Allyn and Bacon, 1963.

Unpublished Literature

11. Cecil, Herbert M. *Fundamental Principles of the Organization, Management, and Teaching of the School Band*, unpublished dissertation, University of Rochester, 1953.

Monographs

12. Pepper, J. W. and Son, Inc. (Don H. Razey, ed.). *How to File and Find Music*, Philadelphia: J. W. Pepper and Son, Inc., 1966.

Appendix I

Selected and Annotated
Lists of Books on Music
for the School Band Library

THE GREAT BOOKS SHELF, MINI STYLE *

or

How You Can Build A Music Library At
Super-Market Prices

by Joan Boucher

I. *Dictionary-types*

Apel, W. and Daniel, R., eds. *The Harvard Brief Dictionary of Music,* Washington Square Press (W589)

Westrup, J.A. and Harrison, F., eds. *The New College Encyclopedia of Music,* The Norton Library (N273)

II. *Music History*

Prentice-Hall History of Music Series, 9 vols., H. Wiley Hitchcock, ed.

Seay, A.: *Music in the Medieval World*

---

* Reprinted from Selmer Bandwagon, Volume 16, No. 4, courtesy of the Selmer Division of the Magnavox Company. Dr. Joan Boucher is Assistant Professor of Music History at Western Michigan University.

Palisca, C.: *Baroque Music*
Pauly, R.: *Music in the Classic Period*
Longyear, R.: *Nineteenth-Century Romanticism*
Salzman, E.: *Twentieth-Century Music: An Introduction*
Nettl, B.: *Folk and Traditional Music of the Western Continents*
Malm, W.: *Music Cultures of the Pacific, the Near East, and Asia*
Hitchcock, H.: *Music in the United States: A Historical Introduction*

Dexter, Dave Jr. *The Jazz Story*, Spectrum Books (S-108)
Dorian, F. *The History of Music in Performance*, The Norton Library

III. *Biographies, auto- and other*

Here the number and your individual choice makes a specific list impossible. Four of the most important publishers turn out some of the best works in this category:

Dover Publications—do not fail to get a catalog of musical works from this firm!
The Norton Library (paperback division of W.W. Norton—reason in itself)
Doubleday Anchor Books—constantly revised reprints. (The great *Haydn, A Creative Life in Music* by Geiringer, formerly an Anchor Book, has just been re-issued by the U. of California Press and is heavily revised)
Collier Books: The Great Composer Series, ed. Westrup
Don't forget the Sullivan biography of Beethoven, a Mentor Book.

IV. *Various and Important Sundry*

Donington, R. *The Instruments of Music*, University Paperbacks (UP-39)
Winckel, F. *Music, Sound and Sensation*, Dover
Simpson, R. *The Symphony*, Vol. 1: Haydn to Dvorak, Vol. 2: Elgar to the Present
Pelican Books, A772 and A773
Copland, A. *What to Listen for in Music* (revised edition) Mentor Books (MP546)
Sessions, R. *The Musical Experience*, Atheneum, College Edition
Newman, W. *Understanding Music*, Harper, Colophon Books (CN109)

A BASIC LIBRARY ON BANDS, BAND HISTORY, AND INSTRUMENTAL MUSIC *

Adkins, Hector E. *Treatise on the Military Band,* rev. ed. London: Boosey and Hawkes, 1945.

Baines, Anthony. *Musical Instruments Through the Ages,* Baltimore: Penguin Books, 1961.

Baines, Anthony. *Woodwind Instruments and Their History,* London: Faber and Faber, Ltd., 1943.

Berger, Kenneth. *Band Bibliography,* Evansville, Indiana: Berger Band, 1955.

Carse, Adam. *Musical Wind Instruments,* London: MacMillan and Company, Ltd., 1939.

Dart, Thurston. *The Interpretation of Music,* rev. ed., London: Hutchinson's University Library, 1955.

Donnington, Robert. *The Instruments of Music,* New York: Pitman Publishing Company, 1949.

Farmer, Henry George. *Handel's Kettledrums,* London: Hinrichsen, Ltd., 1950.

Farmer, Henry George. *Military Music,* London: Max Parrish and Company, 1950.

Garcia, Russell. *The Professional Arranger Composer,* Hollywood, California: Barrington House Publishers, 1954.

Geiringer, Karl. *Musical Instruments: Their History from the Stone Age to the Present Day,* Trans. by Bernard Miall, London: George Allen and Unwin, 1943.

Holz, Emil A. and Roger E. Jacobi. *Teaching Band Instruments to Beginners,* Englewood Cliffs, New Jersey: Prentice-Hall, Inc., 1966.

Lang, Philip J. *Scoring for the Band,* New York: Mills Music, Inc., 1950.

Langwill, Lyndesay G. *The Bassoon and Contrabassoon,* New York: W.W. Norton and Company, Inc., 1965.

Ledarie, Siegmund and Ernst Levy. *Tone, A Study in Musical Acoustics,* Kent State University Press, 1968.

Lehman, Paul R. *Tests and Measurements in Music,* Englewood Cliffs, New Jersey: Prentice-Hall, Inc., 1968.

Leidzen, Erik. *An Invitation to Band Arranging,* Bryn Mawr, Pennsylvania: Theodore Presser Company, 1950.

---

* This list is in addition to the titles given in the Bibliography.

Marcouiller, Don R. *Marching for Marching Bands*, Dubuque, Iowa: Wm. C. Brown Company, 1958.

Miller, Ray M. *Practical Instrumentation for the Wind Band*, Detroit: Wayne University Press, 1948.

Norton, W.W. and Company, Inc. *Instruments of the Orchestra Series:*
Bate, Philip. *The Oboe*
Bate, Philip. *The Trumpet and Trombone*
Morley-Pegge, R. *The French Horn*
Rendall, F. Geoffrey. *The Clarinet*

Oxford University Press *Technique Books Series:*
Blades, James. *Orchestral Percussion Technique*
Camden, Archie. *Bassoon Technique*
Chapman, F.B. *Flute Technique*
Rothwell, Evelyn. *Oboe Technique*
Rowland-Jones, A. *Recorder Technique*
Schuller, Gunther. *Horn Technique*
Thurston, Frederick. *Clarinet Technique*

Porter, Maurice M. *The Embouchure*, London: Boosey and Hawkes, Ltd., 1967.

Reed, H. Owen and Joel T. Leach. *Scoring for Percussion*, Englewood Cliffs, New Jersey: Prentice-Hall, Inc., 1969.

Sachs, Curt. *The History of Musical Instruments*, New York: W.W. Norton and Company, 1940.

Schuller, Gunther. *Early Jazz: Its Roots and Musical Development*, New York: Oxford University Press, 1968.

Sousa, John Philip. *Marching Along*, Boston: Hale, Cushman, and Flint, 1928.

Spohn, Charles L. and Richard W. Heine. *The Marching Band*, Boston: Allyn and Bacon, Inc., 1969.

Wagner, Joseph. *Band Scoring*, New York: McGraw-Hill Book Company, Inc., 1960.

Weerts, Richard. *Developing Individual Skills for the High School Band*, West Nyack, New York: Parker Publishing Company, 1969.

White, William Carter. *A History of Military Music in America*, New York: The Exposition Press, 1944.

Whybrew, William E. *Measurement and Evaluation in Music*, Dubuque, Iowa: Wm. C. Brown Company Publishers, 1962.

Appendix II

Music Copyright Law Guide*

WHAT YOU *CAN* DO AND
WHAT YOU *CAN'T* DO UNDER
THE UNITED STATES COPYRIGHT LAW

Introduction

The source of the United States Copyright Law is the Constitution, Article 1, Section 8, which provides, "The Congress shall have Power. . . To promote the Progress of Science and useful Arts, by securing for limited Times to Authors and Inventors the exclusive Right to their respective Writings and Discoveries." Thus empowered, Congress enacted the Copyright Law to effectuate the intent of the Founding Fathers. It is this law which governs, and which must be our guide in our treatment and use of the works of authors who properly seek the protection afforded by copyright. This is so, whether the work created by the author be music or literature or indeed, any other form which enjoys the protection of the copyright law.

By providing protection to authors and composers it was the intention of the Congress and indeed the Founding Fathers to benefit the public by promoting creation of a larger, better body of literary and artistic works for its use, instruction, and pleasure.

In the music field, perhaps as in no other, because of the inherent nature of music and the multiplicity of ways of utilizing it, there has been practiced by the users thereof a great number of abuses in derogation of the authors' rights and in violation of the law. It is in the belief that many of these abuses are founded in misunderstanding rather than in malice, that we have made available this (guide) which it is hoped will clarify the uses which can and cannot be made of copyrighted music.

A. Even though music is protected by copyright under the United States Copyright Law there are various things which you can do without securing permission of any type and without fear of infringing.

You may purchase a copyrighted musical composition, orchestration or other form of published music and do the following with it:

1. You may sell it or give it away.
2. You may perform it in private, or in public for non-profit.
3. You may use it for teaching in a classroom, at home or in a pupil's home. Solely for teaching purposes you may write symbols and indicate instructions upon it.
4. Provided the composition has already been recorded by others, under the authorization of the copyright owner, for the manufacturer of phonograph records serving to reproduce the same mechanically, and provided further that you notify the copyright owner by registered mail of your intention to make such use (with a duplicate of such notice to the Copyright office, Washington, D.C. 20540), you make similar use thereof upon making monthly payments of the statutory royalty, to the copyright owner.

B. If you wish to make some other type of use which is not described above, you should write to the copyright owner for specific permission in each instance. The following are some of the things you cannot do without specific permission:

1. Reprinting, duplicating or copying the work or any part of it by any method or means whatsoever.
2. Arranging, adapting, orchestrating, translating or making any new versions of the work or any part of it.
3. Photographing or reproducing the work or any part of it by any method or means, including on film, or slides by opaque projector.
4. Performing the work in public for profit.

5. Recording the work by any method or means or for any use or purpose, other than as provided in A.4 above, including in synchronization with motion pictures or for television, and whether on records, film or tape.
6. Writing of parodies upon lyrics.

To avoid infringement, the right to do each or any of these acts must be cleared, and the clearance of one particular right does not clear any of the other rights. All rights are separate, distinct and independent. For instance, the clearance for broadcast does not carry with it the right to copy, or to arrange, or to record; clearance of the right to record does not carry with it the right to perform. The obligation is upon you to make certain that the right involved in the act you intend to do has been cleared.

C. If you have occasion to perform a musical composition publicly for profit, in a manner other than set forth in D below, guide yourself as follows:

If the performance is to be in a theatre or over a radio or television station, in all likelihood the theatre, radio or television station will have a license for you to perform the musical composition publicly for profit. However, it is your obligation to make certain of this and to secure a license if there is none.

If the performance is to take place elsewhere, there is less likelihood that the establishment has a license for you to perform publicly for profit and in such event a license must be secured. There are three important performing rights societies which license the great majority of copyrighted musical compositions: American Society of Composers, Authors and Publishers (usually referred to as "ASCAP"), One Lincoln Plaza, New York, New York 10022; Broadcast Music, Inc. (usually referred to as "BMI"), 589 Fifth Avenue, New York, New York 10017, and SESAC, Inc., 10 Columbus Circle, New York, New York 10019.

D. If you have occasion to present a musical play or other dramatic work or a musical composition from a musical play, with costumes and/or dialogue on the stage at your school, church or elsewhere, whether for profit or non-profit, you must secure from the owner of the work or his agent a license or permission. Such uses are not licensed by the performing rights societies referred to in C above.

E. When you see the word "Copyright" or the distinctive © printed on a piece of music, it is the notice that protects the copyright owner of the work and authorizes him to exclusively exercise and enforce all rights secured to him under the United States Copyright Law, and at the same time it is the notice that informs *you* that the exercising by you of any such acts, including those described in B, C, and D, above, *unless authorized*, will subject you to liability under such law.

A printed copy of a musical composition published in the United States, bearing no copyright notice, or one with a copyright notice dated more than 61 years ago, indicates that the composition is in the public domain in the United States and may be used freely. However, if an arrangement, adaptation or other version of such a work has been copyrighted, utmost caution must be exercised in treating the same as you would any other copyrighted work. But notwithstanding such copyrighted arrangement, adaptation or other version, of a work in the public domain, you are still free to treat the basic composition as being in the public domain. A work in the public domain reprinted in a compilation is not protected, even though the compilation itself is copyrighted, unless the reprint is a copyrightable or copyrighted arrangement, adaptation or other version thereof.

Philip B. Wattenberg, Counsel for the Music Publishers' Association, points out that "The latest copyright law is still the law of 1909." The 89th Congress made considerable progress toward the formulation of a new copyright law. Subcommittee number 3 of the House of Representatives Judiciary Committee worked on bill H.R. 4347 which was introduced on February 4, 1965. After hearings and subsequent executive sessions, the subcommittee submitted a revision of the bill. When the new law is finally written, music educators will need to study it to be sure (a) that they are not depriving copyright holders of their just due, and (b) to make sure that they are making the best educational use of materials that the law allows.

Appendix III

Key to Publishers

Alfred Music Co., 145 W. 45th Street, New York City
AMP—see "Associated"
Associated Music Publishers, 609 Fifth Avenue, New York City
Avant Music Co., 1825 Orchard, Los Angeles, California
Band Guild—see "Omega"
Bandland—see "Belwin"
C.L. Barnhouse, Inc., 110 B Avenue, Oskaloosa, Iowa
Belwin, Inc., 250 Maple, Rockville Centre, L.I., New York
Berklee Press, 284 Newberry St., Boston, Mass.
Irving Berlin Music Corp., 1650 Broadway, New York City
B.H.B.—see "Boosey & Hawkes"
Big Three Music Corp., 1350 Avenue of the Americas, New York City
BMI—see "Associated"
Boosey & Hawkes, Inc., P.O. Box 418, Lynbrook, New York
Boston Music Co., 116 Boylston St., Boston, Mass.
Bosworth—see "Chappell"
Bourne, Inc., 136 W. 52nd St., New York City
George F. Briegel, Inc., 17 W. 60th St., New York City
Brodt Music Co., P.O. Box 1207, Charlotte, N.C.
Silver Burdette Music Publ., Boston, Mass.
Byron Douglas, 3812 W. Palmaire Dr., Phoenix, Arizona
Carlin Music Pub. Co., Oakhurst, California
Chappell & Co., 609 Fifth Avenue, New York City
Church—see "Presser"
M.M. Cole Pub. Co., 251 E. Grand Avenue, Chicago, Illinois

Charles Colin, 315 W. 53rd St., New York City
Franco Colombo, 16 W. 61st St., New York City
Crescendo Music, 444 W. Barry, Chicago, Illinois
Cundy-Bettoney Co.—see "Carl Fischer"
Ditson—see "Presser"
Educational Music Bureau, South Wabash, Chicago, Illinois
Elkan-Vogel Co., 1716 Sansom St., Philadelphia, Pa.
Henri Elkan Music Pub., 1316 Walnut St., Philadelphia, Pa.
Famous Music Corp., 1619 Broadway, New York City
Feist—see "Big Three"
Fillmore—see "Carl Fischer"
Carl Fischer, 62 Cooper Square, New York City
H.T. Fitzsimons Co., 615 N. LaSalle, Chicago, Illinois
Harold Flammer, Inc., 251 W. 19th St., New York City
Charles Foley Co., 67 W. 44th St., New York City
Forster Music Pub., Inc., 216 S. Wabash, Chicago, Illinois
Sam Fox Pub., Co., 11 W. 60th St., New York City
Frank Music Corp., 119 W. 57th St., New York City
Samuel French, 25 W. 45th St., New York City
Galaxy Music Co., 2121 Broadway, New York City
Gordon Music Pub. Co., 408 N. Rodeo Dr., Beverly Hills, California
David Gornston, 117 W. 48th St., New York City
Charles H. Hansen Music Corp., 119 W. 57th, New York City
Harms—See "MPH"
Highland Music Co., 1311 N. Highland Avenue, Hollywood, California
Instrumental Music Co., 1418 Lake St., Evanston, Illinois
Edwin F. Kalmus, P.O. Box 47, Huntington Sta., L.I., New York
Kendor Music Inc., Delevan, New York
Karl L. King Music House, Box 763, Ft. Dodge, Iowa
Neil A. Kjos Music Co., 520 Busse Avenue, Park Ridge, Illinois
Kuchen Publications, 2198 Monroe, Rochester, New York
Lavell Publishing Co., 128 N. 40th, Omaha, Nebraska
Lawson—see "Schirmer"
G. Leblanc Corp., 7019 30th Avenue, Kenosha, Wisconsin
Leeds Music Corp., 322 W. 48th St., New York City
Hal Leonard Music Inc., 64 E. 2nd, Winona, Minnesota
Ludwig Music Pub. Co., 557 E. 140th, Cleveland, Ohio
Edward B. Marks Music Corp., 136 W. 52nd, New York City
MCA—445 Park Avenue, New York City
Mercury—see "Presser"
Mills Music Co., 1619 Broadway, New York City
Edwin H. Morris & Co., 31 W. 54th, New York City

Music Publishers Holding Corp., 488 Madison Avenue, New York City
Edition Musicus, 333 W. 52nd St., New York City
New World—see "MPH"
Omega Music Edition, 19 W. 44th St., New York City
J. W. Pepper & Sons, Inc., 231 N. 3rd St., Philadelphia, Pa.
C. F. Peters Corp., 373 4th Avenue, New York City
Plymouth Music Co., 1841 Broadway, New York City
Theodore Presser Co., Presser Place, Bryn Mawr, Pa.
Pro Art Publications, 469 Union Avenue, Westbury, L.I., New York
Remick—see "MPH"
Ricordi—see "Colombo"
Robbins—see "Big Three"
Rubank, Inc., 16215 N.W. 15th Avenue, Miami, Florida
G. Schirmer, Inc., 609 Fifth Avenue, New York City
Schmitt, Hall & McCreary Co., 527 Park Avenue, Minneapolis, Minne-
sota
Shapiro-Bernstein, 666 Fifth Avenue, New York City
Shawnee Press, Inc., Delaware Water Gap, Pa.
Southern Music Company, 1100 Broadway, San Antonio, Texas
Southern Music Publishers, 1619 Broadway, New York City
Staff Music Pub. Co., 374 Great Neck Rd., Great Neck, New York
Summy-Birchard Pub. Co., 1834 Ridge Avenue, Evanston, Illinois
Volkwein Brothers, 632 Liberty, Pittsburgh, Pa.
Warner Brothers Music, 488 Madison Avenue, New York City
Williamson Music Inc., 1270 Sixth Avenue, New York City
Willis Music Corp., 124 E. 4th, Cincinnati, Ohio
Wingert-Jones, 1211 Walnut St., Kansas City, Missouri
Witmark—see "MPH"
Wynn Music Pub., 615 Spruce, Berkeley, California

Bibliography

BOOKS

American Library Association. *Anglo-American Cataloging Rules (North American Text)*, Chicago: American Library Association, 1967.

Andrews, Frances M. and Joseph A. Leeder. *Guiding Junior High School Pupils in Music Experiences*, New York: Prentice-Hall, Inc., 1953.

Bessom, Malcolm E. *Supervising the School Music Program*, West Nyack, New York: Parker Publishing Company, 1969.

Birge, Edward Bailey. *History of Public School Music in the United States*, Boston: Oliver Ditson Company, 1928.

Bradley, Carol June (ed.). *Manual of Music Librarianship*, Ann Arbor, Michigan: Music Library Association, 1966.

Bryant, E.T. *Music Librarianship: A Practical Guide*, London: James Clarke and Company, Ltd., 1959.

Colwell, Richard J. *The Teaching of Instrumental Music*, New York: Appleton-Century-Crofts, 1969.

Davis, Ennis. *More Than a Pitch-Pipe*, Boston: C.C. Birchard and Company, 1941.

Duvall, W. Clyde. *The High School Band Director's Handbook*, Englewood Cliffs, New Jersey: Prentice-Hall., Inc., 1960.

Dvorak, Raymond Francis. *The Band on Parade*, New York: Carl Fischer, Inc., 1937.

Dykema, Peter W. and Hannah Cundiff. *School Music Handbook* (new ed.), Boston: C.C. Birchard and Company, 1955.

Dykema, Peter W. and Karl W. Gehrkens. *The Teaching and Administration of High School Music*, Boston: C.C. Birchard and Company, 1941.

Edelson, Edward. *The Secondary School Music Program from Classroom to Concert Hall*, West Nyack, New York: Parker Publishing Company, 1972.

Fennell, Frederick. *Time and the Winds,* Kenosha, Wisconsin: G. Leblanc Corporation, 1954.

Foster, William Patrick. *Band Pageantry,* Winona, Minnesota: Hal Leonard Music, Inc., 1968.

Goldman, Richard Franko. *The Band's Music,* New York: Pitman Publishing Company, 1938.

Goldman, Richard Franko. *The Concert Band,* New York: Rinehart and Company, 1946.

Goldman, Richard Franko. *The Wind Band: Its Literature and Technique,* Boston: Allyn and Bacon, Inc., 1961.

Green, Elizabeth A.H. *The Modern Conductor,* Englewood Cliffs, New Jersey: Prentice-Hall, Inc., 1961.

Hartshorn, William C. *Music for the Academically-Talented Student in the Secondary School,* Washington, D.C.: M.E.N.C., 1960.

Haydon, Glen. *Introduction to Musicology,* New York: Prentice-Hall, Inc., 1941.

Hind, Harold C. *The Brass Band,* London: Boosey and Hawkes, Ltd., 1934.

Hindsley, Mark. *School Band and Orchestra Administration,* New York: Boosey and Hawkes, 1940.

Hjelmervick, Kenneth and Richard Berg. *Marching Bands: How to Organize and Develop Them,* New York: The Ronald Press Company, 1953.

Hoffer, Charles R. *Teaching Music in the Secondary Schools,* Belmont, California: Wadsworth Publishing Company, Inc., 1964.

House, Robert W. *Instrumental Music for Today's Schools,* Englewood Cliffs, New Jersey: Prentice-Hall, Inc., 1965.

Hovey, Nilo W. *The Administration of School Instrumental Music,* Rockville Centre, L.I., New York: Belwin, Inc., 1949.

Illinois Curriculum Program, The. *Music in the Secondary School,* Springfield, Illinois: Office of the Superintendent of Public Instruction, 1966.

Jones, Archie N. (ed.). *Music Education in Action,* Boston: Allyn and Bacon, Inc., 1960.

Jones, Bruce L. *Building the Instrumental Music Department,* New York: Carl Fischer, Inc., 1949.

Kuhn, Wolfgang. *Instrumental Music: Principles and Methods of Instruction,* Boston: Allyn and Bacon, Inc., 1962.

Labuta, Joseph. *Teaching Musicianship in the High School Band,* West Nyack, New York: Parker Publishing Company, 1971.

Lee, Jack. *Modern Marching Band Techniques,* Winona, Minnesota: Hal Leonard Music, Inc., 1955.

Leeder, Joseph A. and William S. Haynie. *Music Education in the*

High School, Englewood Cliffs, New Jersey: Prentice-Hall, Inc., 1958.

Leonhard, Charles and Robert W. House. *Foundations and Principles of Music Education,* New York: McGraw-Hill Book Company, 1959.

McColvin, Lionel Roy, Harold Reeves, and Jack Dove. *Music Libraries* (2 vols.), London: Andre Deutsch, Ltd., 1965.

Moses, Harry E. *Developing and Administering a Comprehensive High School Music Program,* West Nyack, New York: Parker Publishing Company, 1970.

Mueller, Kenneth A. *Teaching Total Percussion,* West Nyack, New York: Parker Publishing Company, 1972.

Music Educators National Conference. *Music Buildings, Rooms, and Equipment,* Washington, D.C.: M.E.N.C., 1966.

Music Educators National Conference. *Music in the Senior High School,* Washington, D.C.: M.E.N.C., 1959.

Music Educators National Conference. *Music in General Education,* Washington, D.C.: M.E.N.C., 1965.

Music Educators National Conference. *The Music Curriculum in Secondary Schools,* Washington, D.C.: M.E.N.C., 1959.

Music Educators National Conference. *Perspectives in Music Education* (Source Book III, Bonnie C. Kowall, ed.), Washington, D.C.: M.E.N.C., 1966.

Music Library Association. *Code for Cataloguing Music,* Washington, D.C.: Music Library Association, 1941–42.

National Education Association. *Contemporary Music Project Catalog for Band* (3 vols.), Washington, D.C.: N.E.A. Publication Sales, 1966.

National Interscholastic Music Activities Commission. *N.I.M.A.C. Manual: The Organization and Management of Interscholastic Music Activities,* Washington, D.C.: M.E.N.C., 1963.

Neidig, Kenneth I. (ed.) *The Band Director's Guide,* Englewood Cliffs, New Jersey: Prentice-Hall, Inc., 1964.

Norman, Theodore. *Instrumental Music in the Public Schools,* Philadelphia: Ditson Company, 1941.

Otto, Richard A. *Effective Methods for Building the High School Band,* West Nyack, New York: Parker Publishing Company, 1971.

Paul, John B. (ed.) *Music Education,* Washington, D.C.: The Catholic University of America Press, 1954.

Prescott, Gerald R. and Lawrence W. Chidester. *Getting Results with School Bands,* New York: Carl Fischer, Inc., and Minneapolis: Schmitt, Hall, and McCreary Company, 1938.

Rainbow, Barnarr (ed.). *Handbook for Music Teachers,* London: Novello and Company, Ltd., 1964.

Redfern, Brian. *Organizing Music in Libraries,* London: Clive Binglen, 1966.

Righter, Charles Boardman. *Success in Teaching School Orchestras and Bands,* Minneapolis: Schmitt, Hall, and McCreary Company, 1945.

Righter, Charles Boardman. *Teaching Instrumental Music,* New York: Carl Fischer, Inc., 1959.

Schwartz, H.W. *Bands of America,* Garden City, New York: Doubleday and Company, Inc., 1957.

Singleton, Ira C. *Music in Secondary Schools,* Boston: Allyn and Bacon, Inc., 1963.

Snyder, Keith. *School Music Administration and Supervision* (2nd ed.), Boston: Allyn and Bacon, Inc., 1965.

Sur, William and Charles Schuller. *Music Education for Teen-Agers* (2nd ed.), New York: Harper and Company, 1966.

Taubman, Joseph (ed.). *The Business and Law of Music,* New York: Federal Legal Publications, Inc., 1965.

Walls, Howard. *The Copyright Handbook for Fine and Applied Arts,* New York: Watson-Goptill, 1963.

Ward, Arthur E. *Music Education for High Schools,* New York: American Book Company, 1941.

Weerts, Richard. *Developing Individual Skills for the High School Band,* West Nyack, New York: Parker Publishing Company, 1969.

Weerts, Richard. *How to Develop and Maintain a Successful Woodwind Section,* West Nyack, New York: Parker Publishing Company, 1972.

Werder, Richard H. (ed.). *Developing Skills in Music,* Washington, D.C.: Catholic University of America Press, 1960.

Werder, Richard H. (ed.). *Music Skills,* Washington, D.C.: Catholic University of America Press, 1958.

Werder, Richard H. (ed.). *Procedures and Techniques of Music Teaching,* Washington, D.C.: Catholic University of America Press, 1962.

Werder, Richard H. (ed.). *Specialized Activities in Music Education,* Washington, D.C.: Catholic University of America Press, 1956.

Weyland, Rudolph. *A Guide to Effective Music Supervision,* Dubuque, Iowa: Wm. C. Brown Company, 1960.

PERIODICALS

Akers, Howard E. "The March Is Music Also," *The School Musician,* Vol. 35, No. 1, Aug.–Sept., 1963.

Akers, Howard E. "The Publisher—Friend of the Music Educator," *The School Musician,* Vol. 35, No. 2, Oct., 1963.

Akers, Howard E., "What Is Good Music?" *The School Musician*, Vol. 37, No. 7, Mar., 1966.

Andrus, Robert. "Marching Band Trends—Good or Bad?" *The School Musician*, Vol. 37, No. 2, Oct., 1965.

Baird, Forrest J. "Let's 'Sell' Our Music Program," *The School Musician*, Vol. 36, No. 1, Aug.–Sept., 1963.

Ballou, Richard. "Preparing for Television Appearances," *The Instrumentalist*, Vol. XXIII, No. 3, Oct., 1968.

Beeler, Walter. "Band Techniques," *Educational Music Magazine*, Nov.–Dec., 1952.

Beeler, Walter. "Know Your Band Arrangements," *The Instrumentalist*, Vol. VIII, No. 2, Oct., 1953.

Beeler, Walter. "More Band Color," *The Instrumentalist*, Vol. XIX, No. 1, Aug., 1964.

Beeler, Walter. "The Next Twenty Years," *The School Musician*, Aug.–Sept., 1968.

Bilik, Jerry H. "A Missing Ingredient in Music Education," *The School Musician*, Vol. 35, No. 8, April, 1964.

Blanton, Robert. "Music Reading and the Marching Band," *The Instrumentalist*, Vol. XXI, No. 8, Mar., 1967.

Bordo, Victor. "Music History Thru Band Literature," *Music Journal*, Vol. XXVII, No. 10, Dec., 1969.

Brendler, Charles. "The March Is the Heritage of the Band," *The Instrumentalist*, Vol. XIX, No. 3, Oct., 1964.

Butler, John H. "Concert Band: Real Hope for New Music," *Music Journal*, Vol. XXVII, No. 7, Sept., 1969.

Butler, John H. "Marching Band Music of the Past," *Music Journal*, Vol. XXV, No. 8, Oct. 1967, and No. 9, Nov., 1967.

Connor, Frank H. "The Publisher Serves Education," *Music Journal*, Vol. XXIV, No. 7, Sept., 1966.

Cooper, Milton L. "An Educational Criteria for Selecting and Evaluating Materials for Band Shows," *The School Musician*, Vol. 38, No. 9, May, 1967.

Dalby, J. Philip. "The Arranger and the High School Band," *Journal of Band Research,*, Vol. IV, No. 1, Autumn, 1967.

Downing, Edward. "Band, Marching," *The Instrumentalist*, Vol. XXI, No. 2, Sept., 1966.

Drake, Alan H. "21 Tips Toward the Production of Successful Marching Band Shows," *The School Musician*, Vol. 39, No. 1, Aug.–Sept., 1967.

Dunn, Earl. "The Marching Show Band, A Medium of Expression," *The Instrumentalist*, Vol. XXI, No. 2, Sept., 1966.

Effinger, Cecil. "A New Look at the Concert Band," *Music Journal,* Jan.–Feb., 1950.

Falcone, Leonard. "Let Us Not Forget the Outstanding Band Literature of Yesterday," *The Instrumentalist,* Vol. XXI, No. 11, June, 1967.

Faulkner, Jeanne Gissenaas. "Taste, Music, and Education," *Missouri Journal of Research in Music Education,* Vol. II, No. 1, 1967.

Feist, Leonard. "Music Publishing," *The Instrumentalist,* Vol. XXI, No. 1, Aug., 1966.

Fennell, Frederick. "As I See It," *The School Musician,* Vol. 40, No. 1, Aug.–Sept., 1968.

Fischer, Irwin. "Contemporary Music—A Problem Child?" *Music Journal,* Vol. XXIV, No. 3, Mar., 1966.

Foster, Donald L. "Using the Library," *The School Musician,* Vol. 36, No. 3, Nov., 1964.

Fowler, Charles B. "The Misrepresentation of Music," *Music Educators Journal,* Vol. 51, No. 5, April–May, 1965.

Fowler, Charles B. "Music Education Through Performance," *The Instrumentalist,* Vol. XIX, No. 4, Nov., 1964.

Freeman, E.L. "The Band and Its Music," *Music Journal,* Jan.–Feb., 1949.

Goldman, Edwin Franko. "The Function of the Band," *Etude,* Nov., 1952.

Goldman, Edwin Franko. "Programs and Repertory of the Concert Band," *Music Journal,* Jan.–Feb., 1949.

Goldman, Richard Franko. "Compositions Written for the Band," *Musical Quarterly,* October, 1950.

Grasso, Benjamin V. "The Music Publishers' Association," *The School Musician,* Vol. 35, No. 9, May, 1964.

Harpham, Dale and Conrad Hutchinson, Jr., Arthur W. Rohr, Robert T. Scott. "From the Four Winds: A Symposium on the Full Band Score in C," *Journal of Band Research,* Vol. III, No 2, Spring, 1967.

Hauser, Arthur A. "The Band and the Publisher," *The School Musician,* Jan.–Feb., 1949.

Herendeen, James F. "Let's Look at Methods" (A Regular Clinical Column), *The School Musician,* Beginning Sept., 1960.

Hohstadt, Thomas. "The Band's Golden Age Debased," *Music Journal,* Vol. XXIV, No. 3, Mar., 1966.

Hullfish, William and Jack Allen. "Let's Teach Music Appreciation in Band," *The School Musician,* Vol. 36, No. 9, May, 1965.

Instrumentalist, The. "100 Most Popular Marches," *The Instrumentalist,* Vol. XIX, No. 3, Oct., 1964.

Ivory, Paul S. "Band Programs in Minnesota," *Journal of Research in Music Education,* Spring, 1953.

Izzo, Christopher *et al.* "Are Halftime Shows Doomed?" *The Selmer Bandwagon,* No. 57, Fall, 1969.

Johnson, William and Donald McGinnis, Gilbert Mitchell, Charles Payne. "From the Four Winds: A Symposium on Audience Reaction to Contemporary Band Music," *Journal of Band Research,* Vol. 1, No. 1, Autumn, 1964.

Kahley, Arlington. "Now Is the Time to Build Your Concert Program for Next Year," *The School Musician,* Vol. 39, No. 9, May, 1968.

Kurtz, Samuel. "On the Other Side of the Counter," *The School Musician,* Vol. 39, No. 7, Mar., 1968.

Labuta, Joseph. "High School Band Curriculum," *The Instrumentalist,* Vol. XXI, No. 2, Sept., 1966.

Long, Johnny. "A Short Evaluation of the Marching Band," *The School Musician,* Vol. 38, No. 1, Aug.–Sept., 1966.

Mathie, Gordon. "Wind Ensemble or Band?" *The Instrumentalist,* Vol. XXI, No. 5, Dec., 1966.

McGuire, Frank. "What Are Sousa's Best Marches?" *The Instrumentalist,* Vol. XXI, No. 4, Nov., 1966.

Music Educators National Conference. "Report On Copyright Legislation," *Music Educators Journal,* Vol. 53, No. 5, Jan., 1967.

Miller, Thomas. "Musical Taste Influences Curriculum," *Music Journal,* Vol. XXIV, No. 3, Mar., 1966.

Nallin, Walter E. "Changing Band Concepts," *Music Journal,* July–Aug., 1949.

Neilson, James. "The Aesthetics of Programming," *Journal of Band Research,* Vol. I, No. 1, Autumn, 1964.

Pascucci, Vito. "Needed: Creative Teaching in Instrumental Music," *Music Journal,* Vol. XXIV, No. 1, Jan., 1966.

Ralston, Jack L. "When Students Ask: Have a Good Basic Music Library," *The School Musician,* Vol. 35, No. 8, April, 1964.

Revelli, William D. "The Band's Repertoire," *Etude,* Dec., 1954.

Revelli, William D. "The Gridiron Marching Band," *The Instrumentalist,* Vol. XXI, No. 2, Sept., 1966.

Revelli, William D. "More Than a Downbeat," *Etude,* Sept.–Oct., 1954.

Revelli, William D. "The Selection and Evaluation of Teaching Materials," *Etude,* Nov., 1954.

Roeckle, Charles A. "Notes on Musical Taste," *Missouri Journal of Research in Music Education,* Vol. II, No. 2, 1968.

Satz, Ralph. "Actions Speak Louder Than. . ." *Music Journal,* Jan.–
  Feb., 1949.
Schaefer, William. "Is There an Emerging Band Repertoire?" *The
  Instrumentalist,* Vol. XXI, No. 9, April, 1967.
Shepard, Wesley. "Interpreting Music of the Classical Period," *Journal
  of Band Research,* Vol. II, No. 1, Spring, 1966.
Slocum, Earl. "Music for Bands," *The School Musician,* Vol. 36, No. 4,
  Dec., 1964.
Sperry, Gale L. "The Importance of a Band Course of Study," *The
  School Musician,* Vol. 34, No. 1, Sept., 1962.
Tauhert, Rudolph. "Publishers Cater to Needs," *Music Journal,* Vol.
  XXIV, No. 7, Sept., 1966.
Thompson, E.D. "Is It Good Music?" *The Instrumentalist,* Vol. XX,
  No. 5, Dec., 1965.
Thomson, Virgil. "The Art of Judging Music," *Music Educators Journal,*
  Vol. 51, No. 2, Nov.–Dec., 1964.
Udell, Budd A. "A Statement of Purpose," *The Instrumentalist,* Vol.
  XIX, No. 4, Nov., 1964.
Wagner, Joseph. "Band Scoring Is Composition," *Music Journal,* Vol.
  XXVIII, No. 2, Feb., 1970.
Wagner, Joseph. "Dilemma of Concert Band Programs," *Music
  Journal,* Vol. XXVII, No. 1, Jan. 1969.
Werner, Robert. "A New Meaning for Marching Bands," *The Instru-
  mentalist,* Vol. XXI, No. 2, Sept., 1966.
Whitcomb, Manley R. "The College Band of the Future," *Music
  Journal,* Vol. XXV, No. 7, Sept., 1967.
Whitcomb, Manley R. "The Future of the College Band," *The School
  Musician,* Vol. 39, No. 3, Nov., 1967.
Whitwell, David. "Attitude Towards the Marching Band," *The Instru-
  mentalist,* Vol. XIX, No. 7, Feb., 1965.
Whitwell, David. "The College Band: Can It Escape Its Heritage?"
  Music Educators Journal, Vol. 51, No. 6, June–July, 1965.
Whitwell, David. "The Contemporary Band: In Quest of an Historic
  Concept of Aesthetics," *The Instrumentalist,* Vol. XXIII, No. 9,
  April, 1969.
Whitwell, David. "Three Crises in Band Repertoire," *The Instru-
  mentalist,* Vol. XIX, No. 8, Mar., 1965.
Williams, Arthur L. "Better Band Music," *Educational Music Magazine,*
  Nov.–Dec., 1952.
Wilson, George C. "Choice of Repertory," *The Instrumentalist,* Jan.,
  1954.

Woodruff, Asahel D. "Concept Teaching in Music," *The Instrumentalist*, Vol. XIX, No. 3, Oct., 1964.

MONOGRAPHS

Bachman, Harold B. *Program Building*, Chicago: Frederick Charles, Inc., 1962.

Hartshorn, William C. and Carleton Sprague Smith. *The Study of Music as an Academic Discipline*, Washington, D.C.: M.E.N.C. 1963.

Music Industry Council. *The Music Educator's Business Handbook*, Washington, D.C.: The Music Industry Council, 1965.

Neilson, James. *What Is Quality in Music?* Kenosha, Wisconsin: G. Leblanc Corporation, no date.

(Pepper, J. W.). *How to File and Find Music*, Philadelphia: J. W. Pepper and Son Music Company, Inc., 1966.

(Southern Music Company). *How to Index Your Band or Orchestra Music Library*, San Antonio, Texas: Southern Music Company, 1945.

UNPUBLISHED LITERATURE

Bachman, Harold B. "Observations of a Veteran Bandmaster," A paper delivered at the College Band Directors National Association 15th National Conference Proceedings, Feb., 1969.

Charles Carter. "The Band's Music," A Report for the College Band Directors National Conference 11th National Conference Proceedings, Dec., 1960.

Cecil, Herbert M. *Fundamental Principles of the Organization, Management, and Teaching of the School Band*, unpublished dissertation, University of Rochester, 1953.

Desidero, Anthony Russell. *Teaching the History of Western Music Through Instrumental Performance in the Secondary School*, unpublished dissertation, University of Southern California, 1966.

Fjeld, Marvin Wendell. *A Survey and Evaluation of Music Performed in Public Concert by Indiana High School Band*, unpublished dissertation, Indiana University, 1959.

Fleury, Robert Myrl. *Objective Measurement of Group Instrumental Music*, unpublished dissertation, University of California, Los Angeles, 1963.

Garner, Gary Thomas. *Transcriptions for School Band of Selected*

Music Written Before 1800, unpublished dissertation, University of Southern California, 1967.

Griffith, Donald N. Remarks in Coordinating Committee, Panel Discussion, College Band Directors National Association, 15th National Conference Proceedings, Feb., 1969.

Haines, Harry Hartman. *Problems in Writing Curriculum Materials for School Bands: A Review of Available Materials with Suggestions for State and Local Curriculum Groups Regarding Methods and Procedures for Implementing Effectiveness,* unpublished dissertation, University of Oklahoma, 1968.

Henderson, Hubert P. "Straws in the Winds," An Address to the College Band Directors National Association 15th National Conference Proceedings, Feb., 1969.

Hindsley, Mark H. "The Concert Band Conductor and the Marching Band," A Report to the College Band Directors National Association, 11th National Conference Proceedings, Dec., 1960.

Hindsley, Mark H. "Future Band Repertoire and Its Influence Upon Our College Bands," A Report to the College Band Directors National Association, 11th National Conference Proceedings, Dec., 1960.

Lang, Philip J. "Band Repertoire," A Report to the College Band Directors National Association, 11th National Conference Proceedings, Dec., 1960.

Pugh, Russell Oris. *The Band Compositions of the Contemporary Music Project for Creativity in Music Education,* unpublished dissertation, University of Arkansas, 1966.

Sampson, Ulysses Thomas. *An Identification of Deficiencies in Past and Current Method Books for Beginning Heterogeneous Wind-Percussion Class Instrumental Music Instruction,* unpublished dissertation, Indiana University, 1968.

Satz, Ralph. "The Future of the Band and Its Music," A Paper for the College Band Directors National Association 11th National Conference Proceedings, Dec., 1960.

Schaefer, William A. and Harold Bachman, David Whitwell, Paul Bryan. "Is There an Emerging Band Repertoire?" Panel Discussion for the College Band Directors National Association 14th National Conference Proceedings, Feb., 1967.

Shaughnessy, Robert M. *Harmonic and Contrapuntal Elements in Selected School Concert Band Compositions,* unpublished dissertation, Boston University, 1963.

Stewart, Robert Louis. *The Musical Taste of the Secondary School Instrumental Music Teacher in Relation to the Character and Suc-*

cess of His Music Program, unpublished dissertation, University of Kansas, 1965.

Tarwater, William H. *Analyses of Seven Major Band Compositions of the Twentieth Century,* unpublished dissertation, George Peabody College for Teachers, 1958.

Wareham, Duane Emerson. *The Development and Evaluation of Objective Criteria for Grading Band Music Into Six Levels of Difficulty,* unpublished dissertation, The Pennsylvania State University, 1967.

Weeks, R. Stanwood. "The College Band—Is It Time To Build A Monument?" Address Delivered to the College Band Directors National Association, 15th National Conference Proceedings, Feb., 1969.

Index

Transcriptions (*cont.*)
idiomatic orchestral features to
consider, 99–100
Leidzen's approach to transcribing orchestral music, 103,
104–105
parallelism in scoring techniques,
103
principal media in selection of
originals, 96
pros and cons of, 92–93
scoring assignments to consider,
104
Tschaikowsky, 33, 63, 96
Twentieth-century music for band,
33–34, 95

U

University of Illinois Bands, 115
card indexing system, 178–179
filing system, 189–190
library order routine, 222–223
system for enumerating selections and file drawers, 191–
193
University of Michigan, 115

V

Van Bodegraven, 57
Vaughan-Williams, 25, 33
Verdi, 96
Vezzetti, 86
Villa-Lobos, 33
Virginia, 111
Vivaldi, 96
von Dittersdorf, 33
von Weber, 96

W

Wareham, 52, 109
Wattenberg, 248
Wagner, Joseph, 80, 101
Wagner, Richard, 33, 63, 96, 99
Webern, 33
Weeks, 85
Whitwell, 32, 33
Wilkinson, 80
Williams, 119
Wilson, 57, 109
Wright, 110

Y

Yoder, 37